Prospects in Trade, Investment and Business in Vietnam and East Asia

Also by Tran Van Hoa

THE ASIA CRISIS: The Cures, their Effectiveness and the Prospects After (*editor*)

THE CAUSES AND IMPACT OF THE ASIAN FINANCIAL CRISIS (*editor with C. Harvie*)

CONTRIBUTIONS TO CONSUMER DEMAND AND ECONOMETRICS (*editor with R. Bewley*)

ECONOMIC DEVELOPMENT AND PROSPECTS IN THE ASEAN (*editor*)

THE MACROECONOMIC MIX IN THE INDUSTRIALIZED WORLD (*with J. O. N. Perkins*)

NATIONAL INCOME AND ECONOMIC PROGRESS (*editor with D. S. Ironmonger and J. O. N. Perkins*)

SECTORAL ANALYSIS OF TRADE, INVESTMENT AND BUSINESS IN VIETNAM (*editor*)

VIETNAM: Market Intelligence and Business Analysis

VIETNAM'S REFORMS AND ECONOMIC GROWTH (*with C. Harvie*)

Prospects in Trade, Investment and Business in Vietnam and East Asia

Edited by

Tran Van Hoa
Associate Professor
University of Wollongong
Australia

Foreword by Pham Ngoc San

First published in Great Britain 2000 by
MACMILLAN PRESS LTD
Houndmills, Basingstoke, Hampshire RG21 6XS and London
Companies and representatives throughout the world

A catalogue record for this book is available from the British Library.

ISBN 0–333–71684–1

 First published in the United States of America 2000 by
ST. MARTIN'S PRESS, INC.,
Scholarly and Reference Division,
175 Fifth Avenue, New York, N.Y. 10010

ISBN 0–312–22656–X

Library of Congress Cataloging-in-Publication Data
Prospects in trade, investment and business in Vietnam and East Asia
/ edited by Tran Van Hoa.
p.   cm.
Includes bibliographical references and index.
ISBN 0–312–22656–X (cloth)
1. Investments, Foreign — Vietnam.   2. Foreign trade promotion–
–Vietnam.   3. Investments, Foreign — East Asia.   4. Foreign trade
promotion — East Asia.   I. Tran, Van Hoa.
HG5750.5.A3P76   1999
332.67'3'09597 — dc21   99–37581
                                                              CIP

This book is printed on paper suitable for recycling and made from fully managed and sustained forest sources.

10   9   8   7   6   5   4   3   2   1
09   08   07   06   05   04   03   02   01   00

Printed and bound in Great Britain by
Antony Rowe Ltd, Chippenham, Wiltshire

*To dearest Souraya, Danielle, Cybele, Aida
and my parents*

Contents

List of Tables and Figures   ix

Foreword by Pham Ngoc San   xii

Acknowledgements   xv

Notes on the Contributors   xvii

1 Trade, Investment and Business in Vietnam:
   An Overview   1
   Tran Van Hoa

2 Trends and Prospects for Trade, Investment and
   Business in Vietnam   6
   Tran Van Hoa

3 Amended Law on Foreign Investment and Investment
   Priorities during the period 1996–2000 in Vietnam   43
   Hoang Tho Xuan and Tran Van Hoa

4 Promotion of Trade, Investment and Business in
   Vietnam   53
   Ho Trung Thanh and Tran Van Hoa

5 The Business Environment for Australian Companies
   in Vietnam   63
   Anne-Marie Humphries

6 Australia's Trade with East Asia: Opportunities with
   Vietnam   82
   Charles Harvie

7 The Mekong Basin Subregion   110
   Anne-Marie Humphries

8 Human Resource Development Issues and Priorities in
   Vietnam: Implications for International Business   129
   Chris Nyland and Eduardo Pol

 9 Business Ethics and Foreign Enterprises in Vietnam   164
    Tran Van Hoa

10 Environmental Regulation and Standards: Implications
    for trade in Vietnam   182
    Subhabrata Bobby Banerjee

11 South Korea's Economic Growth, Trade and
    Development: Contemporary Problems and prospects   200
    Charles Harvie

12 General Comments and Conclusions   240
    Tran Van Hoa

Index   245

List of Tables and Figures

Tables

6.1   Australia – balance of payments on current
     account AUD bn (balance of payments basis)
     1989/90–1995/96   85

6.2   Vietnam – balance of payments on current
     account US$ bn   87

6.3   Breakdown of Australia's merchandise exports
     (per cent of total): by country groups   90

6.4   Australia's major exports (merchandise) markets –
     top ten   92

6.5   Breakdown of Australia's merchandise imports
     (per cent of total): by country groups   93

6.6   Australia's major import (merchandise) sources:
     top ten (AUD bn)   95

6.7   Australia's major trading partners – 1995–96
     (AUD bn)   96

6.8   Australia's trade with Vietnam (AUD mn)   96

6.9   Australia's trade balance by commodity and country
     grouping (AUD bn) 1995–96   97

6.10 Australia's main exports to Vietnam (AUD bn) –
     top ten   100

6.11 Australia's main imports from Vietnam (AUD mn) –
     top ten   101

8.1   Distribution of human capital between the PECC
     economies, 1992   136

8.2   Distribution of the human development index
     between the PECC economies, 1992   139

8.3   Distribution of the gender-related development
     index between the PECC economies, 1992   140

8.4   Selected indicators of child education: by number
     of children in family, unadjusted and adjusted for
     background characteristics   144

8.5   Number of persons attending school within country   148

8.6	Percentage who ever attended school and percentage currently attending school, by age	149
8.7	Average income per household member by regions in 1993	156
8.8	Comparison of some demographic indicators between poor and average households	158
11.1	The OECD's largest economies, 1995	201
11.2	East Asian economies' GDP per capita and real growth rates (%), 1970–1996	202
11.3	Macroeconomic indicators, 1990–95	212
11.4	Trade, balance of payments and the exchange rate (US$ bn), 1990–95	214
11.5	Hourly labour costs in manufacturing (US$), 1985 and 1995	222
11.6	Korea's exports and imports by commodity groups	226
11.7	International tariff barriers, 1988 and 1996	228
11.8	World's major exporters by value, fob, 1995 (US$ bn)	229
11.9	World's major importers by value, cif, 1995 (US$ bn)	230
11.10	Major trading partners (percentage of total trade)	230
11.11	Foreign direct investment in Korea (US$ mn)	231
11.12	Korea's outward foreign investment (US$ mn)	232
11.13	Australia–Korea trade by commodity, 1995–96	235

Figures

2.1A	Exports from Australia to European Union	24
2.1B	Imports from European Union to Australia	25
2.2A	Exports from Australia to USA	26
2.2B	Imports from USA to Australia	27
2.3A	Exports from Australia to Japan	28
2.3B	Imports from Japan to Australia	29
2.4A	Exports from Australia to China	30
2.4B	Imports from China to Australia	31
2.5A	Exports from Australia to Latin America	32
2.5B	Imports from Latin America to Australia	33
2.6A	Exports from Australia to India	34
2.6B	Imports from India to Australia	35
2.7A	Exports from Australia to ASEAN	36
2.7B	Imports from ASEAN to Australia	37

2.8A	Exports from Australia to Indochina	38
2.8B	Imports from Indochina to Australia	39
2.9	Actual exports and imports in (USD mn), Vietnam: 1981–1995	40
2.10	Actual and predicted exports (in USD mn), Vietnam: 1981–1995	41
2.11	Actual and predicted imports (in USD mn), Vietnam: 1981–1995	41
2.12	Actual/forecast imports, exports and trade balance, Vietnam: 1981–2020 (in USD)	42
10.1	Factors influencing environmental strategic focus in business firms	187
10.2	Example of an environmental policy	192

Foreword: Vietnam – A Dynamic and Competitive Market for All

Vietnam, a country with a population of 76 mn people in 1996, has been increasingly emerging as a huge open market that is both very dynamic and competitive in South East Asia.

In the field of economic activities, the average gross domestic product growth rate was 8.2 per cent while the figure of 1996 was 9.5 per cent. The output in agriculture, forestry and fishery increased by 4–8 per cent per annum, and food production reached 29 mn tons in 1996. Vietnam has become one of the largest rice exporters after the US and Thailand. In 1996, more than 3 mn tons of rice were produced. The industrial output grew considerably: 8 mn tons of crude oil, 7.3 mn tons of cement, 1 mn tons of steel. The services industry grew on average by 12 per cent per annum and exports by 20 per cent per annum for the past five years. The 1996 export volume was US$7 bn, an increase of 32 per cent from the previous year. The registered capital in foreign direct investment reached US$26 bn and the figure for 1996 only was about US$7 bn. Inflation had continued to go down and stood at 5 per cent in 1996, and the consumer price index was kept stable. The living conditions of the people have been improved. Those achievements have enabled us to move out of the stage of socioeconomic crises which started in the late 1980s and provided us with sufficient conditions and premises to advance into a higher stage of development, realizing gradually the national objectives of industrialization and modernization, turning Vietnam into an industrialized country by the year 2020.

We advocate a policy of multilateral cooperation and diversification of international relations with the motto: 'Vietnam wishes to befriend all countries in the world community, striving for peace, independence and development', and we have reaped encouraging fruits. At the end of 1996, Vietnam had established relations with 164 countries, normalized its ties with the US, signed the Cooperation Agreement with the European Union, become a full member of the Association of the South East Asian Nations (ASEAN) and taken part in the process of Asia–Europe economic cooperation. We now are preparing the groundwork in order to join the Asia-Pacific Economic Cooperation (APEC) and the World Trade Organization (WTO).

We are very pleased to see the fine growth in our bilateral relations with Australia over the past decades. Australia is one of Vietnam's important investment and trade partners. The two-way trade volume between the two countries had grown rapidly to reach nearly US$400 mn in 1996. In investment, Australia is listed among the ten largest investors in Vietnam with 50 projects for a total amount of nearly US$900 mn. We highly appreciate the goodwill of the government of Australia who, despite financial constraints, continues to give Vietnam substantial aid and keeps implementing, among other important projects, the North My Thuan bridge across the Mekong River in the southern part of Vietnam. This is indeed a practical contribution to the causes which will support economic and social development in Vietnam. As a result of these developments and relationships between the two countries, Vietnam has enjoyed a growing awareness on the part of the people from the research institutes, universities, colleges and business circles in Australia. Seminars and workshops have been held in Vietnam and Australia on aspects and issues of Vietnam's trade and investment. Books and newspapers have been published in these areas. However, at the international workshop on the trends and prospects of trade, investment and business in and with Vietnam in Sydney,which was held in November 1996 and organized by Professor Tran Van Hoa of Wollongong University, a number of well-known Australian and Vietnamese speakers provided a wealth of important and current information that will update the state of our knowledge about this bilateral trade, and presented their ideas in relation to the current situation and the prospects in Vietnam in the political, economic and social spheres. This provided the audience interested in Vietnam with more food for thought in furthering their explorations, research, and designs of business strategies for mutual economic, commercial and social benefits in Vietnam and Australia.

This workshop was held with the sponsorship and association of the Australian Research Council of the Department of Employment,

Education and Training, the Research Institute for Trade, the Ministry of Trade in Vietnam, the Vietnam Trade Office in Australia, the Research Institute for International Business, Department of Economics, and the Applied Economic Modelling Research Group, University of Wollongong.

I strongly believe that this workshop, the papers presented and discussions made by authoritative experts in the areas will contribute significantly to raising international trade, investment and cooperation in Vietnam and enhancing prospects for trade, investment, and business for Australian and other foreign corporations or individual business people outside Vietnam.

This book, which contains papers presented at the workshop and other relevant contributions, is strongly recommended to the people who are interested in Vietnam's market and who wish to do business successfully there in the near future.

PHAM NGOC SAN
Commercial Counsellor
Vietnam Trade Office
Sydney, Australia

Acknowledgements

The book is a collection of the invited papers presented at an *International Workshop on Trade, Investment, and Business in Vietnam,* convened and organized by Professor Tran Van Hoa of the University of Wollongong, and taking place on 20 November 1996 at the University Conference Centre, Sydney, Australia.

The idea behind the organization of the workshop is a formal venue in which academic staff from the universities, senior government officials from Australia and Vietnam, executives from private and public organizations, and interested members of the business community can get together to present new findings from their current work on identification of trends in trade, investment and business in Vietnam and East Asia, to discuss the implications and prospects arising from these trends, to take stock, to exchange experience, to find ways to avoid pitfalls and to develop and promote commerce in the region.

As reflected in the title of the workshop, the topics covered in the papers and the issues raised in subsequent discussions are wide-ranging and current, and they are capably dealt with by some of Australia's best known experts and writers in the fields. The topics include current and future trends in commodity trade and their prospects for the business community between Australia and all of the major trading blocks in the world, the areas of priority set by the government of Vietnam for expansion in trade, investment, and business, identification of the sectors in Vietnam for immediate development and promotion for investment, the problems business people may encounter in doing business in Vietnam and how to deal with them in an effective and productive way, the ethics and good corporate governance of enterprises operating in Vietnam, a survey of prospects for trade, investment, and business beyond Vietnam and into the Greater Mekong Basin region, a study of macroeconomic trends affecting commerce in Vietnam and East Asia, the implications of the World Trade Organization labour standards on companies operating in Vietnam or the ASEAN, and the environmental impact of the various activities in commerce.

The editor wishes to thank the speakers and participants at the workshop for their enthusiastic cooperation and for the high quality of their important contributions to the present book. Thanks are also due to the Australian Research Council – Collaborative Research Program, the Research Institute for International Business and the Applied Economic Modelling Research Group at the University of Wollongong for partially funding the workshop. The Vietnam Institute for Trade of the Ministry of Trade and the East Asia Analytical Unit of the Australian Department of Foreign Affairs and Trade, have provided useful and interesting insights with their participation and reports. Last but not least, the Vietnam Trade Office in Sydney and the New South Wales Vietnam Chamber of Commerce have contributed much valued time and resources to the organization of the workshop.

The present writer alone is responsible for any editorial errors or omissions that may remain in the book.

TRAN VAN HOA
Melbourne

Notes on the Contributors

Subhabrata Bobby Banerjee is a lecturer in the Department of Management at the University of Wollongong. Dr Banerjee's research interests include environmental management, public policy, sustainable development, and indigenous perspective on ecology. He has published in *Journal of Marketing* and various conference proceedings, among others.

Charles Harvie is an Associate Professor in the Department of Economics, University of Wollongong. He has teaching experience at Loughborough University, UK, and Wollongong University. His research covers energy, macroeconomics, monetary economics, and development and transition economics. Professor Harvie has published in *International Journal of Energy Research, Energy Economics, Journal of Economics and Finance*, among others.

Anne-Marie Humphries is Assistant Secretary of the East Asia Analytical Unit, Department of Foreign Affairs and Trade (DFAT), Australia. Her current interests include studies on the development issues in the countries in the ASEAN and their impact on Australia's business, investment, and trade.

Chris Nyland is the Director of the Research Institute for International Business, University of Wollongong. His teaching experience includes at Adelaide, Flinders and Wollongong Universities. His current research interests include the impact of globalization on the rights of labour; the history of human resource development strategies in developed and developing nations and the regulation of labour utilization. Professor Nyland has published widely in the history of economics and labour rights etc. in *History of Political Economy, British Journal of Sociology,* and *Journal of Economic Issues,* among others.

Eduardo Pol is a former Professor of Microeconomics at the University of Buenos Aires, Argentina, and currently a Senior Research Fellow in the Centre for Research Policy, University of

Wollongong, where he has been carrying out research in the fields of technological innovation, human capital, and economic growth. He has published papers in the *Review of Economic Studies, Economic Analysis and Policy, Atlantic Economic Journal,* and *Australian Economic Papers.*

Ho Trung Thanh received his ME from the University of Ukraine, Kharcov, Ukraine, and a graduate diploma from the Institute of Social Sciences, USSR. During 1986–1992, he taught at the Hanoi University, Vietnam. His fields of interest include advertising, marketing, trade promotion, and foreign investment. Currently Mr Thanh is Head of Research Unit, International Research, Consulting, and Training Center (ICTC), Vietnam Institute for Trade, Ministry of Trade, Vietnam.

Hoang Tho Xuan is Deputy Director of Vietnam Institute for Trade, and formerly the Director of the Domestic Trade Department, Ministry of Trade, Vietnam. Dr Xuan's research interests cover trade and marketing, and his teaching and training experience includes the University of Commerce, the National Economics University, and the National Center for Social Sciences and Humanities, Hanoi.

Tran Van Hoa is Associate Professor of Economics at the University of Wollongong, Australia. He has taught widely in universities in Australia, Asia and the USA. He has published numerous books and over 100 articles in the major applied and theoretical areas of economics, business, finance, energy and econometrics in Australian and international professional economics, finance and statistics journals. He is listed in *Who's Who in the World, Who's Who in Asia and Pacific Nations, Who's Who in Science and Engineering, 2000 Oustanding People of the 20th Century* and in the *Dictionary of International Biography.*

1
Trade, Investment and Business in Vietnam: An Overview

Tran Van Hoa

I. Introduction

Vietnam is an emerging, developing and transition economy in South East Asia with a market of 76 mn people (as recorded in 1996), vast untapped natural and human resources, and having a strategic location on the trade sea route from the Subcontinent to North East Asia. With the introduction of the economic reforms (known as *Doi Moi* or renovation) in 1987, Vietnam has embarked on a national programme of open-door and free-market policy to promote growth and development, to seek cooperation and assistance from non-socialist countries, to modernize the economy, and to encourage trade, investment, and business.

Vietnam is also a member of the Association of the South East Asian Nations (ASEAN) which, from a commercial perspective, can provide a bridge for outside trading countries to this regional economic trading block of seven countries and more than 400 mn people. Geographically and historically, Vietnam shares a long land border with Southern China, is one of the five countries controlling and using the great Mekong river and, being part of the former Indochina, can provide easy access to trade in Laos and Cambodia. Politically, Vietnam is one of the two major transition economies in Asia (the other one is China) with a traditionally strong economic cooperation and link between themselves and with other transition economies in Eastern Europe. This aspect can help to expand trade potential not only to Vietnam but also to other important markets in Asia and Europe.

II.   Scope of the book

The present book recognizes the important commercial potential and other cooperative and political considerations of Vietnam in this regional and global context. It aims first and foremost to contribute, by means of rigorous analytical and quantitative studies on main indicators and aspects of international commerce, to development and promotion of trade, investment and business between Vietnam and Australia and other foreign trading countries for mutual economic and social benefits in the short and long term. More specifically, the book brings together in one volume the major work of recent significant research on important trends, commercial prospects, and potential pitfalls and problems for developing and promoting trade, investment and business in Vietnam and some other important countries in East Asia. It also reports the pertinent findings for informed discussions, further studies, policy analysis, formulation and implementation by the research and business community in Australia and in other countries. Some of the features of the contributions to the book are described briefly below.

In Chapter 2, Professor Tran Van Hoa provides a detailed analysis of the trends and prospects for trade of up to fifty tradeable commodities between Australia and each of the major trading blocks in the world from the 1960s to the present day. These trading blocks include Australia's post-World War II traditional markets such as Europe, North America and Japan, and other new or non-traditional markets such as Latin America, India, China, South East Asia and Indochina. Using a comprehensive international trade databank (that is, France's CEPII-CHELEM), the analysis shows that the trends in trade of the traditional markets have been declining substantially both in the level and in the rate of change in the recent years, and Australia's chief prospects for trade expansion in the future lie unmistakably with the new trading blocks in Asia and the Subcontinent. Some forecasts of trade between Australia and the major country in Indochina, namely Vietnam, are calculated using latest official bilateral trade statistics, and recommendations on its development and promotion in some promising areas are also made.

In Chapter 3, Dr Hoang Tho Xuan and Professor Tran Van Hoa first give an overview of foreign investment in Vietnam since the introduction of Doi Moi in the country in 1987 and its projected trends by official estimates to the year 2000. They then discuss the relevant parts of the November 1996 amendments to the Law on Foreign Investment and their implications for both domestic and foreign investors. Specific areas of investment priorities in Vietnam and their capital requirements abroad within the government's master planning programme for the period 1996–2000 are also analysed.

Further analysis of the trends in foreign investment are given by Mr Ho Trung Thanh and Professor Tran Van Hoa in Chapter 4, separately and in more detail for the 20 sectors of the Vietnamese economy and their prospects for trade and business for Australian and other foreign companies and organizations in some significant sectors. In this chapter they also discuss various aspects and opportunities in business cooperation and official and semi-official ways to promote Australia's comparative advantages in commerce and expertise in Vietnam. One of these important opportunities is in the human resource development (HRD) area of training and consultancy provision.

In Chapter 5, Anne-Marie Humphries reports, as part of her findings on the new ASEAN countries, on the realities, the characteristics, the trends and the required strategies of the business environment in Vietnam. The findings are based on private surveys and official observations by Australian representatives in the country. Opportunities, benefits, problems and pitfalls in doing business in Vietnam are presented and evaluated. Experience gained and practical hints useful for more successful business cooperation between Australian and Vietnamese enterprises are also described in detail.

Chapter 6 is written by Professor Charles Harvie who has focused on the fact that the significance of Australia's traditional markets has declined in recent years and that developing economies have become Australia's major and most important trading partners and will continue to be so. Prospects for trade and business with Vietnam in a large number of sectors with great growth potential are in this context excellent for the wary who are aware of possible obstacles in doing business in Vietnam, want to know how to accommodate them and who have in mind not short-term profitability but sound long-term commercial strategies.

In Chapter 7, Anne-Marie Humphries looks at a new and major market (230 mn people) of the six countries in the Greater Mekong Basin subregion (Vietnam, Burma, Cambodia, Laos, Thailand and the Yunnan province of Southern China) and provides the background for its inception and development and the role played by the Australian government in it. Further explanations are also given as to why this 'corridor of commerce' offers excellent prospects for business development and expansion by foreign enterprises in the years to come.

Chapter 8 is written by Professor Chris Nyland and Dr Eduardo Pol and is devoted to a study of human resources in Vietnam and the five-point development strategy the government is committed to implement in the next five years to expand and enrich a labour force that will be suitable for the country's industrialization and modernization processes and improve the climate for foreign investors. The chapter also discusses Vietnam's human resources within an international context and labour standards, and examines how the government manages its four key strategic objectives in human resources development: effective management of population and health, education and training, poverty alleviation and job generation.

In Chapter 9, Tran Van Hoa discusses the role of ethics in doing business which has gained increasing importance and emphasis in recent years. He argues that, with the advent of information technology, we can witness the use of ingenuity, innovation and creativity in the people to produce advancement in sciences and in the way we do business (the so-called electronic commerce), but we can also witness situations where these characteristics can be used to produce (and detect) more easily any transgressions, initially for corporate interest but ultimately for personal gains. Two other aspects of modern commerce and industry have also brought about the rise of business ethics: the globalization of business via transnational corporations and the introduction of Total Quality Management (TQM) where total quality does not mean simply high quality but acceptable quality and responsibility in the management of a business organization in each stage of operation .

In Chapter 10, Dr Bobby Banerjee focuses on the problem of economic development and its possible impact on the environment in Vietnam, and explores ways the government can manage sustainable growth with adequate environment protection. The chapter also explains how the International Standards Organization (ISO) series 14 000 and 9000 can be used by Vietnam to develop policies that preserve its bio-diversity, create public awareness of environmental issues, promote sound environmental management systems in business organizations, develop and enforce appropriate environmental legislation, and focus on sustainable agriculture practices in the rural sector.

In Chapter 11, Dr Harvie surveys the economic achievements and problems of an East Asian dragon, namely South Korea, in recent years and attempts to bring to our attention the lessons of pluses and minuses in a developing economy with strong government intervention and emphasis on big enterprises (the chaebols) at the expense of a truly free-market operation and small- and medium-sized businesses. Economic, industrial and administrative reforms, he suggests, are the key to sustainable growth in the country.

III.   Further aspects of doing business

Finally, Chapter 12 sums up the findings of the main areas of investigation and report covered by the contributions to the book, and surveys emerging conclusions which are useful to policy formulation and implementation in trade, investment and business by government agencies, institutions, and the research and business communities. The chapter also contains provocative ideas for further studies and research which will form a natural extension of the work presented in this book and which will provide further contribution to development and promotion of trade, investment, and business between Vietnam and its trading countries in the world.

2
Trends and Prospects for Trade, Investment and Business in Vietnam

Tran Van Hoa

I. Global trends in Australia's trade

1. Australia's traditional market for international trade (that is, the United Kingdom [UK] and other European Union [EU] countries), started to decline since 1989 after a surge of activity during the years 1984–88 (see Figures 2.1A and 2.1B). Of the 10 categories of exported commodities (construction products, basic metals, textiles, wood paper, metal products, chemicals, mining, energy, agriculture, and food and beverages), the major categories are agriculture, energy, mining and metal products. According to the statistics collected for France's 1995 CEPII (Centre d'Etudes Prospectives et d'Informations Internationales) CHELEM (Comptes Harmonisées sur les Echanges et l'Economie Mondiale) international trade database, trade in agriculture to the EU alone fell from US$1833.9 mn in 1988 to US$991.1 mn in 1993. Total trade was US$4397.2 mn in 1992 but only US$3991.5 mn in 1993.

Imports from the European Economic Community (EEC) to Australia saw, on the other hand, a steady rise since 1967 with a total of US$1202.9 mn in 1967 and US$9682.9 mn in 1993. The largest categories are metal products (US$5019.6 mn in 1993), chemicals (US$1997.9 mn), wood paper (US$1146.7 mn), and food and beverages (US$447.1 mn).

2. For the US market, the trend in Australia's exports also started to fall since 1990 (see Figure 2.2A). The largest category, namely food and beverages, fell from US$1017.4 mn in 1990 to US$900.7 mn

in 1993. Australia's exports to the US were at the peak of US$3007.7 mn in 1990, but decreased to US$2460.3 mn in 1993.

Australia's imports (see Figure 2.2B) from the United States totalled US$813.9 mn in 1967 and reached US$8046.2 mn in 1993. The largest category is metal products but this has declined from US$5632.9 mn in 1990 to US$4929.7 mn in 1993. The categories with a constant light growth rate during the period 1967 to 1993 are chemicals and wood paper.

3. Australia's exports to Japan (see Figure 2.3A) had had a steady rise since 1967 with US$692.5 mn in 1967 and US$10 466.9 mn in 1993. The largest exported categories are energy and food and beverages, with US$4154.2 mn and US$1954.5 mn respectively in 1993.

Australia's imports from Japan since 1967 had been dominated by a single category 'metal products' with US$145.9 mn in 1967 and US$6345.1 mn in 1993 and showed a generally rising trend (see Figure 2.3B). The second largest category is chemicals with US$42.1 mn in 1967 and US$549.3 mn in 1993. The third largest category is wood paper and basic metals which have shown a declining trend since 1988 (with US$332.1 mn and US$371.0 mn respectively in 1988 and US$290.5 mn and US$227.7 mn respectively in 1993).

The above analysis of trade between Australia and the EEC, the US and Japan seems to indicate that exports from Australia to the EEC and the US have declined substantially, and exports to Japan have stagnated. A strategic solution is obviously to look for other markets with potential for trade with Australia.

4. Trade between Australia and China also saw a steady rise since 1972, with exports from Australia totalling US$27.5 mn in 1972 and US$1105.3 mn in 1993. The largest categories are agriculture (US$7.1 mn in 1972 and US$498.9 mn in 1993) and mining (with no export in 1972 and US$323.7 mn in 1993).

The data extracted from CEPII-CHELEM also reveal that exports from Australia to China have subsided since 1986 (see Figure 2.4A). The reasons may be that China has found other trading partners, Australia does not still have the comparative advantage in its commodities to export to China, or the political situation in China has created uncertainty in its demand for imports from Australia and other countries. These are important issues for trade agencies and business councils in Australia to discuss, evaluate and find appropriate solutions. This is particularly true when the income level of the

Chinese population has been growing fast and the market is huge with over 1.2 bn people.

Australia's imports from China (see Figure 2.4B) show an exponential growth between 1967 and 1993 with a total of US$27 mn in 1967 and US$1947.3 mn in 1993. The largest categories in descending order are textiles (US$948.4 mn in 1993), metal products (US$461 mn), wood paper (US$278.3 mn), chemicals (US$120.7 mn) and construction products (US$47.5 mn).

5. Exports from Australia to the Latin American countries (see Figure 2.5A) have an explosive growth since 1983 totalling US$102.3 mn in 1983 and US$358.5 mn in 1993. The largest exported categories are energy (US$178.9 mn in 1993), agriculture (US$57.9 mn), food and beverages (US$54.0 mn) and metal products (US$31.9 mn).

Again with the exception of energy, exports from Australia to the Latin American countries appear to be declining. Trade prospects here are therefore not attractive. Solutions to the problem should be explored.

Australia's imports from the Latin American countries (see Figure 2.5B) saw a rise between 1967 and 1989 (with total exports of US$16.2 mn in 1967 and US$605.3 mn in 1989) but the trend has declined since then (US$443.7 mn in 1993). One interesting feature of Australia's imports from the Latin American countries is that the value of all categories of imports widely fluctuated between 1967 and 1993. Basic metals have a spectacular fall from US$136.1 mn in 1989 to US$29.2 mn in 1993.

6. Australia's exports to India reveal a highly fluctuating pattern with a total of US$36.4 mn in 1969 and US$540 mn in 1993 (see Figure 2.6A). The largest category of exports is energy (US$332.7 mn in 1993) and agriculture (US$91 mn). Exports of metal products were US$42.5 mn in 1993 but these fluctuated widely and reached only US$8.3 mn in 1991.

India as a market for exports from Australia needs further promotion on the part of the public and private sectors in Australia both to increase and to stabilize trade.

Australia's main imports from India (see Figure 2.6B) are textiles and these had shown a steady rise (US$25.1 mn in 1967 and US$133.3 mn in 1993). Total imports from India were US$32.6 mn in 1969 and US$250.4 mn in 1993. Australia also imported agricultural products (US$31 mn in 1993), metal products (US$29.8 mn), and chemicals (US$20.3 mn) from India.

7. Australia's exports to the ASEAN (see Figure 2.7A) have a faster growth pattern since 1972, totalling US$172.8 mn in 1967 and US$3644.7 mn in 1993. The major categories of exports in descending order are basic metals (US$762.7 mn in 1993), energy (US$711.19 mn), metal products (US$640.0 mn), agriculture (US$500.3 mn), food and beverages (US$485.0 mn), chemicals (US$260.4 mn), and wood paper (US$147.5 mn).

From these trends, we believe ASEAN is a good market and will remain so for Australia's exports of all 10 categories of tradeable commodities used in this chapter. More efforts by the public and private sectors in Australia to develop and promote exports to the ASEAN should be undertaken as a priority.

One category of Australia's imports from the ASEAN (see Figure 2.7B) with a steady rise since 1967 is metal products (US$0.1 mn in 1967 and US$1063.1 mn in 1993). The import of energy had its peak in 1982 (US$1008.9 mn) but in 1993 it stood at US$681.4 mn. All other categories of imports, however, show a rising trend.

8. With the countries in Indochina, exports from Australia (see Figure 2.8A) had had a steady rise since 1985 with a total of US$2.7 mn and US$85.3 mn in 1993. The largest exported categories are wood paper (US$45.2 mn in 1993) and metal products (US$22.2 mn).

Apart from wood paper, all other categories of tradeable commodities appear to have good prospects for Australia's exports to Indochina. Particularly important for promotion in terms of their larger share of the exports chart are metal products, basic metals and chemicals. It appears from the trend of exports, however, that there exist good prospects for trade between Australian and Indochina in all categories of tradeable commodities.

Australia's imports from Indochina (see Figure 2.8B) started in 1970 (US$0.1 mn) but now (1993) stood at US$171.0 mn. The single most important category (since 1991) is energy (US$140.7 mn in 1993). However, food and beverages and agriculture have shown a continuing rise since 1985 (US$1.5 mn and US$6.4 mn respectively in 1985 and US$7.2 mn and US$14.3 mn respectively in 1993).

II.   Vietnam's trade: general survey

For many years before 1989, international trade in Vietnam was small in volume and value, and limited to the Commonwealth of the Independent States (CIS) and other socialist countries. The recorded explosion of imports and exports from and to non-CIS countries took place in 1988 and 1989. Exports rose from R-US$854.2 mn in 1987 to R-US$1038.4 mn in 1988 (achieving a growth rate of 21.6 per cent annually) and R-US$1946.0 mn in 1989 (87.4 per cent). Non-CIS (US$-area) imports rose from US$523.3 mn in 1987 to US$804.3 mn in 1988 (53.7 per cent) and US$897.4 mn in 1989 (11.6 per cent) (see Vietnam Statistical Yearbook 1994).

Coupled with this growth in trade is, through the multiplier effect in the economy, an accompanying increasing trend in investment and business, and subsequently in the output growth and the standard of living.

A reason for this spectacular increase in international trade (which favoured exports especially more than imports) – in investment and business – is the introduction of Doi Moi in 1986 emphasizing, in our judgement, what are essentially microeconomic reforms, and the passing of the Law on Foreign Investment by the National Assembly in 1987. More importantly, the active implementation of this law by the Vietnamese government and its agencies both in the North and especially in the South also contributed to the increase.

A further prospect of expanded international trade which follows the lifting of the embargo by the US on 4 February 1994, and a subsequent relaxation of trade in products involving US copyrights and patents through the third countries having business in Vietnam, is considered by many economic analysts to be an outstanding impetus to growth by all trading companies. The trend in 1995 and 1996 is further supplemented by Vietnam's membership of the Association of the South East Asian Nations (ASEAN) and its ensuring regional trade expansion in July 1995.

Our own calculations of future trends in Vietnam's trade, which are based on an estimated dynamic model using the time series data from the 1995 World Bank database and the Australian Department of Foreign Affairs and Trade (DFAT) statistics, reveal a significant exponential growth pattern for both exports and imports during

1981 to 1995 (see Figures 2.9, 2.10 and 2.11). More importantly, this strong upward trend in trade is found to continue well into the twenty-first century (that is, from 1996 to 2020, see Figure 2.12). Our calculations also predict, at the 1981–1995 rate of economic development, a permanent trade deficit (imports exceeding exports) for Vietnam ranging from US$11 641.21 mn in 2000 to US$71 862.91 mn in 2010 and US$218 531 mn in 2020, both at current prices.

In fact, more recent trade data statistics compiled by Vietnam's Ministry of Trade indicated that during the period 1991–1995, total turnover of exports reached US$17bn and that of imports US$22bn. For 1996 the statistics (up to 31 December 1996) also indicated that the volume of exports was US$7bn (an increase of 32.1 per cent over 1995 and 6.2 per cent higher than the average growth rate of exports during the period 1991–95). Also in 1996, rice was one of the commodities with a high growth over 1995 (56.8 per cent) – in 1997, Vietnam has set a target of exporting 3 mn tonnes of rice. Next in the list were shoes for export the growth rate of which was 50 per cent over 1995, followed by textiles for export with an increase of 29.4 per cent over 1995. Of Vietnam's total exports, only 30 per cent are for manufactured goods, with the rest for raw materials and primary products.

Foreign invested enterprises exported twice as much as in 1995 and made up 11 per cent of the turnover of exports and 18.2 per cent of the turnover of imports. Total turnover of imports in 1996 reached US$11bn or 30 per cent higher than in 1995. The main components of imports were machinery, equipment and material. Consumer goods shared only 9.3 per cent of total turnover of imports.

Unless exports, especially manufactured goods (imports), from Vietnam increase (decrease) substantially in the next decade or so, the implications of this permanent or long-term trade deficit at least to 2010 are far-reaching for overseas trading companies and government foreign trade agencies, as well as investing individuals who want to do business in Vietnam. The weak representation of the manufacturing industry in the exporting sector, as mentioned earlier, also has a strong influence on the industrialization and export expansion policy of the government of Vietnam.

These developments are entwined with the present and future international trade policy in Vietnam as promulgated or implied in the public statements after the recent 8th National Congress in Hanoi, and the impact of regional (such as ASEAN and European Union) and international (such as the World Trade Organization [WTO]) trade policy abroad towards Vietnam. More importantly, the strong competition in trade, investment and business from the growing free-market or transition economies in the Asia Pacific and China provides another obstacle or challenge for economic policy-makers in Vietnam.

III.   Vietnam's actual and forecast demand for trade

The demand for overseas commodities (imports), capital and transfer in Vietnam rose from R-US$1314.2 mn in 1980 to R-US$5000 mn (including FDI) in 1994 and US$7500 mn in 1995, achieving an annual growth rate of 35.7 per cent. This demand comes from the central and local administrations with the former having a greater share (59 per cent). However, in recent years, the demand by local administration has grown faster. In 1993, imports totalled R-US$3924 mn, and the largest share of total demand for imports is in factors (means) of production with R-US$3311.2 mn or 83.4 per cent of imports, of which fuel and raw materials account for 72.1 per cent, machinery 19.2 per cent, and complete (finished) and petroleum equipment 8.7 per cent.

Geographically, in 1993, the largest share of imports was from non-ASEAN Asian countries totalling R-US$1400.3 mn or 35.7 per cent, followed by ASEAN countries and Laos and Cambodia with R-US$1318.5 mn or 33.6 per cent, by Europe with 17.6 per cent, and then by the Oceania (Australia and New Zealand) with 8.4 per cent.

In terms of individual countries, in 1993, Singapore has the largest trade with Vietnam at 27 per cent of total imports, followed by Japan at 11.6 per cent, and then by France at 6.8 per cent.

In 1994, imports by Vietnam totalled US$5000 mn, chalking up a growth rate from 1993 of 27.4 per cent. By our conservative estimates, however, total imports by Vietnam could, based on the recent official trade statistics, rise to at least US$25 360.44 mn in 2000, US$127 512.15 mn in 2010, and US$364 156.03 mn in 2020, all at current prices.

IV. Vietnam's actual and forecast supply of trade

In contrast to the growth rate of imports, exports (or supply of trade) from Vietnam since 1980 has grown more rapidly, from R-US$338.6 mn in 1980 to R-US$3600 mn in 1994, and US$5200 mn. This gives an extremely high annual growth rate of 95.98 per cent.

A remarkable feature of Vietnam's export value is that such a high growth rate was achieved even though the export price index actually fell by as much as 4.5 per cent during the period 1991–1993.

During the years 1995 and 1996, Vietnam's exports, at the annual growth rates of 22.2 per cent and 23.5 per cent respectively, have been predicted to exceed the increases in exports of all major ASEAN countries such as Indonesia, Malaysia, the Philippines, Singapore and Thailand (Tan, 1996).

In fact, these export growth rates exceed those in all newly industrialized countries (NIC), the North America Free Trade Area (NAFTA), and the Closer Economic Relation (CER) economies, as well as Japan, China, Chile, Colombia and Peru (Tan, 1996, p. 4).

In 1993, exports totalled R-US$2985.2 mn in which central management shared 57.5 per cent, and local management 42.5 per cent. The largest commodity group in these exports is heavy industrial products and minerals which at R-US$1014 mn accounts for 34 per cent of the total value, followed by agricultural products for 30.8 per cent, and then by light industries and handicraft goods for 17.6 per cent. Seafood products have a reasonable share at 14.3 per cent.

Timber and other forestry products have, on the other hand, a declining trend since 1991, falling from R-US$175.5 mn (8.4 per cent) of all exports in 1991 to R-US$97.5 mn (3.3 per cent) in 1993.

Geographically, Asian countries purchased, in 1993, a total of R-US$2167.5 mn or 72.6 per cent of all exports from Vietnam. This group is headed by Japan with R-US$936.9 mn (31.4 per cent), followed by Singapore with R-US$380.3 mn (12.7 per cent), and Hong Kong with R-US$169 mn (5.7 per cent). Taiwan and China bought R-US$141.9 mn (4.8 per cent) and R-US135.8 mn (4.5 per cent) respectively from Vietnam in 1993. The latter is ranked equally with Russia with purchases at R-US$135.4 mn. Other countries with an import value of approximately R-US$100 mn from Vietnam in 1993 are South Korea, Cambodia and France.

Our conservative estimates which are based on recent official trade statistics would predict that, following the same pattern of growth during 1981 to 1995, Vietnam's exports will reach US$13 719.236 mn in 2000, US$55 629.24 mn in 2010, and US$145 624.11 mn in 2020, all at current prices.

The growths of both exports and imports and their imbalance in the economy of Vietnam will have important implications for trade between Vietnam and other countries including especially Australia. Some of these trade issues and prospects are discussed in more detail below.

V.   Vietnam's prospects for trade to 2010

1.   Current trends

In the financial year 1992/1993, statistics collected by the Australian Bureau of Statistics (*Foreign Trade in Australia: Merchandise Exports and Imports, Detailed Country Tables*, Australian Bureau of Statistics cat. nos 5436.0 and 5437.0, various issues) show Australia's imports from Vietnam were worth AUD237 mn. In return, Australia's exports to Vietnam were worth only AUD76 mn. The trend also indicates a remarkable growth in trade between Australia and Vietnam, with imports from Vietnam increasing from AUD18 mn in 1990/1991 to AUD79 mn in 1991/1992, and exports from Australia increasing from AUD25 mn in 1990/1991, to AUD50 mn in 1991/1992.

According to 1995 estimates by Vietnam's Ministry of Trade, trade openness (exports plus imports) between Australia and Vietnam totalled AUD366.8 mn in 1993, and this consists of AUD251.3 mn in exports and AUD115.5 mn in imports. The increase of this trade level over that in 1990 is 900 per cent. This is a remarkable achieve- ment and a significant contribution to the country's high growth rate even though the US embargo on Vietnam was in force during the period.

In 1994, trade openness rose by 23.5 per cent to AUD452.9 mn with AUD289.4 mn in exports (a rise of 15 per cent) and AUD163.5 mn in imports (a rise of 41.5 per cent). This rapid growth in trade between Australia and Vietnam is among the fastest rates of growth in the world during this period. In 1995, there was a trade openness of AUD474.8 mn of which Australia's exports to Vietnam (including trade through third countries) accounted for AUD188 mn and Australia's imports from Vietnam accounted for AUD286 mn (see *Vietnam Country Brief,* April 1996, DFAT).

In view of the increasing rate of growth in trade between Vietnam and other Asian countries in general and between Vietnam and Australia in particular in the next fifteen years or so, there exists a huge prospect for further trade, investment and business expansion between the two countries. This 3-level expansion is particularly in favour of Australia's potential exports to Vietnam. At present, the major commodities exported to Australia from Vietnam are crude oil and refined petroleum and oils, textiles, coffee and coffee substitutes, and seafood, estimated by DFAT to be AUD286.8 mn in total in 1995.

2.   The prospects and implementation proposals

Five elements in the current status of Vietnam's international trade provide a good prospect for trade expansion by Australia in Vietnam:

(1) The trade imbalance with Australia in favour of Vietnam at this stage,
(2) The small share of Vietnam's imports from Australia total imports,
(3) Vietnam having a long-term trade deficit overall into the twenty-first century as described above,
(4) Vietnam as a conduit to the ASEAN and greater Indochina markets,
(5) Vietnam as a bridgehead to the huge market in southern China across the border in the north of Vietnam.

These would indicate that greater efforts in a number of specific areas of activity on the part of the private and government trade sectors in Australia can be made to expand their exports of goods, capital and expertise to Vietnam.

These efforts necessarily involve investment by Australia in Vietnam. The investment is either in terms of capital or funds (foreign direct investment [FDI]), human resources (training, consulting and education), and expertise and technology (technology transfer) on the part of the Australian business and institutional community, and overseas aid or loan programmes on the part of the Australian government.

The type of investment (joint ventures, wholly owned, subsidiaries, BOT [build, operate and transfer] and its variations) is dependent on the specific case under consideration. The feasibility of the investment also depends on:

(1) Vietnam's physical infrastructure (telecommunications, roads, power, buildings and offices and other utilities),
(2) Human infrastructure (skilled labour and qualified personnel),
(3) Legal infrastructure (laws and by laws on FDI and foreign ownership, land lease etc), and
(4) Regional or international competition in capital fund allocation and in trade and business.

Below, we identify and discuss only in general terms the broadly defined areas in which Australia has, from our own information sources, econometric estimates and official predictions, good prospects in terms of the current and capital accounts of the balance of payments (including profits), and some specific activity and strategy it can take or adopt to exploit these opportunities. Details on the specific sectors of the Vietnamese economy are discussed in our sector-by-sector and category-by-category study on FDI, trade and business to be reported elsewhere.

(a)   Trade, investment and business promotion

This can be achieved through trade promotion, exhibition of products, niches-identification, partner-identification, capital-raising, and contract-signing efforts of both the Australian government agencies (such as Austrade) and the private business sectors.

In a recent report on Vietnamese companies' knowledge about Australia and its trade activity, it is found that almost all of the Vietnamese companies interviewed in our survey in Hanoi during February–April 1995 and covering 12 major sectors of the economy, indicate that they do not know anything about Australia and wish to make contact with Australian companies for business purposes.

Contact through trade associations or chambers of commerce and industry in both countries (Vietnam Chamber of Commerce and Industry, Australia–Vietnam Business Council, the national and state chambers of manufactures and commerce and other trade organizations in Australia) can be made in order to introduce likely business investment partners.

This contact could help to avoid mismatched, misrepresented, or ill-suited connections with damaging results to both parties and to further prospects of trade, investment and business as many overseas companies operating in Vietnam have reported in recent years.

(b) Specialist training in trade and business

With the introduction of a stock exchange centre or even a commodity market centre (in the mould of the Chicago or London commodity trade centre) in Hanoi in the near future, the capital and commodity market will have better facilities for attracting capital inflows or engaging in derivatives operation and for the distribution of these funds into profitable industries in an efficient manner.

An obstacle to this interesting development is an acute shortage of skilled manpower and administrators to manage physical and financial commodities in Vietnam. An opportunity for Australia's training in this area is further enhanced by the recent decision by the government of Vietnam to retrain wholesale 20 000 of its senior cadres or officials. The areas of training are management, manufacturing technology, food processing, hi tech and finance, to name a few.

Specialist training in this area of human resources development is a priority in the commodity and capital markets and also in the financial, non-financial, education and banking systems in Vietnam. This type of training has been identified recently by Vietnam's Ministry of Trade and the Office of the Government (the prime minister's department). It is in this type of activity that Australia has a fair and historical comparative advantage and it could provide much needed expertise for Vietnam in the future.

Three recent initiative in this respect are

(a) a programme of short course (4-week) training in Health Services Provision,
(b) regional (such as ASEAN) and global (such as WTO) economic integration, and
(c) Commodity Market Operation.

These initiatives are for government officials and business people in Vietnam.

The initiatives were proposed by Professor Tran Van Hoa from Wollongong University with the collaboration of the College of Advanced Health Studies in Nam Dinh, the International Consulting and Training Center (ICTC) of the Vietnam Institute for Trade in Hanoi, the National Economics University, the Foreign Trade University, and the Economic Modelling and Forecasting Program at Chulalongkorn University in Bangkok, Thailand.

Other initiatives include

(a) a programme to look at advances in information technology (IT), its implications for developed countries and its potential adaptations to developing economies in the Asia Pacific, and
(b) a programme to use applied business and economic practice for policy analysis, policy formulation and implementation in other ASEAN countries to adapt it for possible applications in Vietnam.

Some training support has been given by the Australian government in this area mainly through AusAID, Department of Employment, Education and Training (DEET) and the Australia–ASEAN Economic Cooperation Program which initiated the research development and training programmes in recent years.

The private sector in Australia at this stage plays a small role in this activity. To bring this business opportunity to the attention of Australian corporations and institutions and interested parties adequately would be a worthwhile effort on the part of trade promoters, public or private.

(c)   International competition in commodities trade and its solution

Another prominent feature of the growth in international trade in Vietnam in recent years is a surplus in exports, especially the surplus of 1992 which was mainly from crude oil exports that year.

In addition to crude petroleum and oils, Vietnam also exports seafoods, coffee and coffee substitutes, clothing, footwear, travel cases and so on. The volume of trade in these commodities is not large, due to strong competition from other countries in the region, especially China with its better quality products and cheaper prices.

Australia and Vietnam could mutually benefit in the form of technology transfer in manufacturing and marketing in the long term, through joint-venture activity, or in the short term through suitably designed training programmes.

It also can provide funds for market research by Vietnamese or Australian experts or consultants to identify suitable new markets, specific areas of market penetration in Vietnam for Australian goods, their substitutions and competitive pricing, and vice versa. These funds can be either independent (without industry partners) or industry-collaborative (with contributing industry partners). Some of these initiatives have been taken up in some of DEET-ARC and DFAT-AusAID research grant programmes in recent years.

(d)   Marketing and commodity regime expansion

Vietnam's imports from Australia include refined oil which accounted for one third of all trade with it in 1994 Other imports from Australia include electrical products, iron steel, civil engineering equipment, heating and cooling equipment, telecommunications equipment, medicaments, machinery and transport equipment, milk and butter, wool and animal hair, chemicals, cereal preparations and foodstuff.

A promotion campaign to introduce other well-known Australian products, such as sugar and wheat, and expertise, such as cold storage technology, high-tech printing and food processing of high quality for export to such third countries as Japan and EU, would certainly enhance trade flows from Australia to Vietnam.

(e)   Pricing policy and transport cost issues

Exports from Vietnam to Australia can also be re-exported to other countries as is the case with crude oil exports in recent years. The market of re-exportation is important and viable in the sense that the products Vietnam imports from Australia are of a better quality and usually in high demand even though they are more expensive.

A difficult problem in this case is the long-distance transport and associated relatively higher costs between Vietnam and Australia. These factors might render Australian products less competitive in relation to similar offered goods from other trading countries with Vietnam. A possible solution is joint ventures between Australian and Vietnamese partners, with production and processing facilities in Vietnam. The marketing of the products made can be handled by the affiliated companies in Australia through the normal channels or through the Internet.

Increased efficiency and productivity through economies of scale and high tech production, management and distribution may also overcome these problems. While joint ventures in Vietnam are standard solutions adopted to similar problems of competition in prices by many transnational companies in other parts of the world, the case may exist for even 100 per cent-owned companies in Vietnam to face competition locally or internationally if they possess comparative advantages.

That is to say, another solution here is to create suitable niches in trade (for example, Telstra in telecommunications, or BHP for oil and gas exploration) for the Australian goods and services that can be identified as having a comparative advantage in Vietnam.

VI.   Forward looking trade strategy in Vietnam

As a by-product of its niche generation in Vietnam, Australia should also expect to have the knock-on effects of its experience and operation in Vietnam in other countries in the region, notably Cambodia, Laos and Myanmar (the so-called Greater Indochina), and other ASEAN countries and Southern China (the Mekong Basin subregion).

This is a long-term strategy on trade, investment and business in a global context and is suitable for large-size companies with adequate internal or external funds for expansion and development.

As part of a niche creation programme, it is interesting to note that plans have been made by Vietnam and Australia to exchange trade information, enhance contact between businesses in the two countries, mount exhibitions of Vietnamese products in Sydney and Melbourne (April 1994) and Hanoi (December 1996), and provide short training courses on market research, banking facilities, commodity market operation, risk management, and so on.

These efforts have helped to improve trade, investment and business between Australia and Vietnam but potential for increasing the level of activity is even higher between Australia and Vietnam.

VII.   General remarks

Our main conclusion would be that while Australia's products and services are well regarded in terms of quality in Vietnam generally, their business potential is not understood by many people and organizations in Vietnam. A solution in this case would be more active promotion, through a variety of media and routes, of Australian goods and services in Vietnam. This can be done via trade exhibitions, mass media advertisement, stronger investment commitments, and wide-ranging cooperation between the two countries.

This action is more relevant when one takes notes that, in the next ten years or so, Vietnam has plans to produce more imports substitution goods and at the same time to promote greater exports. To achieve this, Vietnam also has plans to train or retrain its core officials and senior business executives in many sectors of the economy.

The prospects for trade in goods and services for Australia are there to exploit given the pattern of growth and economic development in Vietnam.

The prospects are further enhanced when it is recognized that a bridgehead in Vietnam for Australian companies and investing individuals would also provide a bridgehead for other countries in Indochina and Myanmar, the ASEAN and Southern China, which together constitute a market of about 700 mn people with a very high output growth rate representing, as a result, the fastest rise in the standard of living and, subsequently, the consumption pattern in the world over the next decade or so.

References

ARC Consultants Reports (1996), *Prospects for Sectoral Trade, Investment and Business in Vietnam*, ICTC, Vietnam Institute for Trade, Hanoi, Vietnam.

Australian Bureau of Statistics, Canberra, Australia, various statistical bulletins.

CHELEM International Trade Database (1995), Paris, France, CEPII and WEFA.

Ministry of Trade, Vietnam, various reports and documents.

NETSCAPE: Internet, *Foreign Investment in Vietnam*, March 1997.

Statistical Yearbook of Vietnam, Hanoi, Vietnam, various issues.

Tan, J. L. H (1996), 'Introductory Overview: AFTA in the Changing International Economy', in Tan (ed.), *AFTA in the Changing International Economy*, Singapore: Institute of Southeast Asian Studies.

Trade and Economic Bulletin, ICTC, Vietnam Institute for Trade, Ministry of Trade, Hanoi, Vietnam, various issues in 1996 and 1997.

Vietnam Country Brief, April 1996, Canberra, Department of Foreign Affairs and Trade.

Appendix I

CHELEM's Classification of Sectors

1. *Construction products*
   - (1) Cement
   - (2) Ceramics
   - (3) Glass

2. *Basic metals*
   - (1) Iron steel
   - (2) Tubes

3. *Textiles*
   - (1) Yarns fabrics
   - (2) Clothing
   - (3) Knitwear
   - (4) Carpets
   - (5) Leather

4. *Wood paper*
   - (1) Wood articles
   - (2) Furniture
   - (3) Paper
   - (4) Printing
   - (5) Miscellaneous manufactures

5. *Metal products*
   - (1) Structural metals
   - (2) Miscellaneous hardware
   - (3) Engines
   - (4) Agricultural equipment
   - (5) Machinery tools
   - (6) Construction equipment
   - (7) Specialized machines
   - (8) Arms
   - (9) Precision instruments
   - (10) Clock-making
   - (11) Optics
   - (12) Electric components
   - (13) Consumer electronics
   - (14) Telecommunications equipment
   - (15) Computer equipment
   - (16) Domestic electric appliances
   - (17) Electronic equipment
   - (18) Electronic appliances
   - (19) Vehicle components
   - (20) Cars
   - (21) Communications vehicles
   - (22) Ships
   - (23) Aeronautics

6. *Chemicals*
    (1) Basic inorganic chemicals
    (2) Fertilizers
    (3) Basic organic chemicals
    (4) Paints
    (5) Toilet
    (6) Pharmaceutical products
    (7) Plastics
    (8) Plastic articles
    (9) Pneumatic tyres

7. *Mining*
    (1) Iron ores S.
    (2) Non-ferrous ores
    (3) Unprocessed minerals n.e.s.

8. *Energy*
    (1) Coals
    (2) Crude oil
    (3) Natural gas
    (4) Coke
    (5) Refined petroleum products
    (6) Manufactured gas

9. *Agriculture*
    (1) Cereals
    (2) Other edible agricultural products
    (3) Non-edible agricultural products

10. *Food, beverages, tobacco*
    (1) Cereal products
    (2) Fats
    (3) Meat
    (4) Preserved meat
    (5) Preserved vegetables
    (6) Sugar
    (7) Animal food
    (8) Beverages
    (9) Manufactured tobaccos

11. *Miscellaneous*
    (1) Jewels
    (2) Gold

Appendix II

Trends in Australia's Trade with Major Countries and Economic Regions in the World 1967–1993

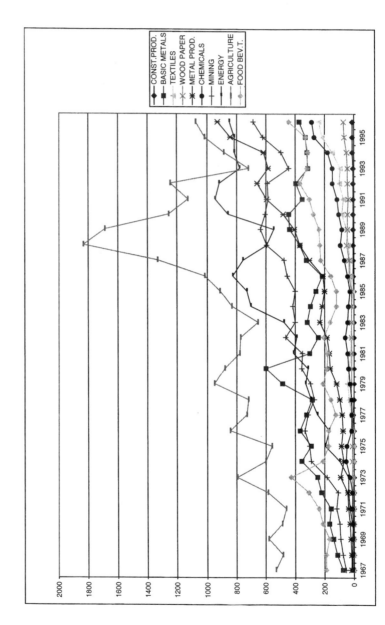

Figure 2.1A Exports from Australia to European Union

25

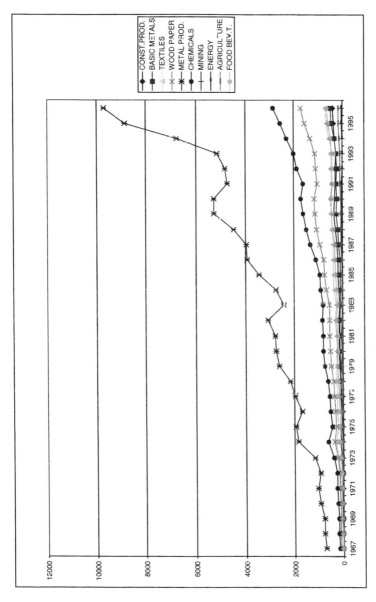

Figure 2.1B Imports from European Union to Australia

Source: CEPII-CHELEM.

26

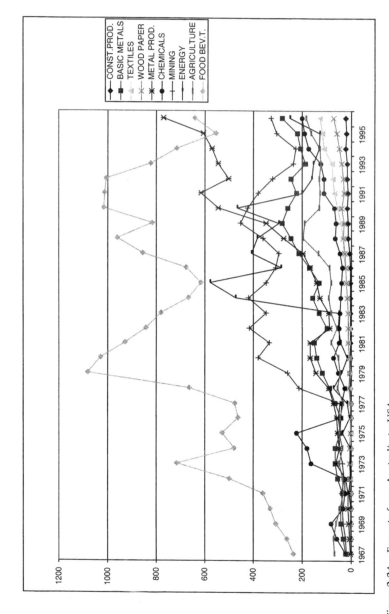

Figure 2.2A Exports from Australia to USA

Source: CEPII-CHELEM.

27

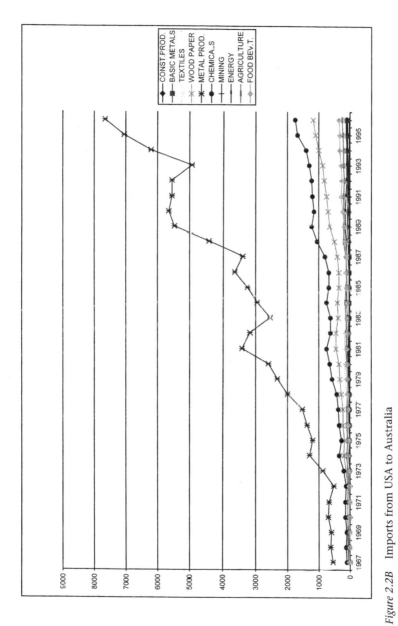

Figure 2.2B Imports from USA to Australia

Source: CEPII-CHELEM.

28

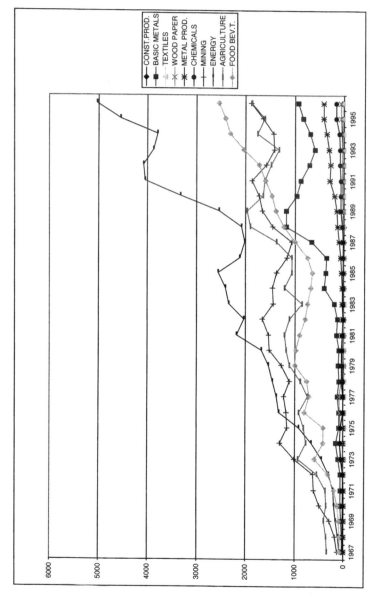

Figure 2.3A Exports from Australia to Japan

Source: CEPII-CHELEM.

29

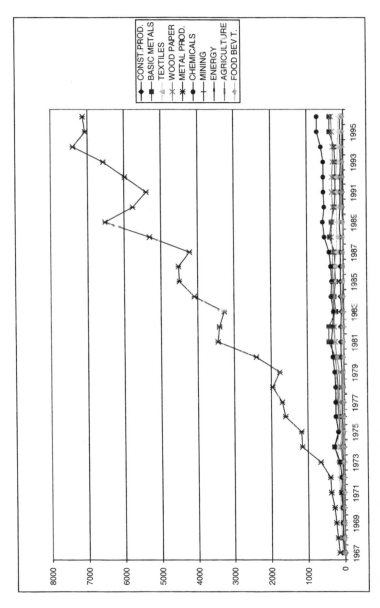

Figure 2.3B Imports from Japan to Australia

Source: CEPII-CHELEM.

30

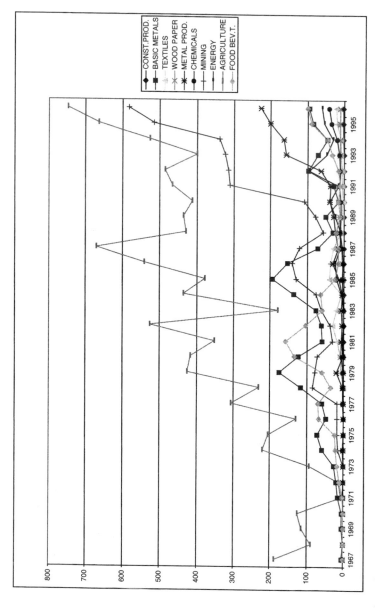

Figure 2.4A   Exports from Australia to China

Source: CEPII-CHELEM.

31

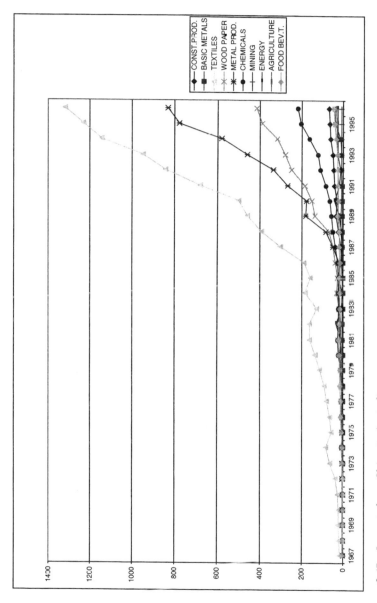

Figure 2.4B Imports from China to Australia

Source: CEPII-CHELEM.

32

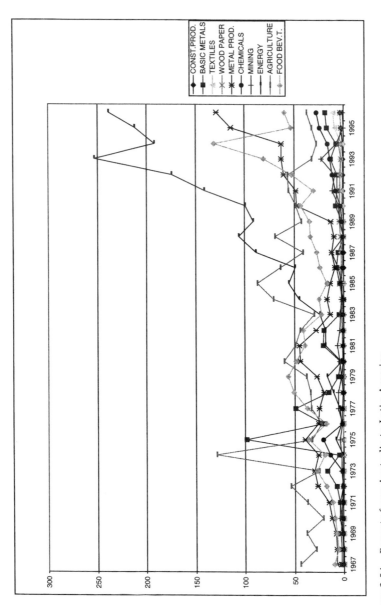

Figure 2.5A Exports from Australia to Latin America

Source: CEPII-CHELEM.

33

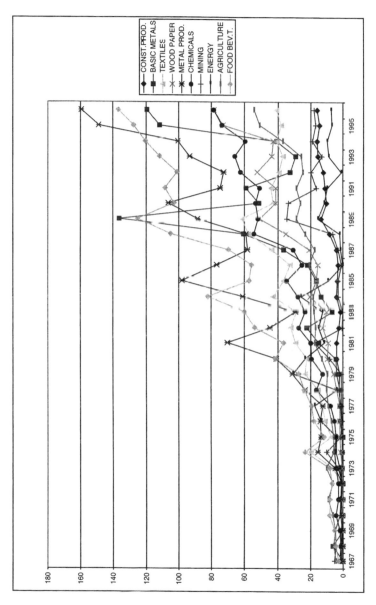

Figure 2.5B Imports from Latin America to Australia

Source: CEPII-CHELEM.

34

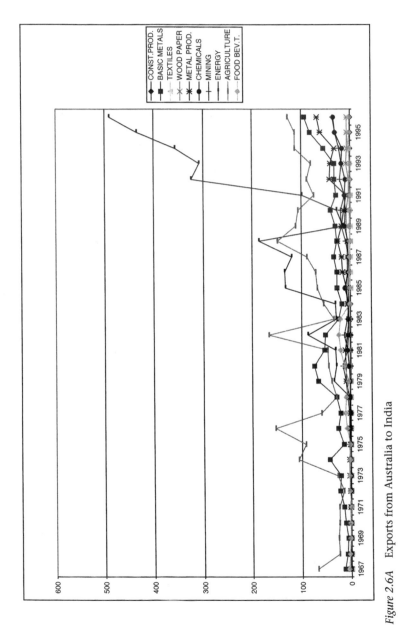

Figure 2.6A Exports from Australia to India

Source: CEPII-CHELEM.

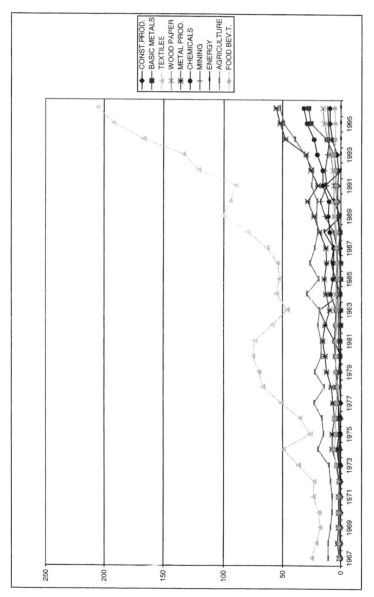

Figure 2.6B Imports from India to Australia

Source: CEPII-CHELEM.

36

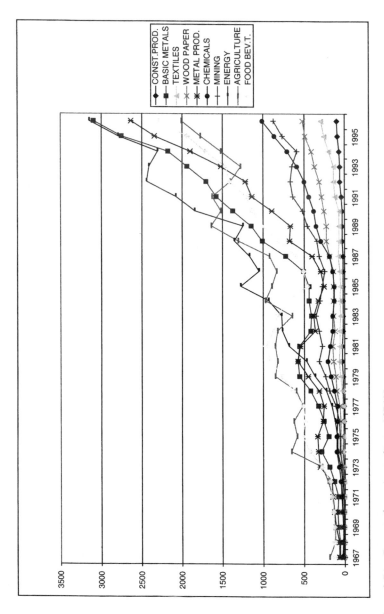

Figure 2.7A   Exports from Australia to ASEAN

Source: CEPII-CHELEM.

37

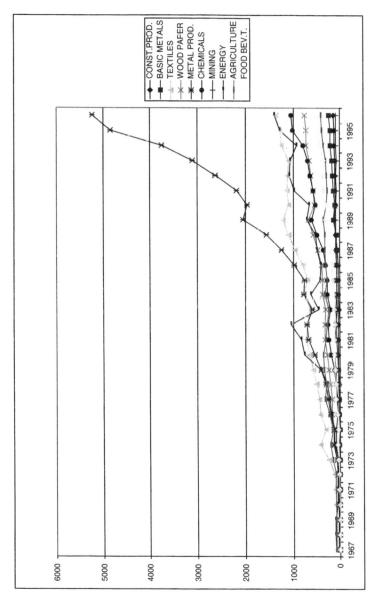

Figure 2.7B Imports from ASEAN to Australia

Source: CEPII-CHELEM.

38

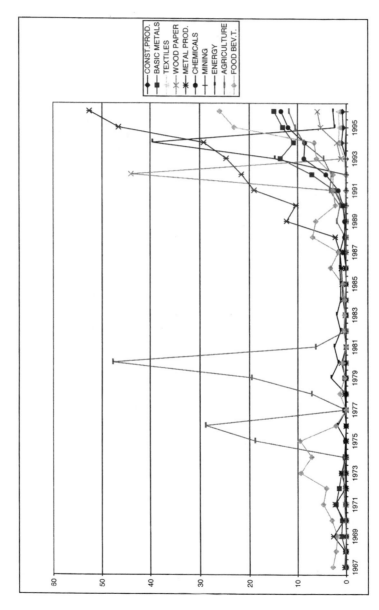

Figure 2.8A   Exports from Australia to Indochina

Source: CEPII-CHELEM.

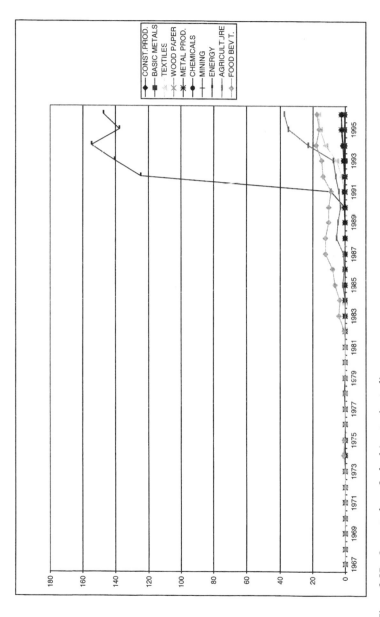

Figure 2.8B   Imports from Indochina to Australia

Source: CEPII-CHELEM.

Appendix III

Graphs: Vietnam's Exports and Imports
Actual and Forecast Values at Current Prices from 1981–2020

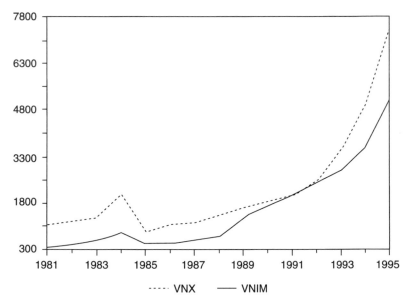

Figure 2.9 Actual exports and imports (in USD mn), Vietnam 1981–1995

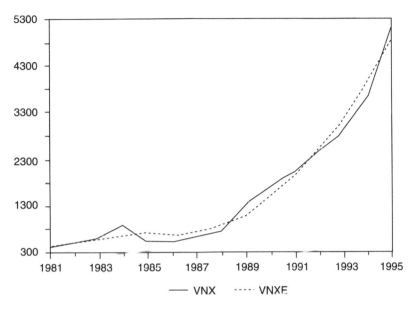

Figure 2.10 Actual and predicted exports (in USD mn), Vietnam 1981–1995

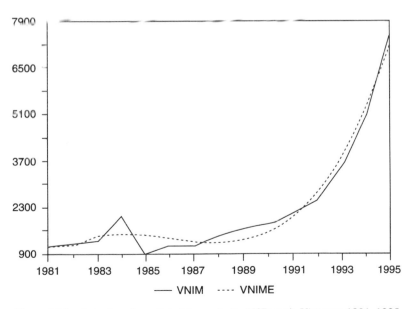

Figure 2.11 Actual and predicted imports (in USD mn), Vietnam 1981–1995

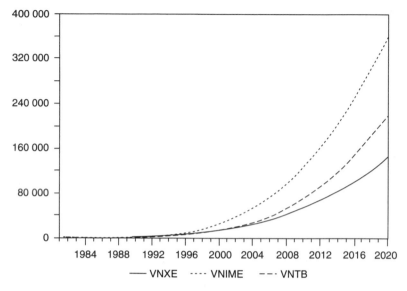

Figure 2.12 Actual/forecast imports, exports and trade balance, Vietnam 1981–2020 (in USD mn)

3
Amended Law on Foreign Investment and Investment Priorities during the Period 1996–2000 in Vietnam

Hoang Tho Xuan and Tran Van Hoa

I.   Introduction

In recent years, Vietnam's economy has achieved great steps forward. The annual growth rate of GDP in the 1991–95 period was 8.2 per cent. It is estimated that, under the same conditions of development, this rate will reach between 9 and 10 per cent per year in the 1996–2000 period. The export-import turnover was US$38.105 bn in the 1991–95 period, and it is estimated to reach approximately US$110 bn, an increase of 300 per cent, in the 1996–2000 period, showing an annual average increase of 28 per cent.

To achieve the above-mentioned projected growth objective and in the face of a low saving ratio in the country, Vietnam necessarily needs foreign direct investment (FDI). This is more so as Vietnam is starting from the status of a less-developed country (LDC). The idea behind the assertion on the role of FDI is based on a time-honoured observation in economic theory and practice that FDI plays an extremely important role in an economy, especially in the LDCs, because it provides the capital and the know-how to help speed up its economic growth rate. That is, in addition to an inflow of capital into the country, Vietnam, through FDI, will be able to absorb scientific achievements and other recent advances and modern tech-nologies. At the same time, FDI will also help Vietnam access new methods of production and management, and help the training, either on the job or through short-term courses, of Vietnamese workers to be familiar with and utilize up-to-date technologies.

Beside its role in the production of goods for exports, FDI also is a tool with which Vietnam can produce competitive goods for exports and expand its export markets to many countries and regions in the world. This in turn will make an important contribution to Vietnam's integration into the global community and accelerate its industrialization and modernization processes.

II.   FDI in Vietnam in the 1988–1995 period

By the end of 1995 or eight years after the introduction of the Law on Foreign Investment, Vietnam had issued 1343 licences to foreign projects with the total investment capital of US$18 128.4 mn (excluding the number of projects whose licences were withdrawn or expired). From this number, 213 projects were valued at US$1794mn in the 1988–1990 period (the average capital of each project was US$8.4mn), and 1130 licensed projects were valued at US$16 334mn in the 1991–1995 period.

1.   FDI and the industrial structure

Though FDI is spread over all the industries, the proportion of investment in the branches or sectors of the economy is in general still inappropriate. Big investment is made in the field of services with 63 projects capitalized at US$6330.9mn, accounting for nearly 35 per cent of the total foreign investment capital. In the field of industries, there are 784 projects worth US$8056.7mn, making up 41 per cent of the total foreign capital. On the contrary, just a very small proportion of investment is available in such fields as agriculture, forestry, aqua-products and education.

2.   Scale of FDI projects

The average scale of a project had gradually increased through the years from 1991–1995, being from US$8.8mn in 1991 to US$11mn, US$11.9mn, US$11mn and US$13mn in 1992, 1993, 1994 and 1995 respectively.

3.   FDI and its distribution

The distribution of investment has become more even over the different localities in Vietnam. By the end of 1995, there were FDI projects in almost all cities and provinces. Ho Chi Minh City is ranked first in terms of the number of projects with 506 projects capitalized at US$5820.8mn, followed by Hanoi with 222 projects worth US$3674mn, and then by Dong Nai with 145 projects valued at US$2379mn.

4. The composition of domestic or local partners in FDI projects

State enterprises account for 98 per cent of the total number of projects, and the rest is held by non-state economic organizations, whose projects only make up less than 1 per cent of the authorized capital. This shows that the scale of FDI-based projects realized in conjunction with state enterprises is much bigger than that of other kinds of enterprises in all economic sectors in Vietnam.

5. The composition of foreign partners in FDI projects

In the beginning, most of foreign investors in Vietnam were small-sized firms. Recently, there have appeared large-sized foreign compa-nies. By the end of 1995, there had been more than 800 companies from more than 55 countries in the world making investment in Vietnam. Taiwan is the biggest investor with 263 projects capital-ized at US$3315.8mn, followed by Hong Kong with 185 projects capitalized at US$2154mn, and then Japan with 126 projects worth US$2030.2mn.

The realized investment capital has also achieved an annual increase. The increase is as follows from 1988–1995: US$620mn in the 1988–1990 period, US$463mn in 1992, US$1002mn in 1993, US$1500mn in 1994, and over US$2300mn in 1995.

The number of employees in foreign invested companies includes 70 000 directly involved workers and 150 000 indirectly involved staff. The level of wages and salaries of the employees in these companies is in general acceptable by the national stan-dards, but other aspects and issues of the labour force, such as work insurance or work care and welfare systems, are not yet well developed.

FDI has made an important contribution to increasing Vietnam's export turnover. Exports of foreign invested companies were US$169mn (excluding crude oil) in 1993, US$300mn in 1994 (accounting for 8.3 per cent of the total export turnover and 20 per cent of the manufactured exports) and increased to about

US$500mn in 1995, making up 10 per cent of the whole country's total export turnover.

III.   FDI in Vietnam in 1996

In the first six months of 1996, the number of foreign investment projects licensed by the government of Vietnam was 160 with a total registered capital of US$3.2 bn and the realized capital of US$1.2 bn. As at 12 December 1996, 162 projects in the industry had been licensed with a total registered investment capital of US$2185.23mn and a prescribed capital of US$901.46mn. The number of these projects and the total capital investment are only 86.6 per cent and 84 per cent respectively of their levels in 1995. Of these 162 projects, 63 are in heavy industries with capitalized investment worth US$1096.64mn covering investment in such areas as automobiles, motorbikes, machinery, chemical, oil and gas, and manufacturing, 67 are in light industries totalling US$470.68 mn and concentrating on garments, leather shoes, consumer goods, plastics and plastic products, 29 are for foodstuff industries valued at US$612.33mn, and 3 for forestry processing and fine arts, capitalized at US$5.58mn.

During the short period from 25–31 December 1996, however, 12 projects totalling US$3.263 bn or more than 38 per cent of total FDI in Vietnam (including two mega urban development projects worth more than US$3 bn) for 1996 were approved by the Ministry of Planning and Investment (MPI). The two mega projects are the Indonesia Ciputra Group's South Thang Long urban development outside Hanoi (worth US$2.11 bn) and the City Horse project outside Ho Chi Minh City (worth US$997mn). The total tally for investment from licences issued by the MPI for 1996 was US$8.538 bn, an increase of 18.2 per cent over that in 1995. The majority of the FDI projects in 1996 was in the production area.

According to the announcement of the Department of Investment of the MPI, implemented investment capital in 1996 was estimated to be US$2.2–2.5 bn. The revenue of operational projects in the year attained US$1.8 bn of which the turnover of exports was about US$700–800mn, or about twice the increase in 1995. This contributes US$350mn to the government's budget or an increase of 75 per cent over 1995.

The year 1996 also showed a remarkable growth in respect of investment from such countries as Japan, South Korea and Western Europe. A number of corporations from Japan (such as Mitsui, Nissho, Iwai and Sanyo), South Korea (Daewoo, Hyundai and Posco), and Germany (Mercedes Benz and Siemens) had quickly changed their status of operation from simple commerce to investment in big projects and planned long-term programmes in Vietnam.

IV.   FDI in Vietnam since Doi Moi: overview

Since the introduction of Doi Moi in 1986 to the end of 1996, Vietnam had issued licences to 772 projects in the industrial sector with a total registered investment capital of US$8839.5mn and a prescribed total capital of US$3810.3mn. Of this total, Vietnam had contributed US$750mn (accounting for nearly 20 per cent of pre-scribed total capital). These projects were focused mainly on heavy industry (290 projects), light industry (312), and foodstuff (109) projects. At present, the industrial sector makes up 42 per cent of all projects with an investment capital equivalent to 31.6 per cent of all investment in the country.

Of the 772 licensed projects above, the number of projects that are still operating is 445 with an implemented investment capital of US$2350.23mn, accounting for about 27 per cent of total registered investment capital. In 1996 alone, US$644.36mn were invested in basic construction accounting for about 30 per cent of total registered investment capital. All this indicates that FDI and capital flow into the business activity in Vietnam were on the increase.

Among the currently operational FDI-based projects, 329 were with a revenue of US$2420.28mn. In 1996 alone, the revenue from these projects was US$1109.6mn the share of which was 46.5 per cent for the foodstuff industry, 29.2 per cent for heavy industry, 20.4 per cent for light industry, and 3.9 per cent for forestry and fine arts.

The export turnover of 227 projects from this group reached US$792mn accounting for 33 per cent of the total revenue in 1996. The biggest share in export revenue was for light industry at 65.8 per cent followed by 13.6 per cent for forestry and handicraft, 12.2 per cent for heavy industry, and 8.4 per cent for foodstuff.

In terms of the distribution of FDI, the Dong Nai area is ranked first in its ability to attract FDI into its industries. It has 137 projects with a registered investment capital of US$2594mn.

In total, 18 projects were with an investment capital of over US$100mn. Dong Nai has six of these projects including the Hualon Fiber Company (US$428mn) and the Vedan glutamate company (US$279mn). However, in terms of licensed industrial projects, Ho Chi Minh City is ranked first with 243 projects having a total registered investment capital of US$1716mn and the highest implemented investment capital of US$672.8mn. Hanoi is ranked third with 75 projects and a registered investment capital of US$1101.4mn. Next in descending order are: Song Be, Ba Ria-Vung Tau, Quang Nam-Da Nang, Hai Phong, Ha Tay, Vinh Phu and Hai Hung with a total of about US$200mn investment capital each, and Tay Ninh, Long An, Khanh Hoa and Ha Bac with a total of about US$100mn investment capital each.

The allocation of implemented FDI over the different areas is not equal, as expected. The areas with the largest share of implemented FDI are Hanoi, Hai Phong, Thanh Hoa, Thua Tien, Hue and Tien Giang which received more than 40 per cent of all registered FDI. Ho Chi Minh City attracted only 39 per cent, Quang Nam-Da Nang 23.7 per cent and Dong Nai 20 per cent. Other provinces such as Song Be, Ba Ria-Vung Tau, Tay Ninh and Khanh Hoa received less than 15 per cent in implemented FDI capital.

V.   Some general comments on FDI in Vietnam

FDI has made important contributions to speeding up Vietnam's economic growth rate and boosting its industrialization and modernization processes in recent years. Thanks to FDI, Vietnam has helped create jobs for the work force, increase the state budget and the export turnover, and train a large contingent of managers for the national economy. However, there still are a lot of limitations in attracting and operating FDI in Vietnam. These are briefly described below.

First of all, Vietnam's legal system is not yet uniform and the laws are not well upheld by the government and business community. State management has not been improved greatly, the administrative procedures are cumbersome, and the 'one-door' policy has not yet been implemented. All this has discouraged foreign investors who wanted to operate in Vietnam. There have not yet been detailed master plans for FDI in Vietnam, and this has led to the situation where different ideas and different implementation methods are being used or adopted by the authorities while assessing and studying potential investment projects. Knowledge about foreign partners is still limited and thus appropriate partners could not be chosen at times, causing many contracts to be cancelled or their licences withdrawn. Staff in joint-venture companies in North Vietnam are in short supply and if they are available they are often incompetent, bringing losses instead of profits to the Vietnamese side. In addition, the infrastructure necessary for a proper operation of FDI-based projects (or any other project for that matter) is still poor, and the land rent and service costs are high, making Vietnam less attractive in the eyes of foreign investors.

VI.   Policy to attract FDI in the period 1996–2000

The amended Law on Foreign Investment which was approved by Vietnam's National Assembly in November 1996 and some priority areas for FDI which were announced by the government of Vietnam have helped create and focus on FDI opportunities in a number of areas for foreign investors. The new law includes 68 articles (as compared to the previous law with 42 articles) of which 26 articles are completely new and 29 articles are amended. While the new law provides more detailed guidelines in the form of required written documents under the law, it is still not as comprehensive or detailed as similar laws in other countries in the region.

The main amendments and the priority areas for FDI are discussed below for the period 1996–2000.

1.   Increasing the effectiveness of licensed projects

- Paying attention to the environmental protection guidelines mentioned in projects, strictly controlling projects which have no method of environmental protection.
- Carefully supervising technological transfer activities, controlling the quality of machines, equipment and materials.
- Strengthening the export capacity of joint-venture companies, encouraging and creating favourable conditions for enterprises with high export turnover.

- Trying to increase the Vietnamese side's capital contribution in joint-venture companies, quickly putting this capital into operation to create favourable conditions for foreign partners.
- In terms of the labour force conditions, continuing to consider and complete policies on salaries and wages, insurance and training to ensure the interests of labourers in joint-venture companies.

2.   Attracting more FDI projects in line with the government's economic policy in the first stage of the country's industrialization and modernization

The total of required investment capital in the period 1996–2000 has been estimated to be US$40–42 bn. The amount of capital to be mobilized from the domestic or local sources is about US$20–22 bn, accounting for over 50 per cent of the required investment capital, and the rest is to be mobilized from the foreign side. The plan to attract FDI includes:

- Establishing a plan of calling for foreign investment capital in line with the national economic development strategy and the master plan.
- Strengthening the evaluation and approval procedures of investment projects, forming a committee directly under the government's control and in charge of these procedures.
- Assess investment projects through the so-called 'inter-branch committee' which has the function of approving big projects in order to ensure that they satisfy the criteria in the interest of the economy, society, environment, science and technology, security and national defence.
- Putting more emphasis on the ability of exporting goods and manufactured products produced in the FDI projects. Projects of the substitution goods should also receive preferential treatment in terms of buying foreign currency to import materials and transferring part of profits abroad in accordance with the government's regulations.
- Creating favourable conditions in terms of simplified legal framework, carrying out the 'one-door' administrative reforms, and improving technical infrastructure so that investors can be assured in terms of the project's profitability.

3. The amendments of the Law on Foreign Investment and priority fields

Article 3 of Chapter 1 of the Law on Foreign Investment in Vietnam stipulates the priority areas and the sectors for attracting FDI as follows:

- Foreign investors are permitted to invest in all sectors of the economy in Vietnam.
- The government of Vietnam encourages foreign investors to invest in the following fields and regions:

(1) *Fields:*
A Producing goods for exports.
B Cultivating and processing agricultural, forestry and fishery products.
C Using high-tech, modern technology, and protecting the ecological environment.
D Using a lot of labour, processing materials and using effectively natural resources in Vietnam.
E Constructing infrastructure and industrial zones.

(2) *Areas:*
A Mountain and remote areas.
B Areas with difficult socioeconomic conditions.

- Priority should be given to those areas which ensure a reasonable structure among the different sectors and territorial regions.
- The incentive structure for FDI attraction can be seen through the fact that the Vietnamese government has exempted and reduced land rent, water surface rent, and given other preferential treatments.
- The exemption period of interest taxes for the priority sectors and areas can be as long as eight years.
- The interest tax reduction period can be as long as four years.
- In addition to the above incentive structure, the Vietnamese government also ensures support of FDI in terms of foreign currency balances.
- The foreign side is allowed to contribute capital in Vietnamese dong, or capital originating from inside Vietnam.

- The government of Vietnam will exempt or reduce export-import taxes in the fields in which investment is encouraged. Import tax exemption is applied to capital contribution in the form of machines, equipment to establish enterprises or to create fixed assets for the implementation of business contracts. The government only exempts taxes for imported materials to manufacture goods for exports or to produce substitute machinery and equipment to serve in joint-venture companies.

IIV.   Sources of investment to support Vietnam's economic development

The investment capital requirements and their shares in total investment in the various sectors of the economy of Vietnam are projected for implementation below for the 1996–2000 period:

- *Sectoral investment shares:* Agriculture, forestry and irrigation account for 20 per cent of total investment of which 7 per cent is to be invested in irrigation; the industrial sector 43 per cent; infrastructure for transport and telecommunications 18 per cent; education, health care, cultural activities and environment, science and technology 14 per cent, and other investment 5 per cent.
- *Investment sources:* Of the total investment requirements, 5 per cent is from the government's budget, 30 per cent from soft credit loan, and 65 per cent from other sources (domestic and foreign).

During this period, the Official Development Assistance (ODA) programme of the international organizations and governments is expected to contribute about 21 per cent of total investment capital requirement in Vietnam, state investment credit capital 16–17 per cent, capital from state-owned enterprises 14–15 per cent, capital from the public and private enterprises 16–17 per cent, and the rest from other sources.

4
Promotion of Trade, Investment and Business in Vietnam

Ho Trung Thanh and Tran Van Hoa

I. Introduction

After more than ten years of renovation, Vietnam has accomplished great economic achievements. The economy has survived many crises and development has been increasing fast in many areas. The annual economic growth rate in the 1991–1995 period was 8.2 per cent, and the rate in 1995 alone was as much as 9.5 per cent. Trade activities have made remarkable progress. The export-import turnover in the 1991–1995 period increased by 3.1 per cent on average per year. The amount of foreign investment is becoming larger and larger. By the end of October 1996 there had been 1730 projects with a total authorized capital of US$23 bn.

Vietnam's economic achievements in the last ten years are mostly due to the implementation of the government of Vietnam's outward-oriented development strategy. Currently there are 120 countries and territories that have established business relationships with Vietnam with nearly 1000 companies investing in Vietnam. Vietnam has gradually integrated itself into the regional and global economic and trading systems. At present, Vietnam is an ASEAN member and is carrying out negotiations to make preparations for its participation in the World Trade Organization (WTO, the former GATT). The Vietnamese government has realized that under the current situation, when economic internationalization is inevitable, it is essential to take advantage of outside assistance and co-operation in order to develop the economy.

According to national and international economic experts' calculations, to reach an annual economic growth rate of 9–10 per cent, Vietnam will need to invest about US$41 bn by the year 2000, of which the domestic capital sources should be approximately US$21 bn. The rest of this capital requirement should be mobilized from foreign countries of which Official Development Assistance (ODA) sources should account for US$7 bn and FDI about US$14 bn. With the capability of attracting FDI in recent years (in 1994: US$6.5 bn and in 1995: US$7.5 bn), the above estimates can be within reach. FDI-attracting strategy has been given great importance by the Vietnamese government and considered one of the main ways to boost the country's industrialization programmes. In addition to the legal documents necessary to create favourable conditions for investors and businessmen, trade promotion activities have made great contributions to speeding up the rate of attracting foreign capital. In parallel to the opening up of the economy, a number of investment promotion organizations have been established.

II.   Promotion programmes for trade, investment, and business in Vietnam

The State Committee for Cooperation and Investment (SCCI) in Vietnam was a ministerial-level organization in charge of evaluating, approving and managing foreign investment projects in the country. It has now been merged with the State Planning Committee to become the Ministry of Planning and Investment (MPI). All ministries and statutory authorities have established their own investment consulting centres or offices to help investors identify the areas of prospective investment. Since early 1995, the Vietnamese government has set up a number of councils responsible for assessing and approving the planning in provinces, including reviewing foreign investment-attracting projects in key provinces and economic zones. So far, a number of provinces and cities in the whole country have listed all foreign investment-attracting projects. The Vietnamese government has formed a foreign capital-attracting programme to operate from now till the years 2000 and 2010.

Among other functions, investment promotion organizations can help foreign investors fulfil local legal procedures relating to their investment projects, look for joint ventures in Vietnam, select effective investment fields, carry out surveys of the Vietnamese market and establish feasible projects for investment.

In addition to investment promotion, trade promotion activities have also been strengthened. In 1989 the Trade Information Center and the International Advertising and Fair Center were established, and in 1993 the International Research, Consulting and Training Center for Foreign Economic Relations (ICTC) of the Ministry of Trade came into being. Together with the Vietnam Institute for Trade, which is directly responsible to the Ministry of Trade and whose main functions are to study Vietnam's trade policies and its foreign trade relationships with other countries, the above-mentioned trade promotion organizations are in charge of a number of important functions. These include providing necessary information about Vietnam's trade activities and policies, making forecasts of exports and imports and studying their markets, and looking for foreign partners for Vietnamese companies exporting and importing goods and technology. At the moment, the Ministry of Trade is preparing to establish a number of trade promotion centres and to expand their activities in the entire nation.

Another big organization that has been set up separately from the Ministry of Trade with the function of supporting trade and investment promotion activities is the Vietnam Chamber of Commerce and Industry (VCCI). The VCCI is the umbrella of Vietnamese entrepreneurs in the process of integrating themselves into overseas economic organizations. Foreign entrepreneurs can carry out a study of potential Vietnamese partners through the VCCI, which acts as a bridge linking Vietnamese enterprises and foreign ones.

Being a state organization with commercial activities under the jurisdiction of the Ministry of Trade, the ICTC undertakes to carry out consulting activities in the economic, commercial and investment fields for foreign and local enterprises which need its services, participates in scientific and commercial research, and supports the application of the research results in the economic, commercial and investment fields. It also organizes seminars and training courses, conferences on economics and trade, and cooperates with local and international organizations, corporations and individuals in the fields of research and information exchange concerning investment and trade. In addition, the ICTC is entitled by law to sign contracts with local and foreign organizations and individuals to implement its duties, to make appropriate arrangements for foreign delegations coming to Vietnam for market surveys or information collection and preparation of investment and business activities in Vietnam.

To date, the ICTC has helped many foreign organizations, companies and individuals looking for business and investment opportunities in Vietnam. Some of these are large companies such as Yokton (Canada), San Miguel (the Philippines), Inter-germ (Belgium).

The ICTC has also received strong assistance and support from academics from such overseas institutions as Wollongong University in Australia to carry out its functions since its formation in October 1993. For example, since 1995 the ICTC has coordinated with the Department of Economics in the Faculty of Commerce of the University to carry out the research work of the ARC Collaborative Scheme-funded research project 'Foreign Investment in Vietnam' to explore and develop prospects for Australian companies. In 1996, we carried out in collaboration with the project leader, Professor Tran Van Hoa, research on investment prospects for Australian companies in Vietnam covering the 20 main economic sectors in Vietnam. The research results have been scheduled to be published in the United Kingdom and an informal reported version of it in Vietnamese will be published in Vietnam.

III.   Prospects for Australian enterprises

In this chapter, we would like to introduce our research findings on some other fields which in our opinion have many prospects for Australian companies. Our research is based on the comprehensive data-set collected since 1988 of the industries in Vietnam, their development strategies until the year 2010, and plausible forecasts for Australia's cooperation possibilities. The research results deal with the 20 economic sectors in Vietnam and involve key categories of exports and imports relating to the Australian market.

The Vietnamese government highly appreciates the cooperation of Australia and it is our hope that from our research results, Australian investors and businessmen will be successful in their business ventures and other cooperation in Vietnam.

Based on Vietnam's economic development strategy for the 1996–2000 period, the sources for foreign direct investment (FDI) will be allocated as follows:

(1)   Building an oil and gas industry with the target of exploiting about 20 mn tonnes of crude oil by the year 2000, establishing an oil-refining factory before the year 2000 and another after the year 2000 with the total capital of US$7.5 bn.

(2)   Building two high-tech industries in Hanoi and Ho Chi Minh City with a total capital of US$600 mn.

(3)   Establishing 12 local industrial zones in Hanoi, Ho Chi Minh City, Hai Phong, Dong Nai, Song Be, Can Tho, Quang Nam, and Da Nang with a capital of US$5 bn.

(4)   Investing about US$2 bn in light industry.

(5)   Investing about US$1.5 bn in heavy industrial factories in the fields of metallurgy, mechanics, electronics and chemicals.

(6)   Building between one and six cement factories with a total output of 9–10 mn tonnes per year with the estimated capital of about US$1.5 bn.

(7)   Investing about US$800 mn in developing agriculture, forestry and processing industries.

(8)   Investing about US$1 bn in transport and communication, telecommunications and infrastructure.

(9)   Building hotels, offices for rent, tourism resorts with a capital of US$1.5 bn.

(10) Investing about US$300 mn in the services industry.

IV.   Sectoral prospects for Australian companies in Vietnam

Infrastructure is a field for which Vietnam is badly in need of improvement and, therefore, large investment capital. Modernizing the infrastructure of the industries in Vietnam, especially the repairs and upgrades of roads, railways, airports and seaports, will help attract foreign investment capital for other fields. The capital source for the construction works will come mainly from the ODA programme. The Vietnamese government is now calling for FDI in this field which has been given first priority. At the moment, there are several specific projects, including the projects on repairing the transport system with a capital of US$100 bn, some upgrading of the transport system which has been valued at US$120–150 mn and some of the new buildings with a capital of US$1.2–1.6 bn.

Another field which has also been encouraged by the Vietnamese government is the post and telecommunications industry. Being a country in the process of industrialization, Vietnam is an attractive market for telecommunications goods and services. According to our forecasts, this market can reach US$700 mn by the year 2000. Currently, there is only 1.05 telephone per 100 people in Vietnam. In order to reach the target of 3 telephones per 100 persons by the year 2000, 500 000 additional telephones must be installed annually. The market for mobile phones is also quickly expanding. For the time being, there are 30 000 mobile phones in Vietnam. It has been estimated that by the year 2000 this market will reach US$250 mn. The capital demand for the construction of earth satellite stations, sea-cable lines, expansion of broadcast and television stations as well as post-industrial zones specializing in telecommunications equipment will be very large. In the 1996–2000 period, Vietnam will need to invest about US$1 bn in the post and telecommunications industry, of which only 30 per cent can be mobilized from local sources and the rest must be from foreign sources.

Australia is an early investor in this field. In 1987, Australia's Telstra signed the first agreement with Vietnam's Post Office. Since then, Australia has always been Vietnam's important partner in the telecommunications field. However, at present, as foreign telecommunications firms are fiercely competing with one another to capture or enter the Vietnamese market, the Australian telecommunications companies should have a long-term and continuous investment strategy in Vietnam for their own benefit.

Informatics is also an attractive field in the eyes of foreign investors. According to the statistics issued by Vietnam's Ministry of Technology and Environment, the supply of informatics equipment has increased by 150 per cent annually in the past few years. The Ministry of Trade's data show that in 1995 the total turnover from hardware supply was US$100 mn, and from software supply US$6 mn. The combined total reached about US$150 mn in 1996. The computers assembled in Vietnam are mainly personal computers. In 1995, 70 000 of these computers were assembled and this figure reached the vicinity of 100 000 in 1996. As a result, by the end of 1996 the total number of personal computers in Vietnam was about 240 000 units. The demand for network servers will also be very high. In the case of the company DEC (USA) which is one of three information firms with the biggest business in Vietnam, its total turnover in 1995 was US$3 mn with 60 per cent of it coming from personal computers, US$1.5 mn or 30 per cent from servers and US$1 mn or 20 per cent from consultancy and services.

In this field of information technology, beside the supply of equipment, Australia can help Vietnam a great deal in training computer experts. According to the master plan for the information technology industry, it has been estimated that by the year 2000 Vietnam will need at least 20 000 experts. About 1500 informatics engineers are trained per year, so, by the year 2000 there will be 6000 informatics engineers in addition to an annual 3000 university graduates in the field of information technology. As a result, Vietnam is still in short supply of informatics technicians, especially technicians in computer software.

Another very promising field for Australian investors and businessmen is in the foods and foodstuff processing industry. It is common knowledge among Vietnam's agricultural decision-makers that Vietnam's agriculture exports in recent years have increased in quantity, but their prices on the global market are still low as they are roughly processed, of not very high quality and are mostly used as raw materials such as seed coffee and rubber. About 25 per cent of sea products are exported to the re-processing markets in the neighbouring region.

The situation which we have described above is due to a number of factors: poor rural infrastructure, and lack of agricultural-forestry-sea product-processing establishments leading to huge losses after the harvest (the post-harvest loss is estimated to be about 15 per cent of the total output). At present, Vietnam's processing establishments, equipment and technologies are too outdated, the production facilities have degraded and have not received proper investment for improvements. As a result, Vietnam cannot yet meet the speed of production requirements, and has to limit the specialization and production consumption. It is forecast that by the year

2000 the productivity obtained in some agricultural branches will be as follows:

Food output: up to 30–32 mn tonnes (2–2.5mn tonnes for exports)
Processed meat of all kinds: 1.8–2 mn tonnes
Sugar and rubber: 180 000–200 000 tonnes
Dried tea: 70 000 tonnes
Sea products: 1.6 mn tonnes with an export turnover of US$4.5 bn

In order to obtain the above targets, beside the expansion of the agricultural consumption market, a planning of agricultural specialized zones such as aqua-product husbandry, fruit planting for exports, and so on, Vietnam needs to attach great importance to investment in this field in order to create competitive products in an open economy. Since Vietnam has joined the ASEAN and broadened its relationships with the nations from the Asia Pacific Economic Cooperation and the World Trade Organization, great attention should be paid to boosting Vietnam's agricultural exports to these regions.

The real situation and development forecast of Vietnam's agriculture have brought about a bright prospect for Australian companies specializing in forest planting, aqua-product husbandry and clean vegetable planting in Vietnam. In our opinion, Australian investors should emphasize promotion of post-harvest technologies related to the storage of processed rice, sea products, vegetables, coffee, tea and rubber. At the moment, Vietnam still has to import such processed agricultural products as canned food and clean vegetables from outside. Investment in processing technologies will help produce competitive products in both the global as well as local markets where there is a big demand for these goods.

V.   Areas of FDI needed from Australia

Vietnam's projects calling for foreign capital investment in the following fields in the 1996–2000 period include:

(1) Projects on aqua-products husbandry and
     processing with the total capital   US$225 mn.
(2) Projects on rice planting and processing   US$62 mn.
(3) Projects on cattle husbandry and processing   US$53 mn.

(4) Projects on coffee planting and processing	US$92.8 mn.
(5) Projects on cotton planting	US$25 mn.
(6) Projects on tea planting and processing	US$15.8 mn.
(7) Projects on vegetable oil processing	US$400 mn.
(8) Projects on sugar processing	US$100 mn.

The government of Vietnam also places great importance on investment in education, training and human resources development in Vietnam. Vietnam is in the transition into a market economy, therefore, there is a great need to improve the present educational system as well as to retrain some officials who work under the old socialist or centrally planned mechanism. Although the number of redundant workers in Vietnam is very large (estimated to be about 5–6 mn people), Vietnam still lacks experts in such fields as informatics, banking, finance, and especially in management. For example, in Ho Chi Minh City annually there are about 3000 university graduates who cannot find jobs while the city has to employ 1500 foreign engineers. Vietnam is speeding up the privatization process, thus, small- and medium-sized enterprises are badly in need of skilled workers. In this field, the Australian government and other foreign governments have helped Vietnam a great deal but the real need is still unfulfilled.

Australia has provided Vietnam with US$12.5 mn to establish an English training centre. With financial assistance from Australia, in 1993 there were 154 Vietnamese students receiving scholarships to study in Australia while the numbers were 216 and 250 respectively in 1994 and 1995. Short-term training courses within the framework of scientific and technical projects have been regularly organized. The ICTC has coordinated with the Australian side to hold short-term courses on trade policy, commodity exchange markets, the international economy, and the security market. Two current short training courses on business economics have been organized at the ICTC with funding from the Australia-ASEAN Economic Cooperation Program of the Department of Foreign Affairs and Trade, and with collaboration of academics from Wollongong University. However, in our opinion, the investment of the Australian private sector in this field is still very limited whereas companies from South Korea, the UK, France, the US, Japan, Hong Kong and Taiwan have worked out significant investment strategies in this field.

First priority is also given to foreign investment in housing development. Currently, the per capita housing area in Vietnam is 7 sq. m. The figure is 7.5 sq. m and 5.8 sq. m in rural and urban areas respectively. Most of the houses and apartments are concentrated in the two big cities of Hanoi and Ho Chi Minh. According to our forecasts, by the year 2000, due to natural and mechanic population growths, the urban population will be in the neighbourhood of 20.5 mn. In order to satisfy the minimum demand for housing of 8 sq. m per person, the urban housing requirement would reach 164 mn sq. m, an increase of 63mn sq. m over the housing stock at the present time. As a result, there should be 16.6 mn squared meters more each year, that is equal to 20 per cent of the existing housing stock. To reach the above-mentioned targets, the domestic capital sources can only meet 60 per cent of the required capital, and the rest must be mobilized from foreign sources.

Other fields such as mineral exploitation, oil and gas, land management, administrative reforms, privatization, banking, financing, forestry and so on also have a great need for foreign investment. The details of our forecast in this field will be reported in the near future in Australia and Vietnam. Those who need this information can contact the ICTC in Hanoi, Vietnam, and Professor Tran Van Hoa of the Vietnam Focus Research Program at the University of Wollongong in Australia.

5
The Business Environment for Australian Companies in Vietnam

Anne-Marie Humphries

This chapter provides an overview of the realities of doing business for Australian companies in Vietnam. It draws on interviews with a number of Australian companies undertaken by a consultant to the East Asia Analytical Unit, Mr Martin Smee, East Asia Analytical Unit staff, and Australian diplomatic representatives in Hanoi and Ho Chi Minh City, as part of the preparation of their report on The New ASEANs: Vietnam, Burma, Cambodia and Laos (1997).

I. Overview of bilateral relations

Australia has a strong and longstanding relationship with Vietnam. Australia was one of the first Western countries to recognize the Socialist Republic of Vietnam more than 20 years ago and over 100 Australian companies are currently engaged in business there.

1. Trade

Australia's trade with Vietnam has expanded strongly in the 1990s, although from a low base. Between 1987 and 1995, Australian exports to Vietnam have increased at an annual rate of almost 50 per cent. In 1995, Australia's exports to Vietnam increased by 65 per cent to AUD186 mn, compared to AUD113 mn in 1994 (making Vietnam Australia's thirty-third largest export market). The major export items are gold, telecommunications equipment, wheat, steel products, medicines and electricity distribution equipment. Australia's imports from Vietnam in 1995 totalled AUD286 mn, a slight fall from AUD289 mn in 1994. The major import item is crude petroleum (most of which is shipped to Geelong for refining); food imports (including coffee and seafood) are also increasing, as are imports of light manufactures (such as clothing and travel goods).

The trade in services between Australia and Vietnam is also developing. Australian companies have established operations in Vietnam across a number of service industries including telecommunications, financial and business services.

2. Investment

Since investment links with Vietnam first started to develop in 1988, Australia has consistently been one of the top foreign investors in Vietnam, ranking third for much of the 1990s. At the end of August in 1996, Australia was the ninth largest investor with over 50 approved investment projects involving a capital commitment of nearly US$700 mn. The companies involved include some of Australia's largest and most experienced – such as Telstra and the ANZ Bank – as well as a range of legal, accounting and other professional service providers, and some smaller innovative businesses. The major concentrations of Australian investment capital in Vietnam are in infrastructure (including civil engineering and construction), natural resources and manufacturing. Most of the investments are valued at under US$5 mn each.

The motivations for Australian companies to invest in Vietnam differ quite significantly from the general proposition regarding Vietnam's attractiveness to foreign investors, according to a survey undertaken of 35 Australian companies with investments in Vietnam (Maitland, 1996). Establishing a long-term presence, the strong growth prospects for the economy, and the size of the Vietnamese market were the major motivations for Australian investors. Low wage costs, access to raw materials, and establishing export bases to China and other Asian countries were not important motivations for investing in Vietnam, according to Maitland's survey.

However, in practice, the situation may be somewhat different. The survey of Australian business in Vietnam undertaken by Smee in 1996 found that the primary customer focus for over 80 per cent of the companies interviewed were foreign customers either in Vietnam or offshore. Very few were focused on servicing the domestic market.[1] This has a number of implications: it limits their exposure to Vietnam's market and hence the development of local knowledge and networks; it makes these companies vulnerable to any significant downturn in foreign direct investment; and it means these companies are in direct competition with each other to supply a relatively small and highly specialized market. However, this may also be partly a matter of timing and, as the local market matures in Vietnam, Australian companies may increasingly diversify their customer base and supply a greater number of Vietnamese customers.

Prior to 1993, most Australian investment in Vietnam was in joint ventures, reflecting the fact that this was the most politically acceptable market-entry vehicle in Vietnam at that time and also the Vietnamese government's promotion of joint ventures with state-owned enterprises. Maitland's survey of Australian companies also identified the main reasons for companies seeking a Vietnamese partner as their 'intangible know-how in the form of cultural, social and political contacts ... and local market knowledge' (Maitland, 1996, p. 101). However, in recent years there is growing evidence of a preference for 100 per cent foreign-owned investment structures, which may partly reflect perceived problems with joint ventures, in particular with establishing good relations with local partners.

It is not clear, however, whether Australia's 'getting in early' into the Vietnamese market has provided any significant advantages for Australian companies. According to Vietnamese statistics, Australian investment projects in Vietnam have one of the highest failure rates of any country This may be partly the result of Australian companies having been a part of the steep learning curve involved, both for the Vietnamese government in its dealings with foreign investors and for foreign investors learning about the realities of doing business in Vietnam.

3. Aid

Australia was one of the first countries to resume aid to Vietnam after the Cambodian settlement. Australia was also active in supporting the renewal of lending to Vietnam by the International Development Assistance agencies. In November 1995, Australia pledged AUD200 mn over four years in development assistance funding to Vietnam at the international donors group meeting, making Vietnam one of Australia's largest aid recipients. Total

Australian aid flows to Vietnam have grown from AUD10 mn in 1990–91 to about AUD72 mn in 1995–96. The bilateral aid programme provides a potential gateway for Australian companies to enter Vietnam's market.

The aid programme covers a number of important areas such as education, health and infrastructure development. Education and training is focused on providing tertiary level education and English language tuition. In the area of infrastructure development, a major project is the My Thuan bridge across the Mekong river, as well as water supply projects.

II.   Key characteristics of the business environment

The business environment in Vietnam is still changeable as the economy continues its transition from central planning to a more market-oriented economic system. Australian business therefore needs to be cautious about overly optimistic and unrealistic expectations but also excessively pessimistic forecasts for the country. Overall, Vietnam is still a high risk business environment. However, the potential to earn substantial profits also exists as economic growth and development generates growing commercial opportunities.

Some of the key themes to emerge from discussions with Australian businesses in Vietnam are that foreign investors need to be there for the long haul, have deep pockets, be flexible and have good local knowledge and contacts (particularly a good local partner). 'Vietnam is no place for the faint-hearted' (Spencer and Heij, 1995, p. 1).

In surveys of business conditions in East Asia, Vietnam is ranked as one of the most difficult places for foreigners to do business. According to the results of a survey undertaken by the Hong Kong-based Political and Economic Risk Consultancy, published early in 1996, of the 12 countries surveyed, Vietnam was judged as the riskiest place to invest on the basis of systemic deficiencies and socio political risk. Frequent policy change also cause uncertainty for investors:

> Vague and contradictory regulations, an underdeveloped legal system, concerns over the adjudication process for economic disputes, a lack of accounting standards, and constant shifts in the

relationships in property ownership leave investors reeling. Above all, stable, cohesive policies will reassure investors that a master plan exists for reforming the economy and fostering development.

For some businesses it may be best to wait until the market becomes less complicated to operate in but they risk 'missing the boat'.

Some of the major challenges to operating in Vietnam that have been raised by Australian companies are discussed below. It should be noted, however, that many of the challenges facing Australian business in Vietnam reflect the country's early stage of development. The importance of understanding the true costs of doing business in Vietnam and the local commercial environment is emphasized by Australian businesses there. Some of the strategies adopted by Australian companies to cope with the challenges to conducting business in Vietnam are discussed in the section on 'Strategies'.

1. Business contracts

There are considerable differences in approach to business contracts between Vietnamese and Australian business. While Australian companies regard contracts as binding obligations, the Vietnamese partners tend to view them more as statements of intent. A common view is that Vietnamese partners seldom keep to the terms of joint-venture contracts signed with Australian companies. Contracts are often one-sided in favour of Vietnamese partners and the ground rules were sometimes changed after an investment agreement had been settled. In addition, Australian companies should not underestimate the length of time needed to negotiate a contract. Many of the companies already in Vietnam describe the negotiation process as 'protracted': this reflects 'Australian inexperience with operating in Vietnam and Vietnamese inexperience in dealing with foreign private companies' (Maitland, 1996, p. 98). Once negotiations were concluded, the approvals process was also long.

2. Dispute resolution

There is also considerable uncertainty about Vietnam's dispute settlement mechanisms. No foreign company has yet tested economic arbitration courts established by Vietnam's government in 1994, reflecting deep mistrust on the part of foreign companies of the entire dispute resolution process which they consider blatantly biased in favour of the Vietnamese side. For example, investigations are one-sided, no foreign company representation is allowed, the verdict is predetermined and there is no right of redress. The dominant view is that 'if you cannot avoid a dispute with your Vietnamese business partner, you are better off walking away altogether, even with financial losses, rather than trying to fight the issue through the Vietnamese legal system' (Spencer and Heij, 1995, p. 4). As a result, many business representatives argue that foreign partners should try to maintain as much leverage as possible in joint-venture arrangements and to ensure the management structure in joint ventures did not give the Vietnamese side too much control.

3.   Legal infrastructure underdeveloped

As discussed in Chapters 2 and 3, Vietnam's commercial laws are very underdeveloped. The situation is improving, however, as 'the increase in the number of laws and the commitment to move to a law-based/appeal-supported bureaucratic system has clearly improved the business situation'. Whereas the early 1990s were characterized by calls from foreign investors for better and more laws and regulations, currently many investors would prefer to see better implementation of existing laws as the profusion of sometimes contradictory decrees, circulars and other legal instruments, with virtually no coordination between the different ministries involved, creates considerable uncertainty for businesses in Vietnam. Larger companies appear most concerned about the risks associated with the rudimentary legal system in Vietnam.

Still, most investors are confident that greater legal and regulatory certainty and transparency will emerge over time and should provide greater certainty for longer-term, high-value investments. Asian investors are generally less concerned with the legal environment and are more comfortable operating in a flexible, administrative-based system than their Western counterparts.

4.   Dealing with the bureaucracy

Complex bureaucratic requirements still create problems for Australian business in Vietnam. A survey conducted by the

Indochina Project Management Company in 1994 found that 44 per cent of the foreign investors interviewed found coping with the bureaucracy their biggest challenge (Dung, 1996, p. 82). This is because the government's philosophy of central control of the economy still permeates many areas of Vietnam's economy: licences and permits are needed for everything. This includes its foreign investment policy: 'Vietnam still views foreign business with suspicion' (Schwarz, 1996, p. 50). At least eight central government agencies, including the Ministries of Industry, Finance and Agriculture, and numerous local government agencies, such as the Ho Chi Minh City's People's Committee, are involved in the investment approval process. Some of the factors they take into account include: whether the firm is offering appropriate (state-of-the-art) technology; whether there is a 'need' for the investment as demonstrated by existing supply and demand in the industry; and whether the investment would threaten domestic firms in the industry. This leads to long delays in the approvals process. According to a survey in early 1994, the licensing of joint ventures took on average about one year and that of wholly-owned foreign enterprises took about twice as long (*Saigon Times*, 1994). There are no recent indications that these time periods have been significantly reduced and 'lead times between project identification and implementation are long'.

There is a basic lack of understanding among many of Vietnam's bureaucrats of free-market mechanisms, modern management or financial practices. Businesses complain about the 'whimsical bureaucracy of communists who are used to setting the rules' (*Asian Business Review*, 1996, p. 24). Moreover, there is a lack of trust of foreign business: 'having spent 2000 years fighting colonisation by the French, the Chinese, the Japanese and the Americans, some bureaucrats are now caught up in a battle to keep Vietnam from being colonised by corporations' (*Asian Business Times*, 1996, p. 24). In addition, government officials often have little appreciation of the need for the risks taken by foreign companies in Vietnam to be matched by rewards in order to justify their investment. This may partly reflect an over-confidence that if individual foreign businesses found the operating environment too difficult, there were plenty more where they came from.

There is also a lack of information flow between the various elements of the Vietnamese bureaucracy. A written assurance from one government agency generally means little to another. This means that almost every rule can be subject to negotiation. Still, over time, 'the transparency and certainty of the control and regulation of foreign investment are improving and 'the whole system is getting better' (Smee, 1996, p. 5). Some suggest that when dealing with the bureaucracy, 'it is better to assume that your paperwork will take a long time to get through the system, and to use patience, tact and persistence to ensure that it does not get bogged down completely' (Spencer and Heij, 1995, p. 4). Many companies are now employing specialist Vietnamese consultants to assist them complete, lodge and ensure prompt processing of their applications.

In many cases provincial, district or village officials have more day-to-day influence over foreign investment projects than central government agencies in Hanoi and changes in provincial powers can have significant effects on foreign investors, especially in terms of the degree of interest in their project and of political patronage. For example, in southern Vietnam the Ho Chi Minh City People's Committee and other provincial authorities have a major role in implementing Vietnamese government policy on foreign invest-ment and are in practice far more powerful than central govern-ment agencies such as the Ministry of Planning and Investment. While the central government approves a licence to establish a busi-ness, provincial level operating departments control the day to day operations of foreign investors. This means that despite the stated intent of the central government to reduce bureaucratic hurdles facing foreign investors, little real improvement has occurred. For example, once a licence is issued, any amendments have to be nego-tiated and reapproved by the Ministry of Planning and Investment which can take considerable time. Foreign investors also experience difficulties and delays in obtaining land use rights, visas and in employing labour.

5.   Corruption

Overall, the bureaucratic red tape referred to above can take consid-erable patience to negotiate. It can also take considerable money as growing corruption is another problem associated with the Vietnamese bureaucracy. This is partly because of very low public service wages, especially compared to the private sector. In 1995, Vietnam's prime minister referred to 'the rising tide of corruption (as) one of the most direct dangers' to the national economy (*Asian Wall Street Journal*, 1996, p. 1).

Businesses talk of an array of 'facilitating procedures' that are required to operate in Vietnam. Some of the strategies they have adopted to cope with them are discussed below. The Vietnamese Customs Service is considered to be especially corrupt, adding to the hidden costs of trading and investing in Vietnam. Some argue that pervasive corruption in Vietnam disadvantages Australian companies who operate in a different ethical framework. Some of Australia's regional competitors, more comfortable with the 'Asian way' of doing business,[2] have been able to get projects approved and in place extremely quickly as they are more adept at the 'art of facilitation'

6.   Foreign currency restrictions

Difficulties in securing hard foreign currency is a major issue of concern to Australian investors in Vietnam. This is another example of differences in Vietnamese regulations and the situation 'on-the-ground'. According to Vietnam's foreign investment law, if a firm is a foreign investor and produces import substitutes or exports it can get a permit from the Ministry of Planning and Investment for the duration of the project to convert local profits into foreign exchange for repatriation once all tax obligations have been met. In practice, however, the State Bank issues case-by-case *ad hoc* approvals for one-year permits, and there is some uncertainty surrounding the security and legal status of these. Some investors complain that the State Bank is not authorizing foreign companies to convert sufficient funds into hard currency to allow them to pay for imports or to repatriate profits. Vietnam's increasing trade and current account deficits are raising concerns about further foreign currency restrictions.

7.   Taxation system

Vietnam's unpredictable and haphazard taxation system also creates difficulties for foreign investors. The tax system is still evolving and is not yet backed in many areas by legislation and interpretations can vary widely. As a result, tax regulations are constantly being changed, taxes are often applied retrospectively and there is a continual process of negotiation on tax arrangements. Moreover, taxes are often arbitrarily imposed. Some business representatives suggest that Vietnamese officials are paranoid about being 'ripped off' by foreign business so therefore try to do the same to foreigners. Foreign companies are also viewed as an easier target for paying tax than Vietnamese ones.

Despite foreign investors being supposed to have access to a wide range of tax reductions and exemptions, in practice these are not guaranteed and generally have to be negotiated with officials on a case-by-case basis. Foreign businesses also face discriminatory costs for many services in Vietnam including higher rents, airfares, hiring local staff, electricity rates, water supply costs and so on.

III. Major trends in the business environment

The increasing number of difficulties being experienced by Australian and other foreign businesses in Vietnam is partly a function of their increasing numbers on the ground as well as of more and more projects reaching the implementation stage. Still, Vietnam undoubtedly has one of the most complex business environments in Asia resulting in significant diversity of views and strategies: 'Vietnam is widely recognised as being one of the world's most difficult investment environments – enormously complex, frustrating and expensive' (Beta Vietnam Fund quoted in Schwarz, 1996, p. 49).

1. Complexity/uncertainty

Uncertainty is a normal part of doing business in Vietnam. This arises from the various factors discussed above including the large number of regulatory changes, extensive bureaucracy and red tape, underdeveloped legal frameworks and so on. In addition, rules and regulations are often contradictory and, sometimes, they may exist on paper only (Spencer and Heij, 1995). In many areas, for example property rights protection, the certainty of application can be as important as the rules themselves.

The complex nature of the business environment in Vietnam is also a result of the interaction of three conflicting economic systems and changes in their relative strength. These are:

- the centrally planned system with its clearly defined power structures and plans which is still the dominant system: 'the party clearly intends to remain in charge' (Smee, 1996, p. 12);

- a flexible market system based on administrative decision-making and informal sanctions and rewards which is increasing in importance; and
- a Western-style market system based on laws and contracts, elements of which are slowly emerging.

The control and regulation of foreign investment in Vietnam has, if anything, become more complex over the past ten years. As the volume of laws and regulations has increased, it has become more difficult for the thousands of middle- and upper-level bureaucrats responsible for making incremental decisions under the administrative based economic system to understand and implement those rules in a consistent manner. This results in an increasing lack of consistency and transparency despite the increasing volume of rules.

2.   Increasing competition

Competition in Vietnam from other countries is accelerating. Australia was one of the 'pioneer investors' in Vietnam, but has since been overtaken by large foreign direct investment inflows particularly from East Asian countries (see Chapter 3). Taiwan, Singapore, Japan and other East Asian countries are now Vietnam's major trading and investment partners. United States and European countries are also increasingly active in Vietnam. In addition, the major multinational companies are starting to invest in Vietnam, for example, in the chemical and pharmaceutical industries. As these companies often have the specific types of technology and product that Vietnam needs for its development, they may be able to increase pressure on Vietnam to improve its investment climate.

So while Australia has a strong relationship with Vietnam, which has the potential to be translated into commercial benefit, there will be strong competition. To meet the challenges posed by this 'Australian companies will need plenty of the qualities for which Australia's are traditionally known, including adaptability and resourcefulness' (Spencer and Heij, 1995, p. 2).

3.   Small companies finding it increasingly hard going

Small businesses are finding it increasing difficult to operate in Vietnam and the window of opportunity for new small and medium investors in some industries in starting to close. Small investors, for example, can experience considerable problems in getting investment licences approved as, depending on the 'need' Vietnam has for a company's technology, products or export capability, the Vietnamese government has little enthusiasm for small foreign companies. 'Before, Vietnam accepted all projects regardless of size ... now we will give priority only to big projects' (Nam, Institute of Economics Hanoi, quoted by Schwarz in *Far Eastern Economic Review*, October 1996, p. 48).

High business costs and risks also affect small companies disproportionately: their 'pockets aren't deep enough'. Often individuals are putting their personal financial resources on the line which, combined with a lack of negotiating strength, makes dealing with Vietnamese authorities difficult. In addition, some small and medium investors in the industry sectors face new challenges as 'the number of local manufacturers is increasing and ... access to raw material import quotas is being restricted'.

4.   Slow pace of microeconomic reforms

In ten years, Vietnam has made significant progress in implementing important economic reforms to make the economy more market-oriented (see Chapter 3). Some of the current challenges facing Australian business in Vietnam are the result of the Vietnamese institutions being unable to cope with the rapid pace of change in recent years. Still, in 1996 signs emerged that the pace of reforms has started to slow. This is partly the result of the more difficult nature of the reforms required but also because of the more vigorous debate surrounding reforms. There is also greater uncertainty about the direction of reform, in particular the emphasis being given to increasing the role of the state in the economy, which creates some disquiet among private sector investors.

IV.   Strategies

Australian companies have adopted a range of strategies in dealing with the challenges of operating in Vietnam's increasingly complex business environment. While there is no guaranteed approach, some of the key themes to emerge from the successful strategies adopted by a number of foreign companies in Vietnam include the following.

1.   Importance of government–government relations

Vietnamese appear to place considerable value on high-level contacts with other governments. It is therefore important that the
Australian government continues to demonstrate at a high level its
close interest in further developing the commercial relationship.
Already the bilateral dialogue between Australia and Vietnam has
expanded significantly with an increasing number of ministerial
and other official exchanges. Australia has good government-to-
government relations with Vietnam at many levels and businesses
can benefit from seeking assistance from government representatives, for example, in arguing its case to senior officials, arranging
introductions or to lobby for changes in government practices that
affect business operations. Australian businesses can also benefit
from participating in trade missions to Vietnam organized by
various federal and state government bodies.

Interviews with a number of Australian businesses in Vietnam
suggested that they already seek to communicate with the
Vietnamese government on industry policy issues through
Australian government representatives in Vietnam. The Vietnamese
government is also gradually accepting the role of business groups,
such as the Australian Business Group, as useful communications
channels with business. It is important that Australian government
and business interests continue to work closely together to achieve
their economic and commercial objectives in Vietnam.

2.   On the ground representation

In order to be able to communicate effectively with the Vietnamese
bureaucracy and local partners, it is important for businesses to
establish a presence on the ground. Australian businesses interviewed emphasized that business cannot be done by flying personnel in and out. 'Vietnamese want to be convinced that foreign firms
are prepared to commit for the long-term and the long term good of
Vietnam, and not just fly in for a quick buck' (Australian
Ambassador to Vietnam HE Susan Boyd, quoted in *Internal Business
Asia*, 1996, p. 9). There needs to be someone on the ground to
follow through on project implementation, to develop personal
relations with business partners and the relevant ministries and to
follow the rapid changes in the business environment that may
impact on the companies activities. Establishing a physical presence

in Vietnam is, however, very expensive. If a company is unable to do so, it is important for someone to travel regularly to Vietnam and this should be the same person each time as Vietnamese do not like to deal constantly with different people.

3.   Personal relations

One of the most effective ways of getting things done in Vietnam (and to some degree anywhere else) is to know the right people. Networks of family and social obligations based on patronage are still important in Vietnam. Personal relationships have become even more important with the shift towards a more flexible administrative system because of greater administrative discretion and the increased importance of personal agendas (partly reflecting the emphasis under capitalism on personal wealth and profits).

Businesses can benefit significantly from developing a genuine personal relationship with their business partners and important government officials as well as with local staff. 'Finding the right joint venture partner (is) vital for any significant business in Vietnam for all the obvious reasons: chemistry, honesty, effectiveness' (Smee, 1996). As Vietnam's economy is still dominated by the state sector, and as the government regulates almost every aspect of business operations in Vietnam, the relationship with government officials is particularly important.

In addition, the legal system in Vietnam, although improving, is still incomplete and often inconsistently applied. Also, in any commercial dispute settlement procedure there is still a strong preference for compromise between the parties involved or for mediation which means that foreign companies need to be flexible and willing to place emphasis on good personal relations rather than a legalistic approach.

Relationship and communication problems between joint-venture partners are identified as one of the most common reasons for investment failures.[3] The major causes of problems identified are that:

• the parties had fundamentally different and conflicting reasons for entering the joint venture which have not been resolved;
• both parties expectations of profit and profit sharing far exceeded reality;

- fundamental differences about how the company should be managed (that is, according to Vietnamese or Australian practice); and
- poor corporate strategies especially regarding communication channels (including with the Vietnamese partner and government and the media).

Australian investors have a good reputation as employers and managers of people in Vietnam and have not attracted the negative press of some other foreign investors (especially from South Korea in the area of employee relations). Most businesses surveyed consciously seek to operate their joint venture in a transparent and honest fashion and have gained the respect of the Vietnamese as desirable partners: the advisability of transparency was a common theme to emerge from interviews with business: 'transparency is vital' (Smee, 1996, p. 8).

4.   Arm's length dealing with the bureaucracy

The strategies used by Australian companies for interaction with the Vietnamese bureaucracy and local partners are becoming increasingly sophisticated. For example, a number of Australian companies have found that it is better to use consultants and agents when dealing with the Vietnamese authorities. This keeps them at arm's length from officials and any direct discussion of 'facilitation arrangements'. Many Australian companies are adopting a conflict minimization model in which a Vietnamese lobbyist or intermediary handles all communication and negotiation, for example to facilitate the provision of a service (such as importing goods or obtaining an investment licence). Even some well-established foreign companies are using lobbyists/consultants to assist them in altering their investment licence conditions. This strategy is increasingly being used in negotiations with the tax department, lobbying to win tenders for projects and even negotiations between joint-venture partners. The minimal direct contact strategy is proving effective for many Australian companies, in both a cost and result sense, as it distances the foreign partner from any suggestion of involvement in bribery and corruption and also avoids the situation where conflict or loss of face might occur. It is highly compatible with the emerging flexible administrative system in Vietnam with its emphasis on case-by-case solutions and non-formal decision-making processes.

5.   Use of Viet kieu

Viet kieu (overseas Vietnamese) from Australia are active in import-export business between Australia and Vietnam and a number have established small- to medium-scale ventures in their former home-land. Some are also employed by non-Vietnamese Australian com-panies as 'facilitators' – to help get business ventures in Vietnam up and running and to handle continuing interactions with the Vietnamese bureaucracy – although opinions vary on the utility of this strategy.

In theory, returnee Vietnamese possess cultural, linguistic, business and technical skills – and a range of local connections – that should make them a valuable asset for most Australian companies operating in the Vietnamese market. As one company commented, 'working with Viet kieu is essential to the success of any foreign company'. The quality, number and range of contacts – rather than other skills – appear to be the key determinants of success in many cases.

On the other hand, Viet kieu, collectively, are often regarded with suspicion, disdain and in some cases outright hostility in Vietnam. The reasons for this attitude – which is widespread – are complex, but a tendency on the part of many returnee Vietnamese to flaunt their recently acquired wealth in front of their poorer countrymen is an important contributor. In addition, many Viet kieu have connec-tions with the former South Vietnamese regime or other 'negatives' in their background that render them unsuitable as business facilita-tors. Companies are well advised, therefore, to exercise a high degree of care and caution in selecting Viet kieu to facilitate their business interests in Vietnam. Particular attention should be paid to verifying – admittedly often a difficult task – an individual's past history in Vietnam and the connections he or she claims in the Vietnamese government and community.

6.   Patience and persistence

'Vietnam is definitely not a place for short-term players, being kinder to people with the patience, the persistence and the purpose that is needed to last for the long haul (Warren Taylor, President,

Australia Vietnam Business Council quoted in the *Asian Business Review*, 1996, p. 25). Things that may be quick to arrange in Australia can be very slow to set up in Vietnam, for example obtaining access to essential utilities such as telephones and electricity, employing staff, even obtaining basic office equipment. These challenges are in addition to coping with inadequate physical infrastructure and the complexities of getting investment licences approved as outlined previously. As a result of increasing pressure on companies to demonstrate why their foreign investment is needed in Vietnam, many companies are also specifying a phased development programme for their investments as a way of indicating there will be ongoing technology transfer. A number of businesses interviewed suggested that it is important to be sensitive to the local culture in Vietnam and have the patience to understand Vietnam's rules, as well as a willingness to compromise and to work within the system. This understanding is required, not only by the Australian representatives 'on-the-ground' in Vietnam, but also by the head offices of these companies in Australia who often lack an appreciation of the realities of doing business in Vietnam.

V. Conclusions

While some of the gloss has gone out of Vietnam as an investment destination in recent years, most Australian businesses interviewed by Smee (1996) are confident about Vietnam's medium- to longer-term prospects. Of the Australian companies surveyed by Maitland, most 'believed that, given their experiences, they would still invest in Vietnam, and none would elect to delay their entry into the country' (Maitland, 1996, p. 104). Maitland also notes the main attraction for Australian companies is not quick profits or cheap inputs for production for export, but in establishing a long-term presence in an economy with strong growth prospects. This is consistent with the view that 'negative corporate stories from Vietnam represent about 3 per cent of the real picture of Australia's investment in Vietnam (*Asian Business Review*, 1996, p. 24).

A number of businesses interviewed pointed to the real improvements that have been achieved in the business environment (such as strong growth, increased consumer spending, improved living conditions, expanding foreign direct investment and better infrastructure) and to positive signs that things will continue to improve (such as more laws, commitment to encouraging foreign investment, membership of ASEAN and so on). But few expect progress to be smooth or rapid: change will take time but the general direction is positive and many businesses are adopting a 'wait and see' approach.

Overall, there is a need for balanced and realistic assessments of business opportunities in Vietnam. Both sides are on a steep learning curve: Vietnam about the complexities of a market economy and Australian business about the complexity of operating in Vietnam.[4] Most businesses on the ground warn against coming to Vietnam with overly optimistic expectations. However, much of the recent media reporting on the business environment in Vietnam has been overly negative, particularly following the withdrawal from Vietnam of some large-scale Australian investment projects, including P&O, Westralian Sands and BHP Petroleum. Vietnam still offers genuine opportunities to Australian companies, partly because of its abundant natural resources, its potentially large domestic market and booming consumer spending 'our sales have expanded by more than 50 per cent per annum over the past three years', its cheap and motivated labour force, and its strategic location with good access to North and South East Asian markets.

Notes

1. This is an interesting development as most companies identify the size of the local Vietnamese market as a critical factor in their investment criteria and many set out with the intention of supplying the local market.
2. The 'Asian approach' emphasizes building long-term relationships and patronage networks which means they are often more prepared to accept short-term facilitation costs in the expectation of obtaining a pay back at a later date.
3. For example, P&O's withdrawal from the Ben Nghe port project in Vietnam cited local partner indifference as a major stumbling block (Freeman, 1996).
4. Some of the blame for the hard luck business stories in Vietnam belongs to the absurd expectations held by some people coming to Vietnam.

References

Beca Investments and Juliette Chen (1995), *Business in Vietnam: Shifting into gear*, Economist Intelligence Unit Research Report, Hong Kong.

Cleary, P. (1995), Survey of Vietnam, *Australian Financial Review*, 10 May, pp. 25–32, Sydney.

Diaz, T. (1995), 'If you're a foreigner in a dispute in Vietnam, settle', *The Australian*, 28 July, p. 37.

Dung, N. T. (1996), 'Foreign Direct Investment in Vietnam' in Leung, S. (ed.), *Vietnam Assessment: creating a sound investment climate*, Institute of Southeast Asian Studies/National Centre for Development Studies, Singapore.

Freeman, N. (1995), 'The reluctantly emerging market', *Business Times Weekend Edition*, 28–29 October, Singapore.

Howard, J. (1996), 'Expats find Vietnam most stressful', *International Business Asia*, March, Sydney.

Leung, S. (ed.) (1996), *Vietnam Assessment: creating a sound investment climate*, Institute of Southeast Asian Studies/National Centre for Development Studies, Singapore.

Maitland E. 1996, 'Foreign Investors in Vietnam: An Australian Case Study', in Leung, S. (ed.), *Vietnam Assessment: creating a sound investment climate*, Institute of Southeast Asian Studies/National Centre for Development Studies, Singapore.

Mansell, T (1996), 'Vietnam breaks eggs to bring home bacon', *The West Australian*, 17 June, p. 49.

O'Flahertie, S. (1996), 'Is Vietnam worth the risk', *Asian Business Review*, June, pp. 24–33.

Schwarz, A. (1996), 'Investment: Vietnam Syndrome', *Far Eastern Economic Review*, 28 March, pp. 50–51.

Schwarz, A. (1996), 'Vietnam: Trade and Investment', *Far Eastern Economic Review*, 24 October, pp. 45–51.

Smee, M. (1996), Consultant to EAAU's Report, Department of Foreign Affairs and Trade, Camberra.

Smee, M. (1997), *The New ASEANs: Vietnam, Burma, Cambodia and Laos* (EAAU, Department of Foreign Affairs and Trade, Camberra).

Spencer, C. and Heij, G. (1995), *A Guide to Doing Business in Vietnam*, Department of Commerce and Trade Western Australia and Asia Research Centre, Murdoch University, Perth.

Turner, D. (1996), 'Vietnam – A Special Feature', *International Business Asia*, 22 July, pp. 6–10, Sydney.

6
Australia's Trade with East Asia: Opportunities with Vietnam

Charles Harvie

I. Introduction

Australia has experienced a further noticeable change in its trade pattern during the period of the 1990s, with an increasing focus being placed upon that with the members of the Asia Pacific Economic Cooperation (APEC) and Association of South East Asian Nations (ASEAN) groupings of nations. This can be seen by an expansion of Australia's merchandise exports and imports to these trading groups. The major objective of this paper is to analyse and interpret these developments focusing upon Australia's trading relationship with East Asia and the opportunities of expanded trade with the emerging Vietnamese economy. The significance of the former group of nations is demonstrated by the fact that eight of Australia's top ten major trading partners are situated in East Asia, with major trading surpluses, with the exception of China, being generated from such trade.

Vietnam has engaged, since the process of economic reform known as 'Doi Moi' was initiated in 1986, in a process of opening up the economy to both international investment and trade, as part of a general movement towards its integration into the regional and global economy. This was further enhanced in February 1994 with the ending of the US trade and investment embargo, and its recognition as an increasingly respected member of regional and international communities, resulting in the normalization of the political relationship with the United States in 1995, its membership of

ASEAN in July 1995 and (at the time of writing) prospective membership of APEC and the World Trade Organization.

Vietnam's strategic locational advantage, its industrious, literate, motivated, inexpensive and adaptable work force makes it a particularly attractive East Asian economy in which to develop long-term trade and investment opportunities for Australian companies, which have to date in general been well received in the country. Although the extent of trade and investment between the two countries is still small – Australia exported only AUD188 mn of goods to and imported AUD286.8 mn from Vietnam in 1995 – it has grown rapidly and there is great potential for a continued expansion in trade and investment between the two countries. While pitfalls for participating Australian businesses in such trade and investment do exist, for the wary and the patient substantial opportunities do, and will, exist in Vietnam's rapidly expanding economy.

The remainder of the chapter proceeds as follows. In section 2 a general overview of trend developments in Australia's and Vietnam's overall current account balances is conducted, in which the significance of trade for the two economics is identified. Section 3 analyses in some depth Australia's changing trade patterns, with particular focus placed upon that relating to East Asia and the contribution of Vietnam within this context. Section 4 identifies the potential opportunities and attractions and the potential pitfalls of engaging in trade and investment linkages with Vietnam, and explicitly identifys key areas of opportunity for Australian compa nies. Finally section 5 presents a summary of the major conclusions from this chapter.

II. Overview of developments in Australia's and Vietnam's trade and current account balances

A dominant influence over the operation of recent macroeconomic policy in Australia have been attempts to reduce the size of its current account deficits, which reached a comparable magnitude to that during the terms of trade collapse of the mid 1980s at 6.1 per cent of GDP in 1994–95. Table 6.1 outlines developments in the current account and its major components over the period 1989/90–1995/96. Over this period of time merchandise exports have grown by some 54.9 per cent while that of merchandise imports by some 51.2 per cent. Generally Australia has a surplus on merchandise trade, although for the period under analysis this only occurred for the years 1990–91, 1991–92 and 1992–93 during which time the economy suffered a severe downturn in economic activity. The strong recovery of the economy thereafter contributed to a deterioration in the merchandise balance culminating in a major blowout of the current account in 1994–95. For the last financial year 1995–96 the size of this deficit has been considerably reduced, falling to 4.2 per cent of GDP. The sum of merchandise exports and imports amounted to some 30 per cent of Australia's GDP which is indicative of the significance of trade to it and that it is a relatively open developed economy.

The net services balance has generally been in deficit during the 1990s although a small surplus was recorded in 1995–96. However, it is the net income balance which presents the major problem for Australia. The period of rising current account deficits during the 1980s, particularly after the resources boom of the early 1980s and the terms of trade collapse of 1985/86, contributed significantly to the build up of Australia's foreign debt, with a consequential increase in debt interest payments. Persistent current account deficits during the period of the 1990s have further exacerbated Australia's gross and net foreign debt, contributing to a further deterioration of the net income account. However, after a noticeable improvement in this balance during the early 1990s it has since further deteriorated to over AUD19 bn by 1995–96. On the other hand, net unrequited transfers are generally positive for Australia and this position has been maintained during the 1990s.

Overall the current account balance has, therefore, been considerably in deficit during the period of the 1990s in absolute terms, however a better indication of the extent of the problem is indicated by the deficit as a proportion of GDP. After the current account blowout of 1994–95 when the current account deficit reached some 6.1 per cent of GDP arising primarily from the rapid recovery of the economy from 1992–93 and the inability to constrain domestic demand, the deficit improved considerably to around AUD20 bn by 1995–96, although still representing some 4.2 per cent of GDP. Government policy has been severely constrained and focused upon the need to improve the country's

Table 6.1 Australia – balance of payments on current account AUDbn (balance of payments basis) 1989/90–1995/96

	1989–90	1990–91	1991–92	1992–93	1993–94	1994–95	1995–96
Exports (fob)	48.6	52.2	54.9	60.0	63.8	66.4	75.3
Imports (fob)	-51.0	-49.2	-51.1	-59.4	-64.4	-74.7	77.1
Balance on merchandise trade	-2.4	2.9	3.8	0.6	-0.6	-8.3	-1.8
Services (net)	-4.1	-2.6	-1.9	-2.2	-1.0	-1.4	0.1
Income (net)	-17.2	-18.1	-15.7	-13.9	-19.8	-18.4	-19.4
Unrequited transfers (net)	2.3	2.4	2.2	0.7	0.2	0.5	1.2
Current account balance	-21.5	-15.3	-11.6	-14.9	-16.2	-27.5	-20.0
Current account balance (% of GDP)	-5.8	-4.0	-3.0	-3.7	-3.9	-6.1	-4.2

Source: ABS Balance of Payments and Investment Position (Catalogue No. 5363.0), 1994–95 p. 12.

current account performance. The terms of trade collapse in the mid 1980s and the banana republic statement made by the then Treasurer, Paul Keating, thrust the current account to the centre of macroeconomic policy. Since this time a key objective has been to reduce this deficit to around 3 per cent of GDP and to stabilize the build-up of foreign debt.

During the late 1980s the twin deficit argument was advanced, which argued that there was a direct, and in its most extreme version effectively a one-to-one, relationship between the size of the public sector deficit and the current account deficit. Focus was therefore placed upon the need to reduce the size of the public sector deficit. Much empirical research was conducted into this issue which effectively discredited any simple relationship between the public sector deficit and the current account deficit. However, with the election of the Howard Government in March 1996 focus again has been placed upon the need to reduce the size of public sector deficits, and thereby to enhance public sector net lending, which would contribute to reduced pressure on domestic savings and a consequential improvement in the current account performance.

Vietnam until the late 1980s experienced a sizeable imbalance in its merchandise trade, in which merchandise imports considerably exceeded merchandise exports. Such a situation was only sustainable through access to foreign savings, specifically financial assistance from the former Soviet Union which at its peak amounted to some US$1 bn annually. The loss of financial assistance from the Soviet Union, as well as the markets of the former Council for Mutual Economic Assistance (CMEA) economies from 1989 onwards, precipitated a radical re-think of the authorities' attitude towards the role and structure of its international trade. Prior to this point, under the centrally planned regime, emphasis was placed upon economic autarchy wherever possible, with exporting seen as a means of obtaining necessities not produced domestically but not as the centrepiece of economic growth and development as in its rapidly developing regional neighbours. The mid 1980s saw a stagnating and inflation-ridden economy unable to feed its population. A further exodus of the population initiated by a further deterioration of the economy precipitated a radical change in policy and the recognition that the centrally planned model of economic development was not working for the country. By the late 1980s, with the traumatic developments in central and eastern Europe, Vietnam was faced with the need to reorientate its trade, particularly to the convertible currency countries of Asia, in order to pay for its imports which now had to be paid for in hard currency at world prices. Over the period 1989–92 Vietnam achieved remarkable progress in this regard. The introduction of a unified and relatively market determined exchange rate in 1989 was of major assistance in boosting trade. Exports expanded rapidly and such was their growth that they effectively offset merchandise imports by 1992. The relative ease with which Vietnam was able to reorientate its exports was primarily due to the fact that they were mainly in the form of crude oil and rice and therefore relatively easy to transfer to the markets of East Asia. However this should not detract from the remarkable achievements attained at this time.

Since 1992 the growth of imports has outstripped that of exports contributing to persistent and growing deficits on the trade and current account balances (see Table 6.2). Such imbalances are not unusual for an economy at the stage of economic development achieved by Vietnam, and in fact could be beneficial by contributing to sizeable inflows of capital that will be essential for the process of growth and development of the economy. Vietnam requires the importation of capital and intermediate goods in the process of meeting its investment requirements, financed primarily in the form of foreign savings (foreign direct investment or overseas development assistance), so as to achieve the modernization of its productive capacities, leading ultimately to the expansion of output and exports. Such a trade imbalance will contribute to downward

Table 6.2   Vietnam – balance of payments on current account US$bn

	1990	*1991*	*1992*	*1993*	*1994*	*1995*
Exports	1.7	2.0	2.5	2.9	3.6	5.2
Imports	1.8	2.1	2.5	3.5	5.0	7.5
Trade balance	–0.1	–0.1	0	–0.7	–1.4	–2.3
Current account (% of GDP)	–4.2	–1.8	–0.7	–8.3	–7.2	–8.0

Source: Department of Foreign Affairs and Trade, *Country Economic Brief*, Vietnam, April 1996.

pressure on the national currency (the Vietnamese dong) which will maintain the country's international competitiveness and enhance further the expansion of exports. Hence, although the trade imbalance is substantial, with the current account deficit equivalent to 8 per cent of GDP in 1995, this should not be perceived as detrimental. The key issue relates to the ability of the country to meet its foreign debt repayments, arising from the accumulation of foreign debt due to the current account deficits. This will crucially depend upon how well the foreign savings inflows are utilized, specifically in terms of the enhanced productive capacity of the economy and the additional exports generated. If this is achieved then the country will have utilized its foreign borrowings well.

The contribution of the external sector, even at this early stage of its economic development, is making a major contribution towards the generation of the country's GDP. Vietnam's trade flows have shown remarkable growth during the past five years. Although in absolute terms merchandise exports and imports only totalled US$5.2 bn and US$7.5 bn respectively in 1995, this foreign trade turnover of some US$12.7 bn represented a record for the country and amounted to 62.5 per cent of GDP (assuming Vietnam's GDP is equivalent to approximately US$20 bn), indicative of both the openness of the economy and the crucial role which international trade will play in the future economic development and growth of its economy. Exports were 23 per cent higher and imports 29 per cent higher than their values in 1994, resulting in a sizeable trade deficit of about US$2.3 bn in 1995. In this same year all of Vietnam's major trading partners were located in the East Asian region, these being Japan (US$2.3 bn), Singapore (US$2.03bn), South Korea (US$1.59 bn), Taiwan (US$1.1 bn) and China (US$1 bn). (These figures being the sum of both merchandise exports and imports). Approximately 70 per cent of Vietnamese exports are now directed to markets in the Asia Pacific region. For Vietnam, Australia remains a middle-sized trading partner.

Official figures, however, on Vietnam's trade levels require to be treated with some caution, particularly due to the fact that they do not include large black market flows of goods from China which also involve Laos and Cambodia. It is estimated that smuggling could account for as much as 30 per cent of Vietnam's total trade, encouraged by Vietnam's high and varied levels of tariffs. The illegal flows of Vietnamese rice to China have been complemented by a steady flow of consumer goods, such as electronics, bicycles and kitchenware from China to Vietnam.

III. Australia and Vietnam's trade developments

This section focuses upon recent developments in Australia's merchandise exports and imports emphasizing the geographical nature of these changes, the relative significance of bilateral trade between Australia and Vietnam, and a brief analysis of the breakdown of Australia's overall merchandise trade balance by commodity and major country grouping.

1. Australia's merchandise exports

Table 6.3 summarises the breakdown of Australia's merchandise exports by country groups and puts into perspective the significance of exports to Vietnam. It is apparent from this table that there is increasing significance of exports to the two trade groups of APEC and ASEAN, where the latter grouping, with the exception of Vietnam itself, is subsumed by the former. The significance of the APEC grouping as a market for Australia's merchandise exports is exemplified by its share rising from just over 60 per cent in 1989–90 to just under 76 per cent by 1995–96. The contribution to this almost 16 per cent share increase over the past six years from the ASEAN grouping alone, with a very small contribution from Vietnam, was equal to 5 per cent. Hence the expansion of Australia's exports has been focused upon the Asia Pacific region, with a significant contribution to this coming from the economies of South-East Asia.

Also observable from Table 6.3 is the declining relative significance of the European Union as a major export market, with its share declining from 14.4 per cent in 1990–91 to 11.1 per cent in 1995–96. This declining significance of the rich industrialized economies of Europe is also reflected in an overall declining significance of industrialized economies in general as markets for Australia's exports. The OECD economies' share of this declining from 59.5 per cent in 1989–90 to 53 per cent in 1994–95. This has been offset by a rising share to the developing economies, which increased from 42.8 per cent in 1993–94 to 47.2 per cent in

Table 6.3 Breakdown of Australia's merchandise exports (per cent of total): by country groups

	1989–90	1990–91	1991–92	1992–93	1993–94	1994–95	1995–96
APEC[1]	60.3	64.0	73.6	74.8	76.2	77.9	75.7
ASEAN[2]	10.4	12.1	13.3	14.4	14.0	15.5	15.4
EU[3]	14.4	12.6	13.0	12.1	11.8	11.2	11.1
OECD	59.5	60.7	57.6	54.5	53.9	53.0	na
Developing countries	–	–	–	–	42.8	44.2	47.2
OPEC	5.8	5.0	5.1	5.0	5.3	4.8	6.0
Vietnam	0.2	0.1	0.1	0.1	0.2	0.2	0.3

1. APEC includes Brunei, Canada, Chile, China, Hong Kong, Indonesia, Japan, S. Korea, Malaysia, Mexico, New Zealand, Papua New Guinea, Philippines, Singapore, Taiwan, Thailand, United States
2. ASEAN includes Brunei, Indonesia, Malaysia, Philippines, Singapore, Thailand, Vietnam
3. EU includes Austria, Belgium–Luxembourg, Denmark, Finland, France, Germany, Greece, Ireland, Italy, Netherlands, Portugal, Spain, United Kingdom

Source: ABS International Merchandise Trade (Catalogue No. 5422.0) June Quarter 1996.

1995–96. The OPEC economies' share of total merchandise exports has barely changed over the period of time under discussion.

Overall it can be concluded that there has been an important structural shift in the composition of Australia's merchandise exports, which in general has shifted from the industrialised economies to the developing economies. The evidence would suggest that it is the developing economies in south-east Asia (ASEAN) and the Asia Pacific region in general which have provided Australia with an expansion in its merchandise export market.

Table 6.4 provides further evidence on the significance of countries in the Asia Pacific region in particular as markets for Australia's exports. Of Australia's top ten export markets nine are in the Asia Pacific region, accounting for 66.3 per cent of total exports, with the UK being the only exception. Closer study reveals further that seven of the top ten are in East Asia with these countries alone accounting for over half (52.4 per cent) of total merchandise exports. Table 6.4 also reveals clearly that the major growth of Australia's exports has been primarily with East Asia, New Zealand being the major exception to this, and particularly with the economies of Japan (Australia's leading export market by a considerable margin), South Korea and China. Of the top ten export markets only that of the USA has experienced a decline over the period of time focused upon. The contribution of Vietnam to total merchandise exports by comparison remains very small at around AUD200 mn in 1995–96, or approximately 0.3 per cent of the total (see Table 6.3).

2. Australia's merchandise imports

Table 6.5 presents a summary of structural developments in Australia's merchandise imports. As with the case of exports Australia has experienced a distinct shift in its sources of imports towards the APEC grouping including that of the ASEAN countries. Unlike the case of exports there has also been a slight shift towards that of the EU economies. In general there has been a movement away from the rich industrialized economies towards the developing countries as sources of imports, however, in saying this it is apparent from Table 6.5 that the industrialized economies still provide over 71 per cent of Australia's merchandise import needs. The contribution of the OPEC economies is relatively small and this is even more so for Vietnam.

Table 6.4 Australia's major export (merchandise) markets – top ten (AUD bn)

	1989–90	1990–91	1991–92	1992–93	1993–94	1994–95	1995–96
1. Japan*	12.8	14.3	14.6	15.2	15.9	16.3	16.4
2. S. Korea*	2.7	3.2	3.4	4.0	4.7	5.2	6.6
3. New Zealand	2.6	2.5	2.8	3.4	4.0	4.8	5.6
4. USA	5.4	6.2	5.3	4.9	5.1	4.7	4.6
5. China*	1.2	1.4	1.5	2.3	2.6	3.0	3.8
6. Singapore*	1.9	2.8	3.2	3.8	3.2	3.6	3.6
7. Taiwan*	1.8	2.0	2.5	2.7	2.8	3.1	3.4
8. Hong Kong*	1.3	1.6	2.1	2.6	2.8	2.6	3.1
9. UK	1.7	1.8	1.9	2.4	2.9	2.3	2.8
10. Indonesia*	1.0	1.5	1.6	1.7	1.9	2.1	2.8
Vietnam	0.1	0.03	0.1	0.1	0.1	0.2	0.2

* East Asian Economies

Source: ABS International Merchandise Trade (Catalogue No. 5422.0) June Quarter 1996.

Table 6.5   Breakdown of Australia's merchandise imports (per cent of total): by country groups

	1989–90	1990–91	1991–92	1992–93	1993–94	1994–95	1995–96
APEC[1]	58.2	57.5	67.3	67.2	69.1	67.4	66.8
ASEAN[2]	5.8	7.1	8.1	8.4	8.2	8.6	9.5
EU[3]	22.4	21.7	20.2	19.5	22.6	24.4	24.9
OECD	76.3	74.2	72.2	70.7	70.5	71.4	na
Developing countries	–	–	–	–	26.5	26.6	27.9
OPEC	3.3	4.5	4.3	4.9	4.0	3.9	4.2
Vietnam	0.03	0.04	0.2	0.4	0.5	0.4	0.4

1. APEC includes Brunei, Canada, Chile, China, Hong Kong, Indonesia, Japan, S. Korea, Malaysia, Mexico, New Zealand, Papua New Guinea, Philippines, Singapore, Taiwan, Thailand, United States. China, Hong Kong and Taiwan are included from 1991–92 onwards. Mexico and Papua New Guinea are included from 1993–94 onwards. Chile is included from 1994–95 onwards

2. ASEAN includes Brunei, Indonesia, Malaysia, Philippines, Singapore, Thailand, Vietnam

3. EU includes Austria, Belgium–Luxembourg, Denmark, Finland, France, Germany, Greece, Ireland, Italy, Netherlands, Portugal, Spain, United Kingdom

Source: ABS International Merchandise Trade (Catalogue No. 5422.0) June Quarter 1996.

Australia's top ten sources of merchandise imports by country is summarised in Table 6.6. From this the continuing significance of the advanced industrialized economies as sources of imports is apparent. Of the top ten sources of imports six can be classified as advanced industrial economies (USA, Japan, UK, Germany, New Zealand and Italy in that order). The USA and Japan alone contribute 36.8 per cent of total merchandise imports and the six previously identified economies contribute some 57.1 per cent of total merchandise imports. The APEC members from this group contributed 56.4 per cent of the total while the countries of East Asia contributed 28.9 per cent of the total. Of particular note has been the very rapid expansion in merchandise imports from the USA, which has contributed considerably to the sizeable imbalance on merchandise trade between the two countries. Vietnams' contribution to Australia's merchandise imports, as with exports, is currently very small amounting to some AUD286.8 mn in 1995–96, representing only 0.4 per cent of total imports.

3. Australia's trade imbalances

Table 6.7 summarises the extent of individual country trade imbalances with Australia, focusing upon that with its top ten trading partners. Of these top ten trading countries six are in East Asia, eight are in APEC, two are in ASEAN, two are in the EU, five are advanced industrial countries who are members of the OECD, and finally four are developing nations. Japan is by far and away Australia's major trading partner followed by the USA, where there is a distinct bias towards merchandise imports. In terms of the overall trade balance, strong surpluses for Australia are recorded with all of the East Asian economies, with the exception of China where a small trade deficit is recorded. Australia's deficits occur with the USA, where a staggering trade deficit of some AUD13 bn was recorded for 1995–96, and the advanced industrial European economies of the UK and Germany with which Australia had trade deficits of AUD2.1 bn and AUD3.8 bn respectively.

Australia has recorded trade deficits with Vietnam since 1992 (see Table 6.8) reaching some AUD176.3 mn in 1994 at its peak, but falling to just AUD98.8 mn in 1995. As previously indicated the magnitude of trade between Australia and Vietnam is still very small, although it has increased substantially, from a very low base,

Table 6.6 Australia's major import (merchandise) sources – top ten (AUD bn)

	1989–90	1990–91	1991–92	1992–93	1993–94	1994–95	1995–96
1. USA	12.3	11.6	11.9	13.0	14.0	16.0	17.6
2. Japan*	9.6	9.0	9.3	11.2	11.7	12.8	10.8
3. UK	3.3	3.3	3.1	3.4	3.7	4.4	4.9
4. Germany	3.4	3.1	3.0	3.4	3.8	4.9	4.9
5. China*	1.2	1.5	2.0	2.5	3.1	3.6	4.0
6. New Zealand	2.2	2.2	2.4	2.8	3.2	3.6	3.6
7. Singapore*	1.2	1.3	1.2	1.5	1.8	2.2	2.6
8. Taiwan*	1.9	1.8	2.0	2.2	2.4	2.6	2.6
9. S. Korea*	1.2	1.3	1.2	1.7	1.9	2.0	2.3
10. Italy	1.6	1.4	1.2	1.4	1.6	2.0	2.2
Vietnam	0.02	0.02	0.03	0.2	0.3	0.3	0.3

* East Asian Economies
Source: ABS International Merchandise Trade (Catalogue No. 5422.0) June Quarter 1996.

Table 6.7   Australia's major trading partners –1995–96 (AUD bn)

	Exports	Imports	Total	Trade surplus/ deficit
1. Japan*	16.4	10.8	27.2	+5.6
2. USA	4.6	17.6	22.2	–13.0
3. New Zealand	5.6	3.6	9.2	+2.0
4. S. Korea*	6.6	2.3	8.9	+4.3
5. China*	3.8	4.0	7.8	–0.2
6. UK	2.8	4.9	7.7	–2.1
7. Singapore*	3.6	2.6	6.2	+1.0
8. Taiwan*	3.4	2.6	6.0	+0.8
9. Germany	1.1	4.9	6.0	–3.8
10. Indonesia*	2.8	1.5	4.3	+0.7
Vietnam	0.2	0.3	0.5	–0.1

* East Asian Economies
Source: ABS International Merchandise Trade (Catalogue No. 5422.0), June Quarter, 1996.

Table 6.8   Australia's trade with Vietnam (AUD mn)

	1991	1992	1993	1994	1995
Total exports	47.0	50.5	107.2	113.1	188.0
Total imports	30.3	202.1	251.3	289.4	286.8
Merchandise trade balance	16.7	–151.6	–144.1	–176.3	–98.8

Source: Department of Foreign Affairs and Trade, *Country Economic Brief*, Vietnam, April 1996.

over the period from 1991–1995. A major objective of the following section will be to identify the commodity areas in which this is currently taking place and the opportunities which exist for expanding trade considerably in the future. However, before doing so, a brief discussion is now conducted again on Australia's trade balance but this time focusing upon its composition by commodity and country grouping. This information is summarised in Table 6.9 for the year 1995–96. In the table six broad commodity categories have been identified as follows: (1) food, beverages and tobacco, (2) crude materials except fuels, (3) mineral fuels, (3) chemicals, (4) manufactured goods and (5) commodities (not elsewhere specified). The trade surplus/deficit for each of these categories by country group-

Table 6.9 Australia's trade balance by commodity and country grouping (AUD bn) 1995–96

	APEC	ASEAN	DCs*	EU	OPEC	Total
1. Food, beverages & tobacco	+6.0	–1.2	+3.3	–0.1	+0.7	+12.4
2. Crude materials except fuels	+6.4	+0.6	–3.2	+2.0	+0.3	+13.1
3. Mineral fuels	+5.2	–0.7	+1.5	+1.0	–1.9	+8.3
4. Chemicals	–1.7	+0.2	+0.2	–2.9	neg**	–5.9
5. Manufactured goods	–23.5	+0.3	–4.7	–12.5	+0.6	–36.3
6. Commodities, nes	+13.1	+2.9	+9.7	+1.5	+1.4	+6.6

* Developing countries
** Negligible
Source: Developed from ABS International Merchandise Trade (Catalogue No. 5422.0) June Quarter 1996.

ing is identified. The broad country groupings consist of APEC, ASEAN, Developing Countries (DCs), the European Union (EU) and OPEC.

It is interesting to observe from Table 6.9 that Australia achieved a strong trading performance in the following categories: (1) food, beverages and tobacco, (2) crude materials except fuels, (3) mineral fuels and (6) commodities not elsewhere specified. These areas together generated a trading surplus of some AUD40.4 bn in 1995–96. With some minor exceptions Australia achieved trading surpluses in these commodities with the APEC, ASEAN, DCs, EU and OPEC country groupings, with sizeable surpluses generated in particular with APEC countries. However, major trading weaknesses can be observed in two key areas, that of chemicals and, more importantly, in the case of manufactured goods. These two areas generated a trading deficit of some AUD42.2 bn in 1995–96 with the extremely poor trading performance in manufactured goods contributing some AUD36.3 bn of this deficit. Most of this deficit arose with the APEC economies, amounting to some AUD23.5 bn (the deficit with Japan contributing AUD8 bn and that with the USA a further AUD12.1 bn), and the European Union economies which contributed a further AUD12.5 bn deficit. However, Australia's trade in chemicals and manufactured goods with the ASEAN countries overall generated small surpluses.

Overall, however, Australia's merchandise trade is in sizeable surplus with the economies of the Asia Pacific region, including the smaller ASEAN group of nations, and is particularly in surplus with developing economies, with a much smaller surplus recorded for trade with the OPEC economies. However, it is considerably in deficit in trade with the EU economies and particularly so in manufactured goods.

In the following section developments, both contemporary and prospective, specifically in merchandise trade with Vietnam will be given focus.

IV.   Australian trade with Vietnam – contemporary developments and opportunities

Trade between Australia and Vietnam has grown rapidly over the past five years, although from a very low base, with, as indicated in the previous section, bilateral trade amounting to some AUD474.8 mn in 1995. Tables 6.10 and 6.11 summarise the major export and import items between the two countries over the last five years. Export development over the past three to four years reflects the rapid development of the consumer market for foreign products and the growing range of new goods and services available in Vietnam. It is estimated that around 10 per cent of Vietnam's 74 mn people are now able to afford at least a limited range of mostly inexpensive imported consumer goods. Consumer demand is higher than might be expected for an economy with an average annual GDP per capita of only US$220–50, due to accumulated wealth, the sharing of income within the family and access to informal credit schemes.

From Table 6.10 it can be observed that Australia's major export items to Vietnam in 1995 consisted of telecommunications equipment, cereals, iron and steel, medicaments, wool, electrical equipment, food and live animals, machinery and transport equipment, heating and cooling equipment and dairy produce. While all of these have grown rapidly over the past five years, in total they still only accounted for 41.5 per cent of total exports in 1995. This indicates that there is considerable diversity in Australia's exports to Vietnam. While exports of telecommunications equipment is by far and away the largest single export item it still only accounted for about 9 per cent of total exports. With the rising interest from Vietnam's regional neighbours in its developing markets, in addition to the lifting of the US trade embargo, there is increasing competition for Australian export sales in areas such as energy and mining technology, telecommunications equipment, building materials, agricultural commodities and consumer goods. However, as the Vietnamese economy continues to expand it will present continued export opportunities for some time to come for Australian companies. Success in this regard will depend upon the ability of Australian exporters: to advertise, package and price their products to meet the demand of the Vietnamese consumer; to account for obvious cultural differences; to recognize that the Vietnamese market cannot be assumed to be the same as in other South East Asian countries; recognize that there are strong internal contrasts in consumer tastes between the north and south of the country and between the city and the countryside.

Table 6.10 Australia's main exports to Vietnam (AUD mn) – top ten

	1991	1992	1993	1994	1995
1. Telecommunications equipment	2.6	4.6	6.1	10.4	17.7
2. Cereal preparations	0.1	0.4	0.9	1.7	10.7
3. Flat rolled iron/steel	0.3	0.9	1.1	3.6	8.2
4. Medicaments (inc. veterinary)	1.3	1.2	7.6	6.5	8.1
5. Wool & animal hair (inc. wool tops)	–	2.1	1.5	7.9	7.5
6. Electrical equipment for circuits	0.02	0.03	2.0	1.2	6.2
7. Food and live animals	0.1	0.2	1.0	2.6	6.2
8. Machinery and transport equipment	0.1	0.5	1.5	2.7	4.5
9. Heating & cooling equipment	2.8	1.4	0.4	1.0	4.5
10. Butter and other milk fats	0.9	0.1	4.9	2.7	4.5

Source: Department of Foreign Affairs and Trade, *Country Economic Brief*, Vietnam, April 1996.

Table 6.11 Australia's main imports from Vietnam (AUD m̄m) – top ten

	1991	1992	1993	1994	1995
1. Crude petroleum & oils	11.0	158.7	207.0	209.3	176.9
2. Coffee & coffee substitutes	2.8	6.4	9.2	27.3	40.7
3. Crustaceans etc.	6.9	11.3	9.7	8.5	10.3
4. Refined petroleum & oil	0	11.8	0	0	9.0
5. Fish	3.5	5.4	9.4	12.5	8.7
6. Footwear	0.2	0.5	1.1	4.3	7.9
7. Manufactures classified by material	0.5	1.4	3.4	4.7	6.7
8. Clothing	–	0.9	3.9	7.1	6.1
9. Travel goods, handbags, etc.	0.3	0.4	1.4	3.3	4.1
10. Miscellaneous manufactured articles	0.2	0.7	1.4	3.6	4.1

Source: Department of Foreign Affairs and Trade, *Country Economic Brief*, Vietnam, April 1996.

On the other hand Australia's imports from Vietnam are quite narrowly focused as indicated in Table 6.11, and mainly in the form of three primary commodity areas: oil (crude and refined), coffee and seafood. Crude petroleum and oil alone contributed 61.2 per cent of total imports, and the three previously mentioned commodities together accounted for 85.6 per cent of total Vietnamese imports to Australia. The top ten items identified contributed 95.7 per cent of total imports suggesting a considerably less diversified range of exports from Vietnam to Australia. The dominance of primary exports by Vietnam to countries such as Australia is not unusual for a country at the level of economic development so far achieved in Vietnam. Of some encouragement to Vietnam has been the considerable recent growth of exports to Australia in the form of manufactured goods, which would be expected to continue as the country achieves a higher level of economic development.

Taking a longer-term perspective, Vietnam offers great trade and investment opportunities for Australian companies. The reason for such business opportunities lies mainly in the fact that the Vietnamese people are very hard-working and determined to improve their standard of living after a prolonged period of war and economic hardship. The government and the labour force recognize the benefits to be derived from education and training and have already demonstrated their ability to be adaptable and flexible. Other factors which make the country an attractive market, as well as recipient of foreign direct investment, include:

- a political environment which is highly stable;
- since 1992 an impressive rate of economic growth has been achieved, and the authorities have made substantial progress in implementing policies for the attainment of macroeconomic stability, having received recognition for doing so by the World Bank;
- the country is strategically located in the fastest growing region of the world economy, is situated close to major shipping routes, and in close proximity to capital-exporting countries such as Hong Kong, Singapore, South Korea and Taiwan;
- the country has an adaptable, motivated, literate and inexpensive work force, making it highly attractive to labour-intensive regional industries in particular;

- the country has substantial proven and potential natural resources, however these are not so substantial on a per capita basis and the country has experienced considerable deforestation due to war and the use of such wood for domestic heating and cooking purposes;
- Vietnam has a large, although still relatively poor, market of some 74 mn consumers, which is still largely untapped and has huge potential;
- the country has an overseas support network of some 2 mn ethnic Vietnamese (Viet Kieu), of which some 150 000 are living in Australia;
- Vietnam's economy has become increasingly integrated with both regional and global markets arising from: the ending of the US trade embargo in 1994 and the normalization of the political relationship between the two countries in 1995; its membership of ASEAN in July 1995, subsequent membership of APEC in 1997 and prospective membership of the WTO. All of these developments have contributed to an ending of its relative isolation, and considerably enhanced opportunities for trade and investment.

Its membership of ASEAN has enabled Vietnam to expand its ties with Australia through the ASEAN–Australia partner dialogue process, the ASEAN Regional Forum (ARF) and the embryonic discussions in regard to forming a partnership between the ASEAN Free Trade Association (AFTA) and the Australia–New Zealand Closer Economic Relations Agreement (CER).

The Vietnamese authorities have clearly emphasized the significance of trade and foreign direct investment in the process of sustaining the country's economic development, based upon the experiences of its successful regional neighbours. Accordingly the government has actively encouraged foreign investment in export-orientated industries, particularly in textiles, oil and gas and agriculture. However, the export promotion activities of Vietnam are not as yet so well developed, although the Ministry of Trade and the Vietnam Chamber of Commerce and Industry (VCCI) are gradually developing some expertise in this area.

Vietnam's import taxes, however, remain relatively high and especially so on consumer goods. The maximum tariff was reduced to 60 per cent from 1 January 1996, but most tariffs are below

20 per cent. Special consumption taxes are placed on many luxury consumer goods such as motorcycles, alcoholic beverages, electronic goods and processed foods. Vietnam presented its first package of tariff reductions under AFTA in January 1996 but only 857 items were listed for the 0–5 per cent preferred tariff level. Most were related to machinery and equipment, followed by other industrial goods and agricultural and forestry products. Negotiations on further reductions will be difficult as Vietnam will request special exemptions to protect fragile local industries. All ASEAN members have declared their intention to cut internal tariffs to 0–5 per cent by 2003, although Vietnam has been given until 2006.

Today few direct controls on imports are imposed by the Vietnamese government, and those which remain are mainly targeted at existing domestic industry which the government perceives are important for national development, such as that of sugar, fertilizer, steel products and automobiles. Other remaining barriers to trade arise primarily from the underdeveloped nature of the Vietnamese economy and from the legacy of the period of central planning. The country's transportation and distribution system is badly in need of upgrading to keep pace with the expanding volume of goods passing through ports, and along roads and railways. Vietnam's excessive bureaucracy also contributes adversely to export-import developments. For example, domestic producers of many commodities, such as rice and coffee, are still unable to sell directly to foreign buyers, and must deal through state-owned trading companies.

From a purely Australian perspective, Australian companies have, in general, been received well in Vietnam. They have benefited from a number of significant advantages including Australia's lack of a colonial image, the decision in 1972 to establish diplomatic relations with the government in Hanoi, Australia's relatively large aid programme and the reputation of Australian business as being reliable and fair. The country is also perceived as being modern and technologically advanced, and located within Vietnam's immediate sphere of interests. In addition, Australian companies are also able to take advantage of a substantial institutional framework for commerce as agreed by the Australian and Vietnamese governments through a number of bilateral agreements and regular official consultations.

Vietnam therefore presents many opportunities for the Australian business sector in terms of both trade and investment, arising from its strategic location in East Asia, its well motivated, literate, adaptable and relatively inexpensive labour force. Many obstacles and pitfalls exist for the unwary, however, including that of excessive national and local government bureaucracy, lack of labour-force skills, lack of skills and knowledge relating to the functioning of a market economy, expensive and poor infrastructure as well as an inconsistent and arbitrary legal system. For the wary, and those prepared to take a longer-term perspective regarding profits, excellent opportunities exist in the areas of telecommunications, banking services, legal services, accounting services, education and training services, resources and mining, construction and infrastructure, building materials, transportation, food processing and medical technology. In particular, excellent opportunities exist in infrastructure and construction projects in Vietnam relating to urban planning, water supply, sewerage, electrical distribution, public transportation and building materials. It has been estimated that the country will require to spend around US$42 bn on its infrastructure over the period 1995–2000, if it is to achieve the government's stated objective of an average annual real GDP growth rate of between 9–10 per cent until the end of the century. It can be anticipated that such a requirement will further increase if the country is to achieve its additional objective of becoming an industrialized economy by the year 2010.

Recently the Vietnamese government announced that foreign direct investment in the medical sector, including that for the building of new hospitals, would be actively encouraged. As the economy develops further, more opportunities are likely to arise for Australian companies, in a variety of additional areas. Business contracts are likely to become available through funding from such sources as Australia's bilateral aid programme, the Japanese Development Assistance Program and by financial institutions such as the World Bank and the Asian Development Bank.

Also worthy of note is the increasing demand for education and training services, particularly in areas such as the English language, business, management, economics and information technology. As the economy develops, an emerging middle class is likely to expand its demand for education and training services. Currently Australia remains a popular destination for Vietnamese students, as indicated by the fact that during the period July 1995 to February 1996 some 563 student visas were issued. Approximately one-third of all Vietnamese students are funded under Australia's aid programme to Vietnam. In addition strong interest has been shown by Australia's universities, vocational education and training institutions, schools, private colleges and training providers in developing links with Vietnamese counterparts.

1.   Vietnam's foreign investment policy

Foreign direct investment plays a central role in the economic growth and development of the Vietnamese economy. This was recognized early on in the process of economic reform, given the insufficiency of domestic savings to meet the country's desperately needed investment requirements. In addition it was recognized that foreign direct investment had the benefits of generating employment, gaining access to Western technology, enhancing labour-force and managerial skills, improving export performance through gaining access to new overseas markets and, finally, providing a new source of taxation revenue. If such investment is successful it will generate economic growth further enhancing trading opportunities with Vietnam.

The Vietnamese government has identified a number of priority areas over the next few years, these being: oil and gas, heavy and light industry, mining, agriculture, petrochemicals, electricity, water supply, roads and bridges, ports and railways. In particular foreign investment will be welcomed where it:

- is in export-oriented industries which generate foreign exchange,
- is in labour-intensive industries with good employment generating prospects,
- is in industries that use Vietnamese raw materials and natural resources,
- contributes to basic infrastructure development,
- is in high-technology industries which encourage skills transfer.

Vietnam's Law on Foreign Investment, first adopted in 1987, allows for foreign investment in three basic forms: joint ventures, business cooperation contracts and 100 per cent foreign ownership.

In addition, production-sharing contracts are permitted in the oil and gas sector, and build-operate-transfer contracts have been approved as an alternative framework for infrastructure projects. Also, special provisions have been established for foreign investment in Export Processing Zones and in Industrial Zones.

The major incentives offered to foreign investors in Vietnam include:

- corporate income tax rates of between 10–20 per cent,
- exemptions or reductions on corporate tax rates,
- waivers on some import and export duties,
- repatriation of profits, subject to 5–10 per cent withholding tax rates,
- constitutional prohibitions on nationalization or expropriation.

In Vietnam about 90 per cent of all officially recognized foreign investment has taken the form of joint ventures with state-owned companies. The foreign partner provides all the capital, technological, management and marketing requirements, while the Vietnamese side generally provides land and labour Such ventures are managed on the basis of strict guidelines, and provide the major advantage of combining the local knowledge of the domestic Vietnamese partner with the capital, technology and managerial and marketing expertise of the foreign investor partner.

2.   Australian investment levels and prospects in Vietnam

Since the Vietnamese authorities promulgated the Law on Foreign Investment in 1987, Australia has been a major foreign investor in the country. In the early 1990s it ranked third on the foreign investors' table, but this ranking has declined to number eight with the expanded interest of the East Asian capital-exporting nations such as Taiwan (which is currently ranked first), Hong Kong, Japan, Singapore, South Korea and Malaysia. The United States currently ranks number six, with a rapid expansion of investment following the ending of the trade and investment embargo and the normalization of political relations between the two countries.

Australia had some 47 licensed foreign investment projects in Vietnam by January 1996, with a total committed capital of US$703 mn. The two major Australian projects have been undertaken by Telstra and BHP Petroleum, whose combined investment is equivalent to around two-thirds of Australia's total investment in Vietnam. The remaining Australian investments cover diverse areas such as mining, hotels, banking, energy development, food processing, building and construction, transportation, legal services and education.

Despite the impressive expansion in foreign direct investment achieved by Vietnam since its active initiation from 1987 and the contribution made to this by Australian companies, and the impressive opportunities which undoubtedly exist in the country, the difficulties facing the business sector in general should not be underestimated. This relates primarily to the continued existence of basic difficulties such as that of the poor state and high cost of utilizing economic infrastructure, excessive bureaucracy and red tape, corruption, inconsistencies in the application of laws and the breaking of commercial contracts.

V.   Summary and conclusions

The period of the 1990s has so far seen a further noticeable shift of Australia's trade towards the countries of the Asia-Pacific region in particular, as reflected in the fact that of Australia's top ten major trading partners eight are situated in this region. In the case of export markets there has been a noticeable increase in the significance of this region and a decline in the significance of European markets. In addition the significance of the advanced industrialized economies has declined whilst that of developing economies has increased. An almost identical development can be observed in terms of sources of imports. The future expansion of Australia's trade is therefore likely to be focused upon the further development of existing as well as the nurturing of embryonic trading relationships, such as that with Vietnam, in the Asia-Pacific region. In regard to Australia's bilateral trade with Vietnam, this has grown impressively over the past five years although from a very low base. Australian merchandise exports are already considerably diverse providing a strong basis upon which to expand such trade further, and to take advantage of the expected rise in consumer incomes as Vietnam's economy develops further. Australia's merchandise imports from Vietnam are much more heavily concentrated upon primary commodities, crude petroleum and oil in particular, which is not surprising given the stage of economic development currently achieved by that country. For Vietnam there will be the pressing need to move away from the export of primary commodities to that of higher value-added products. There are already signs that this is happening in trade with Australia as the significance of manufactured exports to this country is already increasing.

References

Australian Bureau of Statistics (1996), *Australian Economic Indicators*, November (Catalogue no. 1350.0), Canberra.

Australian Bureau of Statistics (1996), *Balance of Payments and International Investment Position 1994–95*, June (Catalogue no. 5363.0), Canberra.

Australian Bureau of Statistics (1996), *International Merchandise Trade – Australia*, June quarter (Catalogue no. 5422.0), Canberra.

Department of Foreign Affairs and Trade (1996), *Country Economic Brief – Vietnam*, April, Canberra.

De Vylder, S. and Fforde, A. (1995), *From Plan to Market: The Transition in Vietnam 1979–94*, Boulder, Colorado, USA, Westview Press.

Fforde, A. and Goldstone, A. (1995), *Vietnam to 2005: Advancing on all Fronts*, Economist Intelligence Unit, Research Report, London.

Harvie, C. and Tran Van Hoa (1997), *Vietnam's Reforms and Economic Growth*, Macmillan, UK.

Quinlan, J. P. (1995), *Vietnam: Business Opportunities and Risks, a Guide to Success in Asia's Next Dragon*, Singapore, Heinemann Asia Business Series.

7
The Mekong Basin Subregion

Anne-Marie Humphries

Economic liberalization and the promotion of foreign trade and investment in the Mekong Basin countries – Vietnam, Burma, Cambodia, Laos, Thailand and Yunnan province of China – have created significant opportunities for subregional economic cooperation in recent years. This has resulted in a range of recent initiatives and large inflows of foreign capital (both overseas development assistance and foreign direct investment) supporting moves to increase economic cooperation and develop the Mekong Basin countries as a 'corridor of commerce'.[1]

The Mekong Basin covers a land area of 2.3 mn square kilometres and a population of nearly 230 mn. As a result of market-oriented economic reforms implemented in recent years, the Mekong Basin countries have generally achieved rapid economic growth while improving macroeconomic stability.[2] In the past five years economic growth in the subregion has averaged over 6 per cent per annum. The total gross domestic product of the Mekong Basin economies was about US$184 bn in 1994 and per capita GDP ranges from around US$225 to US$2450, for an average of US$805 for the subregion, according to Asian Development Bank estimates.

I.   The Greater Mekong Subregion

One of the economic cooperation initiatives currently underway is the Greater Mekong Subregion initiative which started in 1992 with the support of the Asian Development Bank. It aims to promote economic cooperation between Vietnam, Laos, Cambodia, Burma, Thailand and Yunnan Province of China.

In addition to shared borders, the countries involved in the Greater Mekong Subregion have close cultural and historical ties. The subregion is also rich in human and natural resources. The Mekong river, which either forms the border or flows through the six countries, offers potential for hydropower development as well as significant navigation, irrigation and fisheries potential. As a result, the Greater Mekong Subregion is considered a 'natural economic area whose complementarities in natural resources, labour and capital, if exploited, could generate more vigorous growth' (Asian Development Bank, 1996a, p. 1).

The Greater Mekong Subregion initiative gained momentum after a ministerial meeting in Hanoi in 1994 agreed to step up efforts to promote economic cooperation in the subregion. Development of the initiative has also been boosted by large overseas development assistance inflows. For example, between 1992 and 1996, the Asian Development Bank has provided over US$280 mn in loans for priority subregional projects, including in the transport and energy sectors. It has provided a further US$7.6 mn in technical assistance grants to support subregional activities aimed at identifying programmes and projects and promoting subregional consultations.

The Asian Development Bank has also worked closely with other multilateral and bilateral donor agencies to mobilize resources for the subregion's development. As a result, bilateral donors from countries like Australia, Japan and the European Union, as well as the other major international aid organizations such as the International Monetary Fund, World Bank, and the United Nations Development Program, are providing large amounts of capital and technical assistance to support the economic development of the countries in the subregion (with the exception of Burma).[3]

Seven priority sectors have been identified for development; transport, tourism, energy, human resource development, trade and investment and telecommunications. The focus initially was on projects designed to enhance economic interaction, particularly on infrastructure and energy. The priority subregional projects are set out in a masterplan for each sector and many of these projects are now at the implementation stage. The projects being given priority for implementation are discussed in the section on 'Priority Projects'.

Because of the large scale of investment required in these projects, the countries of the Greater Mekong Subregion and the Asian Development Bank increasingly have recognized the importance of and are encouraging the participation of the private sector. For example, the Bank has sought, through its technical assistance grants, to create a more conducive environment for private investors through the development of appropriate legal, institutional and administrative frameworks. In addition to providing capital, the private sector is expected to contribute expertise, management skills and technology.

II.   Mekong River Commission

The Mekong River Commission plays an important role in promoting the sustainable development of the Mekong river's resources, particularly in the lower Mekong Basin. The Commission was re-established in 1995 under 'The Agreement on the Cooperation for the Sustainable Development of the Mekong River Basin'.[4] It is the latest incarnation of the Mekong Committee that was first established in 1957 and is therefore the oldest Mekong subregional cooperation initiative. The Commission also works closely with the Asian Development Bank in initiating and identifying projects for the development of the area's resources.

With the support of donor countries (including Australia) and international development agencies, the Commission/Committee has undertaken a large number of programmes and activities to develop the potential of the Mekong's resources. It provides principles for the sustainable development, utilization, management and conservation of the water and other resources of the Mekong river basin, to optimize the multiple use and mutual benefits of these resources and to minimize the harmful effects that might result from natural occurrences and man-made activities (Lim, 1996).

The Commission coordinates water resources development, management and environment protection in the region. In mid-1996, it had nearly 50 programmes or projects under implementation and another 50 had been proposed but were still seeking donor support. The total cost of these projects amounts to more than US$200 mn – about half this amount has already been secured. To implement programmes or projects the Commission publishes each year the Mekong Work Program. Programmes cover the environment, irrigation, hydropower, hydrology and human resources development. The Commission is also involved in the preparation of a Basin Development Plan to provide a long-term framework for the development of the Mekong river's resources.

III.   Other subregional cooperation initiatives

The high level of international interest in the Mekong Basin countries, for example among governments, businesses and development assistance agencies, particularly in East Asia, is reflected in an expanded number of economic cooperation initiatives (independent of the Greater Mekong Subregion initiative and those of the Mekong River Commission). These new initiatives are outlined below. They aim to promote economic development in the subregion and are sponsored by a number of different countries and organizations.

1.   ASEAN–Mekong Basin Development Cooperation

Although the details of ASEAN–Mekong Basin Development Cooperation have still to be worked out, the concept is a Malaysian initiative arising out of the ASEAN Summit in Bangkok in December 1995. A basic framework for cooperation in the development of the Mekong Basin was agreed in June 1996 and focuses on agriculture, tourism, infrastructure, utilities, energy, telecommunications, and trade and investment generating projects. The objectives of the initiative are: to accelerate economic growth and development of the Mekong Basin and to improve living standards; support moves to more market-oriented economies; garner support from donor countries and multilateral organizations; and help prepare Cambodia, Laos and Burma for their forthcoming entry into ASEAN. This represents the first time that ASEAN has made a collective effort to assist in the economic development of a subregion.

How the initiative is to be funded remains undecided. One idea under consideration is to establish a Mekong Fund to promote investment in the subregion by providing soft loans to governments in the subregion and to private investors. It has been proposed that the Mekong Fund be replenished through voluntary contributions from ASEAN countries, internal donors and multilateral aid organizations. Thailand is currently working to develop ideas for the funding of ASEAN's initiative.

2. The forum for the comprehensive development of Indochina

This Japanese initiative was formally established in Tokyo in 1995. The Forum seeks to coordinate the development activities of the large number of countries and multilateral agencies engaged in the development of Vietnam, Laos and Cambodia, and to enhance the efficiency and effectiveness of such aid. It includes working committees on infrastructure and human resource development and a private sector advisory group. It commissioned a compendium of all aid project in the three countries – compiled by the Asian Development Bank – as part of its efforts to prevent duplication and to identify areas that have been left out of aid programmes.

3. Golden quadrangle

This comprises northern Thailand, the south-west of Yunnan Province in China and neighbouring areas of Laos and Burma. The initiative dates from the mid-1980s when provincial and chamber of commerce officials from Chiang Rai Province in northern Thailand attempted to forge closer economic links with adjoining areas of Yunnan, Burma and Laos. As part of these efforts they proposed the formation of an economic or golden quadrangle consisting of the four countries of the upper Mekong Basin. The proposal gained a national profile in Thailand in early 1993 and meetings of high-level officials agreed to promote economic cooperation between the four countries. However, since late 1993, this has been left to the private sector. As a formal inter governmental initiative, this proposal has largely been overtaken by other initiatives, in particular the Asian Development Bank's Greater Mekong Subregion initiative.

4. Initiative overload?

The plethora of initiatives reflects the enormity of the task of developing the Mekong Basin countries. It does, however, also provide some grounds for optimism as it suggests that a large number of countries and organizations stand ready to assist in the development of the Mekong Basin countries. The large number of initiatives in the subregion has generated concerns about 'initiative overload' mainly because of the strain it is imposing on the limited resources of the countries involved. Concerns about possible resource waste and duplication prompted the six countries forming the Greater Mekong Subregion to agree on the need for coordination among these various initiatives. They have requested the Asian Development Bank to play a coordinating and facilitating role.

IV. Priority projects

Plans for the development of the Mekong Basin countries vary enormously in terms of their size and practicability. The aim is to provide the foundations for sustained rapid growth and modernization of the economies of the Mekong Basin countries, particularly through infrastructure development.

For example, the masterplan for the development of the Greater Mekong Subregion prepared by the Asian Development Bank identifies a number of projects for development across a range of sectors including transportation, telecommunications and energy. Over 100 projects have been endorsed by the participating countries in the Greater Mekong Subregion. Some of these projects are already being carried out, others are still being studied. The masterplan calls for US$40 bn to be spent over the next twenty-five years on infrastructure development alone to provide the basis for the Greater Mekong Subregion's economic development.[5]

The costs associated with the Subregion's enormous need for infrastructure, however, exceed the financial capacity of the six governments and official development assistance commitments. This implies that many of the proposed projects will require development agency support and participation from the private sector. At present, only 10 per cent of infrastructure investment is being funded by the private sector: it is hoped that over half of the US$40 bn can be raised through international investors. Unless dramatic improvements occur in the investment climates of the Mekong Basin countries, however, this level of private sector involvement appears unlikely.

Many of the projects identified in the Asian Development Bank's masterplan have already progressed to implementation. For example, projects such as the US$280 mn Theun Hinboun Hydropower project involving Laos and Thailand, and the upgrading of subregional roads in Yunnan, Laos and Cambodia, are already being implemented. Other projects are entering the implementation stage, having already been the subject of detailed engineering and feasibility studies. Some projects in the environment, tourism, human resource development and trade and investment sectors are also being implemented with regional technical assistance grants from the Asian Development Bank and co-financing from other donors.

1. Transport infrastructure

A major area of focus is transport infrastructure – especially roads, ports and airports – required to facilitate cross-border trade in goods and services in the subregion.[6] The road network, in particular, will be an important means of linking the countries involved. At this stage, the quality of road infrastructure in the subregion is very poor.

Some of the priority projects agreed to in the transport sector focus on upgrading existing infrastructure rather than building from scratch. The priority road transport projects are:

- the construction and upgrading of a road passing through Bangkok, Phnom Penh, Ho Chi Minh City and ending in the Vietnamese coastal city of Vung Tao, estimated to cost US$207 mn – currently entering the implementation stage with detailed engineering studies being undertaken;
- the development of a Thailand–Laos–Vietnam east–west corridor involving routes 8, 9 and possibly 12, including the construction of associated bridges and ports, estimated to cost US$192 mn – the feasibility study is currently underway;
- a road link between Chiang Rai in Thailand and Kunming in Yunnan Province of China via Laos and Burma, estimated to cost US$108 mn; and
- upgrading the Kunming – Lashio (Burma) road system at an estimated cost of US$817 mn.

In addition, there is some longer-term interest in developing and upgrading railways in the subregion. The existing rail system is limited and has deteriorated because of a lack of maintenance. Malaysia has offered to underwrite a feasibility study on a railway running from Singapore to Kunming in Yunnan Province of China.[7] There are other proposals for subregional rail projects including: the Yunnan–Laos or Burma–Thailand railway project estimated to cost between US$1.2–1.8 bn; the Thailand–Cambodia–Vietnam railway project costing US$735 mn; and the Yunnan—Burma railway project costing US$600–700 mn (Asia Times, March 1996). Railway construction appears to be a long-term option because of the high costs involved and the current lack of railway infrastructure, although the Malaysian government is giving it very high priority.

The Subregion's port infrastructure is also generally run down with poor berthing facilities, dilapidated cargo-handling equipment, and inefficient port operations. So priority is being given to upgrading ports and to developing inland water transport projects (linking southern Laos and north-eastern Cambodia) as well as improving navigation in the Mekong Delta.

The Asian Development Bank has also proposed a number of airport improvement projects and projects to establish new subregional air routes to facilitate transport, business and tourism links.

Increasing attention is also being paid to the improvement of 'soft' infrastructure in the transport sector, for example the liberalization and harmonization of rules and procedures governing cross border access

2. Energy

The development of the energy sector is being given priority for investment as part of the Greater Mekong Subregion. Hydroelectricity generation from the Mekong River is thought to offer considerable potential to link the economies of the subregion. Although the Subregion is well-endowed with energy resources, their utilization is low and their distribution uneven. For example, the Mekong hydropower potential lies in Laos and Cambodia. Thailand is also interested in obtaining power from an upper Mekong Grid: in Yunnan province in China large-scale dam construction is already underway.[8] In addition to the subregion's hydropower potential there are abundant coal deposits and promising oil and natural gas reserves.

Present levels of electrification in the subregion are very low. For example, only about 10 per cent of the total number of households in Vietnam, Cambodia and Laos have electricity. At current rates of growth power demand in these countries will increase eight-fold between 1993 and 2020. Many of the proposed projects in the energy sector in the Subregion involve power transmission. A number of projects also aim to strengthen energy ministries and agencies in these countries. Priority hydro electricity and electricity projects are:

- Xe Kong and Se San Basin hydropower project in Cambodia, Laos and Vietnam, with transmission interconnection among these countries and with Thailand;
- feasibility study of the Nam Tha hydropower project in Laos, including transmission interconnection with Thailand;
- transmission interconnection with Thailand of the Jinghong hydropower project in Yunnan;
- Nam Theun Basin hydropower development in Laos, with transmission interconnection with Thailand and Vietnam; and
- Salween Basin hydropower development in Burma and Thailand, including interconnection between the two countries;
- Theun Hinboun hydropower project in Laos including interconnection with Thailand – currently being implemented.

A longer-term priority is to develop subregional power generation and transmission systems. A recent initiative in this area is a proposal by Laos for the Asian Development Bank to coordinate a study of an interconnected high voltage transmission network which could provide the basis for a subregional transmission network in the future.

3.   Telecommunications

The development of a modern telecommunications sector in the Subregion is considered to be essential to meet the needs of business and to promote the move towards more open and market-oriented economies. The state of telecommunications in each of the countries involved varies, although the international telecommunications structure is generally much better than the domestic structure. Cambodia's telecommunications infrastructure requires urgent investment in both urban and rural areas. In Laos, expansion and modernization of the telecommunications system is taking place although this is heavily concentrated in urban areas with very few lines available in rural areas. In Vietnam, considerable advances in telecommunications have been made in recent years, especially in international communications. Local communications, however, are still weak. In Burma and Cambodia telecommunications infrastructure is very poor.

Given the generally poor state of telecommunications in the Subregion, large-scale investments are required to modernize telecommunications infrastructure and services. Considerable priority is being given to mobilizing private sector capital for telecommunications development. For example, telecommunications projects in Phnom Penh, Hanoi and Ho Chi Minh City are being implemented with private sector participation, often in joint ventures with the state sector.

4.   Water resources management

The sustainable use of the water resources of the Mekong river and its tributaries is another area of priority. These resources are still largely under-utilized and could be further exploited to generate power, provide irrigation for increased food production, and for increased navigation links. The Mekong River Commission has developed a comprehensive plan for joint development activities along the river in areas such as hydroelectricity generation, irrigation, flood control, drainage, navigation improvement, watershed management, fisheries and tourism. Five major subregional projects are proposed involving hydrological studies of the Mekong basin, flood forecasting, control of soil erosion and development of water management models. There are, however, still serious problems surrounding the degree of political support for genuinely subregional projects and mechanisms through which they can be implemented.

V.   Opportunities

The development of the Mekong Basin countries offers a range of potential opportunities for business. As outlined above, there are major opportunities in the development of infrastructure as part of the Asian Development Bank's Greater Mekong Subregion initiative, particularly in the transportation, telecommunications and energy sectors.

Many of the business opportunities in the Mekong Basin countries are directly related to the activities of international aid agencies. The other major category of opportunities in the subregion are independent of aid activities (although benefiting indirectly from them).

1.   Large potential market

While 'extremely low incomes prevail in most of the Mekong subregion ... the potential is great and economic growth is beginning to surge' (Asian Development Bank 1996b, p. iii). Over 230 mn people offer the potential (in the longer term) of a huge market and some of the cheapest labour in South East Asia. As a result, international interest in the trade and investment potential of the subregion has increased markedly in recent years.

The process of economic reform is likely to continue in the Mekong Basin countries, although it may be an uneven and increasingly difficult process. In the longer term, the trend to greater economic openness and to rapid economic growth that has characterized the development of other economies in East Asia, is likely to take hold in the subregion: this is certainly the aspiration of the Mekong Basin countries and the inspiration for many of the initiatives evolving for the development of the subregion. This means that the subregion could be an increasingly attractive market with an expanding population and rising per capita incomes.

2.   Enormous resources

There is also considerable development potential based on the Mekong basin's natural resources. For example, the area is rich in energy resources such as coal, oil and natural gas, has considerable potential for the development of hydroelecticity, and has extensive mineral reserves. It also has vast agriculture resources and in a number of countries large aquaculture and fisheries potential. An increasing trend is to process these products domestically, adding value to the exported product. So opportunities may emerge in the medium- to long-term for investment in food processing, packaging and shipping industries.

The subregion's human resources are also extensive and opportunities exist for a subregional division of labour, for example labour costs in Thailand are over 250 per cent higher than in Laos or Cambodia. Expanded power supplies, improved transport infrastructure, combined with relatively low labour costs and high literacy and education rates in some of the subregion's countries, makes labour-intensive manufacturing in the subregion an increasingly attractive new area of opportunity.

Human resource development will also be a key new business frontier, particularly in the fields of education and training, as these countries will have to improve skill levels as part of the overall transition towards market economies as well as to attract foreign direct investment and upgrade existing industries. This is also an important component of institutional strengthening in the Mekong Basin countries.

3.   Tourism potential

The tourism sector is a major area already benefiting from subregional economic cooperation. The Mekong Basin countries have considerable tourism potential based on their natural attractions and cultural sites of great interest. A number of efforts are already underway to promote the Greater Mekong Subregion as a single destination for tourists. However, these are currently constrained by the lack of international hotels and developed tourism attractions, continued security problems in some parts of the Subregion (for example, in Burma, Cambodia and Laos), lack of developed transport links, and government red-tape controlling movements across borders. Many of these constraints, however, are being overcome, for example road and air transport links are improving, and a considerable amount of foreign investment is flowing into the construction of new hotels. Although each country is already becoming established as a tourism destination – the number of visitors to Vietnam, Burma, Cambodia and Laos has doubled in each of the past five years – 'their potential as a distinct grouping is far greater than that of any one on its own' (*Asian Wall Street Journal*, 1996, p. 4).

4.   Subregional corporate strategies

A number of companies are adopting subregional strategies for their business activities in the area by establishing operations in two or more of the countries involved. This is because 'a successful project

in one country, winning the trust and support of the national government, can be a serious door-opener to a neighbouring state'
(Brinsdon, 1996a, p. 3). With considerable investment in large projects in the subregion currently underway or planned for the near
future, already in the construction industry the 'same select names
keep appearing as new projects are launched around the Greater
Mekong Subregion' (Brinsdon, 1996b, p. 3).

MORE FIRMS GOING REGIONAL

Some of the companies that are adopting a regional strategy to
their operations in the Greater Mekong Subregion include:

- 3M – consumer and industrial products
- Accor group – tourism and hotels
- Daewoo group – manufacturing and trading
- Krung Thai Bank, Citibank, Standard Chartered Bank –
  financial services
- Bank Pakong – real estate and industrial parks
- Telstra – telecommunications services
- Kodak – film products

Source: The Brooker Group 1996.

This is because there are a number of common fundamentals in
each market which mean that for many businesses there may be
advantages to adopting a total perspective on the market of the
Greater Mekong Subregion, even if implementation is on a phased
country-by-country basis. For example, with the exception of
Thailand, each economy is in the process of moving from closed to
open, market-oriented economies and the overall pattern of development is largely similar so that experiences gained and techniques
developed in one market can be successfully transferred to others.

The needs of each market are also broadly similar for both goods
and services. Significant opportunities exist for economies of scale
in product and services support across the subregion. And improvements in transportation and communications links, and harmonization of documentation and controls on cross-border movements, are
creating opportunities for integrating distribution networks in the
subregion (Brinsdon, 1996a). This suggests that treating the sub-

region as a whole may prove far more profitable than would have been possible by adding the sum of the parts (Asia, Inc. 1996)

5. New partnerships

New partnership opportunities are emerging, for example ASEAN companies are increasingly active in all of the Mekong Basin countries. This can be expected to gain momentum as Laos, Cambodia and Burma follow Vietnam in becoming members of ASEAN and as the ASEAN initiative to develop the Mekong Basin gets underway. The associated commitment to the reduction of barriers to intra-ASEAN trade under the ASEAN Free Trade Area are likely to boost private sector cooperation still further. The emerging private sectors in each of the countries of the Subregion also offer opportunities for the development of new partnerships, particularly in supplying the expanding domestic markets of each country.

6. Large development assistance inflows

Governments, including Australia, Japan, the European Union, and elsewhere in East Asia, as well as the major financial institutions, are committed to their efforts to promote development in the Mekong Basin countries. So large aid inflows into the subregion are likely to continue. This offers direct and indirect opportunities for private sector involvement. The Asian Development Bank is particularly proactive in promoting the Subregion's development, for example it has hosted seminars in Tokyo, Bangkok and Seoul to brief potential investors on the various transport projects on the drawing board as well as initiatives in tourism development, trade and investment, and environmental management. And Japan's Forum for the Comprehensive Development of Indochina hosted a meeting on infrastructure needs in the subregion (held in Sydney in September 1996) and published a compendium of all of the aid projects in three of the Greater Mekong Subregion's countries – Vietnam, Laos and Cambodia – to help potential investors identify areas of opportunity.

IV. Challenges

The Mekong Basin countries are still poor developing countries: per capita incomes in the subregion are among the lowest in the world. The area remains a mix of complex cultures and politics, and this complexity is further heightened by the rapid socio economic change that is occurring. This is creating a competitive environment which may complicate efforts to promote economic cooperation.

1.   Inadequate infrastructure

Poor roads, power, telecommunications and water supplies are common problems in the six Mekong Basin countries. These can add to the costs of projects, for example, as investors have to provide back-up power, water and other utilities. In addition to the need to improve the 'hard' infrastructure, there is also a need to address important areas of 'soft' infrastructure, for example removing the non-physical barriers restricting the movement of goods and people across borders. As a result, increasing attention is being given to liberalizing and harmonizing rules and procedures governing cross-border trade.

2.   Financing projects

Turning the vision for the development of the Mekong Basin countries into reality represents an enormous challenge. In particular, mobilizing resources to finance the development requirements of the subregion is one of the most important challenges facing the countries involved. Neither the governments of each of the countries nor the international development agencies are able to finance the scale of investment required as part of subregional development plans.

As a result, there is increasing interest in attracting private sector investment in the development of infrastructure. This will only happen, however, against a background of political stability, coherent and consistent industrial, investment and economic policies, clear and transparent legislation allowing for the involvement of the private sector in specific areas of the economy, and the availability of foreign exchange for the repayment of offshore debt and repatriation of profits. Each of the Mekong Basin countries still have a long way to go in order even partially to meet these requirements.

Given the massive demand for capital in the subregion, obtaining project finance will therefore be a major challenge facing investors in these countries. The legal systems in these countries in particular are still being developed and the vague nature and differences in the interpretation of laws create considerable uncertainty for investors.

This makes partnerships and personal relationships more important than legal frameworks, particularly in the early years of development in these countries. The complexity of operating across more than one country, as proposed in many of the subregion's projects, is also associated with increased political risk and makes obtaining finance approvals even more difficult. In addition, many of the returns on infrastructure projects are very long-term and it may therefore be difficult to attract private sector investors on the scale that is required. Moreover, the rates of return required by private investors will often conflict with the subsidized tariffs on many existing infrastructure services, for example, electricity tariffs.

This implies that the implementation of many infrastructure projects may therefore be slower than currently envisaged. These challenges, however, are also creating new opportunities as banks and professional advisers, accountants and lawyers are now moving into the markets of the Greater Mekong Subregion in increasing numbers to help businesses deal with these issues.

3. Large bureaucracies

Bureaucratic obstacles and delays also create challenges for business in the Greater Mekong Subregion. Large government bureaucracies still exist in many of these countries and many bureaucrats remain unfamiliar with many of the concepts of a market economy. Foreign businesses complain about an 'attitude problem' among people accustomed to a centrally planned system (Thaitawat and Marukatat, 1996) and 'businessmen talk wearily of bureaucracy, delays, lack of clear rules, and uncertainties over contracts and property rights'. This can cause significant delays in the approvals process and in getting things which can add significant costs and risks to development projects. In the Greater Mekong Subregion each country has different approvals processes and all are very time-consuming. In addition, lack of certainty regarding land ownership and the transferability of land use rights, and poor legal infrastructure translate into a lack of security for financiers.

Many of these challenges can be viewed as part of the learning curve of developing economies but this is made even more complex in the Subregion because they are also in the process of transition from closed, centrally planned economies to more open, market-oriented ones. Alternatively, some businesses in the subregion argue that 'of course, there are problems out there, but if you wait until they are solved, you will have missed the boat' (Asiamoney, 1996, p. 61)

VII. Implications for Australian business

The opportunities in the Greater Mekong Subregion are enormous and very real. Regional governments, established foreign investors, local businessmen and regional analysts all agree that the region has considerable potential for growth: 'prospects are excellent – given the strategic location of the Subregion and the sweeping structural reforms that have created a very positive environment for domestic and foreign investment' (Asian Development Bank, 1996b, p. iii). The Subregion's human resources are also extensive and offer potential for development based on the availability of low-cost unskilled and semi-skilled labour.

So the area is worth watching: by 2010 the combined GDP of the subregion is forecast to reach US$863 bn. If population growth is held to about 2 per cent per year, the subregion will have 314 mn people by 2010, with an average per capita GDP of US$2700 or more than triple the 1994 level (Asian Development Bank, 1996b). In addition, subregional economic cooperation is likely to help to promote the investment attractiveness of the participating countries as a group, that is 'the whole is becoming greater than the sum of the parts' (The Brooker Group, 1996, p. 3).

Australian businesses have considerable expertise in a number of areas being given priority for development in the Greater Mekong Subregion. This includes telecommunications, infrastructure development, natural resource development, environmental management, and legal and financial services.

Despite recent improvements, doing business in these countries is still not easy. A number of business opportunities exist for potential traders and investors prepared to show patience in getting to know and understand prospective partners as well as the business and cultural environment. It is also important to observe local regulations and commercial practices. Many of the proposed infrastructure and other development projects make sense, but it remains to be seen how many will attract foreign private sector capital. So there needs to be some caution shown about some of the more ambitious development plans for the Mekong Basin countries and expectations need to be kept at realistic levels.

Notes

1. A term used by Asia Inc. in August 1996 in an article on the Mekong called 'River of Dreams'.
2. There is some uncertainty about the real economic situation in Burma where reforms have been more limited and recent signs have emerged of increased macroeconomic instability.
3. Current aid inflows to Burma are very limited. Most nations, including Australia, suspended their aid programmes to Burma in 1988. The major multilateral and bilateral aid donors also do not currently provide significant aid to Burma, although the World Bank is completing some projects, the Asian Development Bank is providing some technical assistance for a subregional transport project involving Burma, and the World Health Organization and the United Nations Development Program have modest aid programmes in Burma.
4. The agreement was signed by Laos, Cambodia, Thailand and Vietnam in April 1995; Burma and China are not yet signatories to the agreement.
5. This is only a small part of the US$1.2–1.5 trillion that the World Bank estimates will need to be invested in infrastructure in the whole of East Asia over the next twenty-five years.
6. Cross-border trade in the area is already considerable, although much of this trade is unregulated and unofficial. Also, in the bordering mountainous regions of China, Burma, Thailand and Laos – the so-called 'Golden Triangle' – there is still a heavy reliance on drug trafficking. However, trade liberalization measures currently being adopted unilaterally by the countries involved in the subregion, and in the future as part of commitments under the ASEAN Free Trade Area, should promote further expansion of legitimate trade in the subregion.
7. Singapore is also interested in the proposed rail project, which is considered to be one of the most ambitious and long-term of the various infrastructure projects proposed for the subregion.
8. China has plans for at least seven dams with a total capacity of 13 700 megawatts. The first of these, the Manwan dam with a 1000 megawatt capacity may be nearing completion. There are growing concerns about the potential negative downstream effects on fisheries and water flows arising from the construction of these dams. A particular area of concern is the potential impact on the flooding of the Great Lake Tonle Sap in Cambodia and the associated impact on rural subsistence communities.

References

Amerasinghe, N. (1996), 'Statement by the Asian Development Bank to the Working Committee on Infrastructure Development Forum for the Comprehensive Development of Indochina', 26–7 September, Sydney.
Asian Development Bank (1996a), 'Economic Cooperation in the Greater Mekong Subregion: An Overview', paper presented at the Greater Mekong Growth Summit, Ho Chi Minh City, September.
Asian Development Bank (1996b), *Economic Cooperation in the Greater Mekong Subregion: Toward Implementation*, Proceedings of the Third Conference on

Subregional Economic Cooperation among Cambodia, People's Republic of China, Lao People's Democratic Republic, Myanmar, Thailand and Vietnam, Hanoi, April 1994, Asian Development Bank, Manila.

Asian Development Bank (1996c), *Compendium of Infrastructure Projects in Cambodia, Lao PDR and Viet Nam Volumes 1 and 2*, Forum for the Comprehensive Development of Indochina Working Committee on Infrastructure Development, September, Asian Development Bank, Manila.

Brady, D. (1996), 'The Last Frontier a Mekong River Holiday? Tour operators see Potential', *Asian Wall Street Journal*, 21 May, Hong Kong.

Brimble, P. (1996), 'The Greater Mekong Subregion: A Private Sector Perspective on Recent Developments', Paper presented to the Greater Mekong Growth Summit, Ho Chi Minh City, Vietnam, September.

Brinsdon, J. (1996a), 'The Greater Mekong Subregion – Opportunities for private sector participation', *Standard Chartered Viewpoints*, August, Singapore.

Brinsdon J. 1996b, 'Sub-regional corporate strategy – opportunities and challenges', Paper presented at the Greater Mekong Growth Summit, Ho Chi Minh City, September.

The Brooker Group, Wellington, New Zealand.

Corben, R. (1996), 'Bank fights for Mekong forests', *The Australian*, 6 August, Sydney.

Crampton, T. (1996), 'Mekong supplies new frontier for regional trade and red tape', *Asia Times*, 16 September, p. 4, Hong Kong.

Dwyer, M. (1996), 'New habits for golden triangle', *The Australian Financial Review*, 4 October, p. 4, Sydney.

Grant, R. L. (1995), 'Greater Mekong', *World Link*, July/August, Singapore.

Lim, K. T. (1996), 'The Mekong River Projects: Present and Future Ones and Potential Impact on Investments', Paper presented to the Greater Mekong Growth Summit by the Mekong River Commission, Ho Chi Minh City, Vietnam, September.

Limeqeco, P. (1996), 'ADB plots course for Mekong', *Asia Times*, 4 March, Singapore.

Mellor, W. and Clewley, J. (1996), 'River of Dreams', *Asia, Inc.*, August, Hong Kong.

Nakajima, A. (1996), 'Statement made at the Working Committee on Infrastructure Development of the Forum for the Comprehensive Development of Indochina', 26–7 September, Ministry of Foreign Affairs of Japan.

Nette, A. and Wallengren, M. (1995), 'Facts about the Mekong River', *Phnom Penh Post*, Cambodia, October.

Spencer, C. (1996), 'Challenge is to tap Mekong without being damned', *The Australian*, 6 September, p. 18, Sydney.

Stewart, I. (1996), 'Mekong guidelines to test regional harmony', *The Australian*, 18 June, p. 26, Sydney.

Thaitawat, N. and Marukatat, S. (1996), 'Caution slows the Mekong', 2 March, *Bangkok Post*, Bangkok.

The Greater Mekong Task Force (1996), 'Strategies for Development of the Greater Mekong Area', July, unpublished report submitted by the Greater Mekong Task Force, Ministry of Foreign Affairs, Tokyo.

8
Human Resource Development Issues and Priorities in Vietnam: Implications for International Business

Chris Nyland and Eduardo Pol

I. Introduction

In an address to a 1996 investment forum organized by the Organization for Economic Cooperation and Development and the Asian Development Bank, Tran Xuan Gia, Vietnam's Vice Minister of Planning and Investment, outlined the 'great efforts' his Government had undertaken to improve the climate for foreign investors. In so doing Professor Tran also sketched his government's development strategy for the next five years. The goal of this strategy is to turn Vietnam into an industrial nation with a modern technological base and economic structure integrated into both the regional and the global economies. This objective is to be achieved by gearing the economic structure of the nation for industrialization and modernization; adopting an incentive policy designed to develop a multi-sector economy; introducing economic reforms which provide the business community with macroeconomic stability; developing science, technology and education as the 'moving force' of the industrialization process; and by concomitantly preserving Vietnam's national culture, heritage and values.

Professor Tran emphasized that this five-point programme is very much dependent on the expansion and enrichment of Vietnam's human resources. Indeed, he asserted that human resources constitute 'the basic factor' in the industrialization and modernization processes and the 'main development factor in implementing a rational redistribution policy to improve society, practice social fairness, and reduce poverty'. The purpose of this chapter is to provide scholars and potential investors with a working knowledge of the human resources of Vietnam and the programme being implemented presently by the government to develop these vital assets. It will begin with a brief discussion of the role of human resources in the development process and some comments about the sources of human resource-related statistics in Vietnam, proceed to situate Vietnam's human resources within an international context, and then conclude by examining how the government is managing what it has described as its four key 'strategic objectives' in the area of human resource development, namely: the effective management of population and health; education and training; poverty alleviation; and employment generation.

II.   Human resources and economic dynamism

The spectacular economic dynamism that has come to characterize the Asia-Pacific Rim nations has stimulated controversy regarding the prime mover of this economic 'miracle'. It is generally agreed that the following four elements constitute the key factors that have induced and shaped this development, though scholars differ concerning the weights that each should be allocated:

(a) liberalization and the opening up of the domestic economy in the context of political stability;
(b) significant investment in infrastructure;
(c) meaningful adoption of advanced technology; and
(d) deep and sustained commitment to the development of human resources.

In this chapter we are mainly concerned with this last issue. Irrespective of the weighting they accord human resource development (HRD) as an element in the industrialization and modernization processes, few observers would deny that 'an impressive commitment to human capital formation' has been fundamental to the recent economic history of the Asia-Pacific Rim nations.[1]

The region has undergone a dramatic demographic transformation over the last quarter century with population growth rates declining rapidly as part of the development process. Evidence suggests that relatively small developmental changes are needed to bring down fertility and that an organized campaign of birth control can have a significant impact on fertility reduction. As a consequence, many developing nations along the Rim have promoted the widespread utilization of modern contraceptive methods and other forms of family planning. As far as HRD is concerned the decline in fertility is a development of vital importance for there is a strong inverse relationship between the fertility rate of nations and their capacity for human resource development. A rapidly declining birth rate tends to induce a favourable increase in both the age distribution of the population and the resources that families can accumulate and invest. Indeed, a decrease in the dependency ratio has been found to have a significant impact on the rate of family savings, the growth of physical capital per worker and the amount spent on education per student at both government and household level. The last correlation suggests that families with few children have greater capacity to educate each child and that an increasing prevalence of smaller families should contribute to the educational enhancement of successive generations. This, in turn, is seen to be highly important given the positive relationship that generally exists between the rate of growth of per capita income and the population's years of schooling.

Declining fertility is also important for human resource development because it increases the time women can devote to non-child rearing productive activities. The rapid decline in fertility in the Asia-Pacific Rim nations has been a critical factor enabling women to increase their rate of participation in the paid work force. Unfortunately, it appears that the adjustment processes introduced by the governments and employers of the developing nations required to facilitate women's participation have seldom been sufficient. Consequently, the industrialization and modernization processes have tended to subject women more than men to greater social and economic vulnerability.

Two other important groups that generally have had insufficient attention paid to their needs are children and the elderly. Child labour and high child mortality continues to be prevalent in a number of nations along the Rim. This constitutes a considerable wastage of human resources with many children either dying or failing to gain the education they need to fully realise their productive potential. Likewise, the elderly have generally been paid inadequate attention and this is emerging as a growing problem given the tendency for life expectancy to increase in all the nations that are managing to effectively embrace the development process.

Ogawa *et al.* (1993) have noted correctly that while demographic transformation is of critical significance there are further vital factors that explain the process of human capital formation along the Asia-Pacific Rim. At least three other important forces have been at work in the region. First, the people of the Rim appear to maintain a higher commitment to human resource development than does much of the rest of the world. This is a characteristic that has a long history exemplified by the fact that compulsory education was introduced in Japan as early as 1872. Second, this cultural commitment to HRD has been materialized in a marked willingness on the part of governments to intervene, with this intervention including the direct subsidization of human resource development and/or the twisting of the terms of trade in order to favour those sectors of the economy where workers can gain important learning-by-doing skills. The success achieved by these forms of intervention suggests that at the early stage of the industrialization and modernization processes it is important that the state invest heavily in HRD even if significant returns are not immediately realized. Third, the sustained commitment to the development of human resources has generated important externalities associated with knowledge accumulation. For example, the widespread dissemination of basic scientific knowledge and an understanding of modes of efficient production have made the region more capable of adapting to advanced technologies, and hence more attractive to foreign investors.

Before leaving these general remarks about the contribution of HRD to the spectacular economic growth along the Asia-Pacific Rim, it is instructive to make contact with the recent developments on the theoretical front. Broadly speaking, the new growth theory explains economic growth through the interactions of ideas: human and physical capital. More specifically, the new growth theorists have formulated models where per capita income grows indefinitely and the rate of economic growth depends on structural and policy parameters of the local and global economy.

In essence, there are three strands within the new growth theoretical framework offering logically coherent explanations of sustained, *policy-sensitive* growth. One approach is a prolongation of the traditional view, namely that capital accumulation is the driving force behind economic growth, but capital accumulation *includes* human capital formation. A second approach argues that when firms and individuals accumulate new capital, *beneficial spillovers* (positive externalities) occur, and sustained economic growth can be obtained by continuing accumulation of both physical and human capital. This externality approach to growth rests on the assumption that human capital can grow without bound. Obviously, this notion of human capital is totally different from the human capital measures such as years of schooling used by labour economists. A third view casts *industrial innovation* as the engine of growth. In this strand human capital is also of absolutely fundamental importance, but plays a different role because it involves a threshold effect. That is, there exists a critical mass of human capital above which growth becomes self-reinforcing but below which the economy is confined to an underdevelopment trap (low growth or stagnation). Quite obviously, all three approaches stress the role of human capital as a major factor explaining economic growth, and therefore the new growth theory offers strong motivation for the focus of our chapter.

It should be emphasized that human capital alone is not sufficient for economic growth. The growth performance of several countries with relatively high levels of schooling compared to the level of development in the 1960s was very poor over the next quarter of a century (Argentina and Cuba are good examples). Human capital is in the nature of a necessary condition for achieving economic development. Furthermore, the question of how much education is advantageous for achieving growth remains open. Education is a multi-level input to be optimized, not maximized. Consequently, the policy recommendation that more education at whatever level will have a greater effect on growth than most alternative investments appears to be generally untenable.

III.   Human resource statistics in Vietnam

The formulation of Vietnam's human resource development strategy is mainly carried out by the Communist Party with implementation being the responsibility of the Ministry of Labour, Invalids and Social Affairs (MOLISA). Basic activities concerning HRD, for example data collection, organization of scientific research, and international cooperation, are dispersed in several sub-agencies of MOLISA, including the Department of Social and Labour Policies, National Centre for Employment Promotion, Centre for Population and Human Resource Studies, Migration Department, Centre for Scientific Information on Labour and Social Affairs, Department of International Labour Cooperation, Department of Social Insurance and Assistance, and Department of Working Conditions. Not surprisingly, there are *coordination* problems (Nguyen, 1992: 24).

The basic source of human resource-related statistics in Vietnam is the *Annual Statistical Year Book*, published by the General Statistical Office (GSO). This source is supplemented by sample surveys carried out on a national scale by government agencies. While the *Year Book* provides rather comprehensive information on topics such as changes to the population and labour force, and wages in the state sector, its value is constrained by two facts: lack of basic information on the quality of the labour force and (generally) failure to report the situation in the private sector (Nguyen, 1995: 3).

A further factor limiting the value of the *Year Book* is that information on such fundamental issues as employment and unemployment are often difficult to interpret as definitions and the classification systems used are rather different from those generally utilized by other nations. Most of the GSO's present employees were trained on the basis of the centrally planned economic statistical system and as a result few are well qualified to meet the requirements of the emerging market economy (Nguyen, 1995: 7). Statistical services moreover suffer from a serious shortage of computing facilities and adequately trained staff. These are problems that the government is urgently seeking to overcome.

In 1995 the Centre for Scientific Information on Labour and Social Affairs published a *Report on Labour Statistics in Vietnam* that evaluated the quality of the present system of collecting and evaluating data relating to the labour market. As part of this report the Centre made a series of important recommendations as to how the collecting and processing of data might be significantly improved. This is a very promising development for scholars, policy-makers and investors and hopefully will soon lead to reforms that will greatly enhance our capacity to analyse the Vietnamese labour market.

IV. Vietnam's human resources: international comparisons

A first look at the available statistics on schooling lends some support to the claim that Vietnam is well endowed with human capital. By focusing on literacy as a measure of human capital, Vietnam ranks remarkably well: in 1992, the Vietnamese *adult rate of literacy* was 91.9 per cent, considerably higher than the average of all developing countries (68 per cent). Thus, the evidence points to the conclusion that the human capital endowment of Vietnam is considerable. This is true as a first approximation, but not as a second for two reasons. First, literacy affords only a rough estimation of the level of human capital (measures of secondary or higher education, or measures of scientists, engineers and technicians, are also important in making cross-country comparisons). Second, the *combined first-second-and-third-level enrolment ratio* locates Vietnam close to the *least* developed countries. In fact, the Vietnamese combined enrolment ratio was only 49 per cent against 47 per cent which is the norm for the least developed countries. More specifically, taking into account South East Asia, the 1992 distribution of the combined enrolment ratio is as follows: Brunei Darussalam (68 per cent), Cambodia (30 per cent), Indonesia (60 per cent), Laos (48 per cent), Malaysia (60 per cent), Philippines (77 per cent), Singapore (68 per cent), and Thailand (53 per cent). That is, Vietnam performs better than *only* Laos and Cambodia. But it is worthwhile noting here that in terms of real GDP per capita (PPP$) the Vietnamese economy comes after Laos and Cambodia.[2]

The foregoing suggests that the proxies for human capital 'adult literacy' (*AL*) and 'combined first-second-and-third-level gross enrolment ratio' (*CR*) provide a mixed picture. One way of comparing the different levels of human capital from country to country – and finding how attractive Vietnam is in terms of human capital – is to make use of a *human capital index (HCI)*, defined as a weighted average of the variables *AL* and *CR*.

From now on, we will use $HCI = (2/3) \texttt{¥} AL + (1/3) \texttt{¥} CR$ as a *proxy* for the level of human capital in a particular country. For example, the HCI for Vietnam is of the order of 78 per cent [$(2/3) \times 91.9 + (1/3) \times 49 = 77.6$]. Clearly, the selection of weights reflects the fact that *AL* is a relatively more important indicator of human capital than *CR*, and is consistent with the approach of the Human Development Report 1995.[3]

To gain further understanding of the Vietnamese relative position in terms of human capital, it is convenient to embed Vietnam in the context of the 21 members of the Pacific Economic Cooperation Council (PECC). Table 8.1 presents the distribution of the key variables *AL*, *CL*, and *HCI* for the PECC economies in 1992. These data do not reveal the *quality* of the education sector, and thereby, the numbers *mask* important qualitative factors. For example, phenomena such as large proportions of underqualified teachers or teachers

Table 8.1   Distribution of human capital between the PECC economies, 1992

HCI rank	AL Adult rate of literacy	CR Combined enrolment ratio	HCI Human Capital Index
1. Canada*	99.0	100	99.3
2. United States*	99.0	95	97.7
3. New Zealand*	99.0	85	94.3
4. Australia*	99.0	79	92.3
5. Japan*	99.0	77	91.7
6. South Korea*	97.4	79	91.2
7. Russia	98.7	69	88.8
8. Philippines*	94.0	77	88.3
9. Chile*	94.5	71	86.7
10. Fiji	90.1	78	86.1
11. Peru	87.3	79	84.5
12. Hong Kong*	91.2	70	84.1
13. Singapore*	89.9	68	82.6
14. Colombia	90.3	67	82.5
15. Mexico*	88.6	65	80.7
16. Brunei*	86.4	68	80.3
17. Thailand*	93.5	53	80.0
18. Vietnam	91.9	49	77.6
19. Indonesia*	82.5	60	75.0
20. Malaysia*	81.5	60	74.3
21. China*	79.3	55	71.2
22. Chinese Taipei*	n.a.	n.a.	n.a.

* Also APEC member economy
Source: UNDP (1995).

having second and third jobs in addition to their regular employment are not rare in nations at Vietnam's level of development.

It should be clear that Table 8.1 conveys three central messages. First, the Vietnamese government has made significant (and *successful*) efforts to eliminate illiteracy from a broad spectrum of the population. The adult rate of literacy is higher than a foreign investor might anticipate in such a less-developed country. Second, inspection of the second column of Table 8.1 shows that in terms of variable *CR* Vietnam occupies the lowest position in the Pacific Rim. Finally, a glance at the third column of Table 8.1 shows that our proxy for human capital locates Vietnam only above Indonesia, Malaysia and China. Thus, the *HCI*'s basic message leads one to believe that there is a *shortage* of well-educated and highly qualified workers in Vietnam.

The General Statistics Office (1996) has reconfirmed the insights provided by Table 8.1. According to the Viet Nam 1994 Inter-Censal Demographic Survey, the Vietnamese government has been successful in providing elementary education to the people during the past half century. For example, the percentages for urban and rural residents with any schooling during the period April–June 1994 were 93 per cent and 85 per cent, respectively; moreover, the corresponding percentages among the cohort ages 15–19 were 98 per cent (urban residents) and 92 per cent (rural residents) (GSO, 1996: 17). Furthermore, the educational strategies have been able to close the gender gap at all educational levels. For instance, with respect to receiving any schooling the gender gap is *negligible* within the cohort aged between 25–29 (GSO, 1996: 21).

Notwithstanding this success, the dropout rate from school has been sizeable, particularly at the upper-secondary level. Moreover, the system of vocational and technical education has never been prepared to absorb the dropouts from the formal education system. As a result, a significant proportion of those who do not finish formal education enter the labour market as *unskilled* workers (GSO, 1996: 48). Quite obviously, this glimpse of the evidence is consistent with the *HCI*'s basic message and justifies the concern expressed in a recent study of educational trends in Vietnam:

> Despite considerable progress in increasing education over the
> past several decades, internal inefficiency within the education

system still persists. This problem merits more attention than ever before from the relevant bodies given the direction of economic change brought about by the recent economic reforms. *At present, a severe shortage of well educated and highly qualified workers has developed* while at the same time the excess of unskilled labourers who are unable to benefit from many new opportunities created by economic reform continues to grow (GSO, 1996: 48, italics added).

Further insight into international comparisons of HRD is afforded by two additional dimensions, namely: the ability to lead a long and healthy life and the ability to have the economic resources indispensable for a decent standard of living. These two variables, in turn, can be lumped together with the human capital indicator to obtain the so-called *human development index (HDI)*. The value of *HDI* is available for a very significant number of countries and indicates *how far* the country is from the desirable goals: access to education for all, an average life-span of 85 years, and an adjusted level of income computed on the basis of the world average income, which in turn is postulated as a 'reasonable standard of living'.

According to this indicator Vietnam occupies position 120 in the world ranking, though its *HDI* rank is *better* than the real GDP per capita (PPP$) rank. Circumscribing the number of countries to the PECC economies, Vietnam occupies the last position, as indicated in Table 8.2.

We now turn to the evidence on gender *inequality* in Vietnam. To this end, it is convenient to use the indicator termed the *gender-related development index (GDI)*, which concentrates on the same dimensions as the *HDI* (that is life expectancy, educational attainment and adjusted real income) but takes into account gender inequality as well as the average achievement of all people taken together. Or, to put it differently, *GDI* is simply the *HDI calibrated* to capture inequality between women and men. Table 8.3 ranks the PECC economies by their performance in relation to gender inequality.

It is to be noticed that the computation of the *GDI* presupposes a given degree of aversion to gender inequality.[4] Inspection of the data corresponding to the year 1992 (see Table 8.3) reveals that a

Table 8.2   Distribution of the human development index between the PECC economies, 1992

HCI rank	Life expectancy at birth	Educational attainment	Real GDP per capita (PPP$)	HDI
1. Canada*	77.4	99	20 520	95.0
2. United States*	76.0	98	23 760	93.7
3. New Zealand*	79.5	92	20 520	93.7
4. Australia*	77.6	92	18 220	92.7
5. Japan*	75.5	94	14 990	91.9
6. South Korea*	78.6	84	20 340	90.5
7. Russia	71.1	91	9 250	88.2
8. Philippines*	73.8	87	8 410	88.0
9. Chile*	74.8	82	18 330	87.8
10. Fiji	74.2	80	20 589	86.8
11. Peru	71.5	86	5 410	86.0
12. Hong Kong*	67.6	89	6 140	84.1
13. Singapore*	70.8	81	7 300	84.2
14. Colombia	69.3	83	5 480	83.6
15. Mexico*	69.0	80	5 950	82.7
16. Brunei*	70.8	74	7 790	82.2
17. Thailand*	66.0	84	3 300	70.9
18. Vietnam	66.3	88	2 550	67.7
19. Indonesia*	62.7	75	2 950	63.7
20. Malaysia*	63.7	71	1 950	59.4
21. China*	65.2	78	1 010	53.9
22. Chinese Taipei*	n.a.	n.a	n.a.	n.a.

* Also APEC member economy
Source. UNDP (1995).

moderate level of gender inequality aversion leaves Vietnam's relative *HDI* standing unchanged.

Due to severe data limitations, this is as far as we can go. For some countries it is possible to compute the *gender empowerment measure* which reflects women's participation in economic, political and professional activities. Regrettably, the information is not available for Vietnam. Disaggregated statistics focusing on Vietnamese human capital are sorely needed. In particular, disaggregation of *HDI* for different population groups would reveal how unevenly human development is shared within Vietnam.

Table 8.3   Distribution of the gender-related development index between the PECC Economies, 1992

GDI rank	Gender-related development index	HDI	HDI rank [minus] GDI rant
1. Canada*	90.1	4	+3
2. United States*	90.1	2	0
3. New Zealand*	89.6	3	0
4. Australia*	89.1	1	–3
5. Japan*	86.8	5	0
6. South Korea*	85.4	6	0
7. Russia	82.2	9	–2
8. Philippines*	82.2	12	+4
9. Chile*	81.2	10	+1
10. Fiji	79.8	15	+5
11. Peru	78.0	7	–4
12. Hong Kong*	76.8	16	+4
13. Singapore*	75.9	8	–5
14. Colombia	74.1	3	–1
15. Mexico*	72.2	11	–4
16. Brunei*	72.0	14	–2
17. Thailand*	63.1	17	0
18. Vietnam	62.5	18	0
19. Indonesia*	59.1	19	0
20. Malaysia*	57.8	20	0
21. China*	53.7	21	0
22. Chinese Taipei*	n.a.	n.a.	n.a.

* Also APEC member economy
Source: UNDP (1995).

V.   Resolving human resources problems

Human resources policy in Vietnam must seek to resolve a number of 'severe contradictions'. First, Vietnam has a young population with those under 15 years of age making up 39 per cent of the total population. Second, 80 per cent of the total population remains in the rural areas despite the fact that there is inadequate farming land. As a consequence there exists a very high level of rural underemployment. Third, the distribution of human resources is very unevenly distributed between regions with mass unemployment and underemployment in some areas and a relative shortage of labour in others. Fourth, while literacy is high only 13 per cent of the work force has any substantial level of training. Fifth, underemployment in the rural sector, high levels of unemployment in the cities (9–12 per cent) and periodic natural calamities have created a situation where poverty and undernourishment are common.

Vietnam does not have a comprehensive HRD strategy for resolving these problems. In January 1997 Pham Minh Hac, First Vice-Chairman of the Communist Party's Central Committee for Science and Education, informed the authors that this was considered a weakness that had to be resolved in 1997. Professor Hac intended to submit a HRD strategy for the Party's approval by November 1997. The approach to HRD taken through the 90s has, however, not been totally *ad hoc*. HRD has been dealt with in a manner that centres on a programme that has four key foci: population and health; education and training; poverty alleviation; and employment generation. The essence and thrust of the programme has been well summarised by Nguyen:

> The strategic objective of human resource development in Vietnam is to step by step improve the quality of population and labour resources, train a contingent of labourers to have high, appropriate levels of education, professional knowledge and skills in order to meet the demand of socio-economic development strategy, create employment generating income and unceasingly improve the quality-of-life, reduce to the minimum unemployment rate and poverty, especially absolute poverty in urban as well as rural areas (Nguyen, 1992: 19).

The factors emphasized in Nguyen's comment reveal an intimate knowledge of the HRD strategies embraced by the more successful of the developing nations of the Asia-Pacific Rim. The one qualification to this general observation that is worthy of mention is that the programme appears more egalitarian than is usual. In short, the degree of emphasis placed on poverty is somewhat uncommon amongst nations at Vietnam's level of development. An outline of how Vietnam is dealing with each of these foci (or 'strategic objectives') is presented below.

VI.   Population and health

The Government of Vietnam accepts that: 'Population control and family planning is an important part of the strategy for national development, one of the most crucial socioeconomic problems, and a basic factor necessary to raise the quality of life of every individual, every family, and the entire society' (SRVN, 1995: 27). Though the rate of population growth remains high the government's determination to curtail this rate has met with considerable success in recent years. Over the fourteen years from 1976–1992 the crude birth rate was reduced on average by 0.47 per cent per annum. The average number of children ever born to a woman has been reduced from 5.9 in 1970–74 to 4.17 in 1985–89 and was 3.6 in 1993. This decline has been accompanied by a decrease in the crude death rate, which has been reduced from 11.6 per cent in 1976 to 8.4 per cent in 1989 and reached 7.1 per cent in 1992, and life expectancy has increased from 63 in 1979 to 65.5 years in 1992. Together these demographic changes have produced a natural growth rate of the population that remains high but is steadily declining, being 2.3 per cent in 1992 and 2.06 per cent in 1994. This level remains well above that of East Asia (1.31 per cent) but is approaching the norm for South East Asia (1.92 per cent).

Vietnam's delay in achieving the regional rate of population growth is explained by the Centre for Population and Human Resource Studies (CPHRS) as being a consequence of the fact that the development process in many areas has had only limited impact on traditional customs and values. This is especially so amongst the 80 per cent of the population who remain in the rural areas where son preference and early marriage remain prevalent. Another important contributing factor is that Vietnam's family planning programme has until recently been severely under-resourced with many family planning clinics being seriously run down, especially in the mountainous and remote regions (SRVN, 1995: 6). In recent years this situation has improved with family planning activities being strengthened and coordinated as part of a national programme. As a consequence the percentage of Vietnamese couples voluntarily accepting contraceptive measures increased from 44 per cent in 1991 to 51 per cent in 1993. Fertility management was further strengthened in June 1993 when the prime minister ratified

Vietnam's strategy for family and population planning through to the year 2000. The broad goal of this programme is for families to have fewer but healthier children:

> Concrete targets are that each family should have only one or two children so that by the year 2015, on average each couple has only two children at the most; and the country's population reach stability by the middle of the 21st century. In the short term, by the year 2000, it is projected that every couple will have an average of 2.9 children and the country's population will be 82 mn (SRVN, 1995: 28).

As observed above, the experience of those developing nations that have managed to industrialize suggests that a decline in the fertility rate has important implications for human resource enhancement. A rapidly declining birth rate tends to increase the resources families can accumulate and invest in education per student at both government and household level. This lesson has been well appreciated by Vietnam's National Committee for Population and Family Planning which has observed that children in small families 'have more favourable conditions for their advancement in studies'. The extent to which this is true for Vietnam has recently been tested by the General Statistical Office as part of its inter-censal demographic survey on social trends.

As can be seen from Table 8.4 the results show a very pronounced negative association between family size and the education of children, with the disadvantage of belonging to a large family being particularly pronounced in terms of higher education. For example, the unadjusted results suggest that children from families with 1 or 2 children have a 50 per cent greater chance of finishing primary school and a 700 per cent greater chance of finishing the upper-secondary level than have families with seven or more children. If the results are adjusted to allow for region of residence, household wealth, parents education, and urban-rural residence the strength of the relationship declines but a clear negative association can still be observed. In brief, Table 8.4 strongly supports the claim that smaller families are more conducive to the enhancement of human resources.

Turning to the issue of health, it should be noted that the physical and mental health of workers is a critical factor determining the

Table 8.4   Selected indicators of child's education, by number of children in the family, unadjusted and adjusted for background characteristics

Adjustment and number of children in family	% currently in school (by child's age)			% finished primary (aged 15–24)	% with any secondary (aged 16–24)	% finished upper secondary (aged 19–24)
	10–14	15–19	20–24			
Unadjusted						
No. of children						
1–2	95.5	52.1	18.7	90.9	85.8	50.3
3	88.4	40.8	12.6	91.2	86.5	48.7
4	83.2	30.4	3.3	87.0	81.7	32.9
5	76.3	22.6	2.4	81.9	74.0	23.8
6	68.4	18.4	1.2	71.7	61.3	15.9
7+	66.5	11.4	1.2	60.7	47.4	6.6
TOTAL	81.3	27.1	3.9	78.9	70.1	23.8
Adjusted						
No. of children	85.5	37.6	12.3	84.0	77.0	30.1
1–2	84.8	33.2	7.9	84.0	77.2	31.8
3	82.5	27.6	1.4	81.9	74.9	25.3
4	79.5	25.0	2.8	80.9	72.7	25.5
5	75.0	24.5	3.1	76.7	67.0	22.9
6	75.5	20.8	3.7	70.4	59.3	17.6
7+	81.3	27.1	3.9	78.9	70.1	23.8
TOTAL						
Eta statistic	0.10	0.11	0.13	0.12	0.15	0.11

Notes: Adjusted results are statistically adjusted by multiple classification analysis (MCA) for region of residence, household wealth score, mother's and father's education, urban-rural residence and age of child
Source: 1994 VNICDS birth history data.

coefficient of worktime utilization, productivity and income level. A study of the relation between population, migration, human resources and employment prepared by the Centre for Population and Human Resources Studies reports that 'Vietnamese workers are weak physically and structurally' (CPHRS, 1995: 13). In particular, malnutrition remains a problem – 51.5 per cent of children under 5 years old are malnourished to some degree with 10.9 per cent and 1.6 per cent respectively suffering second- and third-degree malnourishment. Further, up to 40 per cent of the population is sick at least once a year, 14 per cent of women do not have breast milk after giving birth and some 42 per cent of women have contracted gynecological diseases.

Given this situation public health care must remain a vital area of concern if Vietnam is to develop the high-productivity labour force needed to compete effectively in the global market. Despite this need, since 1989 there has been a decline in medical services as a consequence of the removal of subsidies. The government accordingly is attempting to restructure the health care sector in ways which will make it possible to meet the demands of a community that is highly diverse because of geographical, economic, social and cultural conditions. In this emerging strategy emphasis is being placed on the production of pharmaceutical and medical equipment, improved training for health workers and the diversification of provision to meet local needs. These targets are to be funded through a combination of state funds, fees charged by hospitals, medical insurance premiums and foreign humanitarian aid.

Even though many of the government's health goals have yet to be realized, the overall health is improving, as indicated by the changing height of the population (this being a measure very much dependent of a country's socioeconomic development). From 1954 to the early 1970s average height increased by 1 cm. War and economic decline subsequently reversed this trend, a reversal that was not halted until the end of the 1980s. Over the past 5–6 years, however, the trend has once again reversed and the average height of the population is again increasing and is expected to further increase by 0.63 cm through to the end of the decade.

VII. Education and training

Recognizing the importance of education and training in the process of industrialization and modernization the government of

Vietnam has made these issues key aspects of its HRD programme. The emphasis the government places on the economic benefits of education and training is clearly manifest in its fundamental educational objective which is to 'provide every citizen with basic education; develop human resources to meet the needs of socioeconomic development; and foster talented people to form a contingent of scientific, technical and managerial specialists and leaders capable of serving the industrialization and modernization of the country' (SRVN, 1995: 26). The three primary education and training objectives to the year 2000 are:

- To radically reduce illiteracy among the labour force, especially for workers between 15 and 35, as well as, to the best extent possible, among older people; complete the universalization of primary education, especially among children between 6 and 14 with more attention given to children in mountainous and remote areas; and promote the universalization of junior secondary education, especially in urban areas.
- To develop vocational education and long-term vocational training courses in order to train a highly skilled work force who will be able to meet the demands of the major economic centres using advanced technologies; meanwhile also develop short-term vocational training courses and develop traditional arts and handicraft production in order to help create employment for young people.
- To reorganize the higher education system including universities and colleges, broaden their scope and renew their curricula and training methods; combine basic training and retraining with the aim of building a contingent of experts, managers and leaders; revise and amend enrolment policies, with special attention to women, and children from ethnic minority groups and poor families at school so as to create favourable learning conditions for young and all other people (SRVN, 1995: 26–7).

1.   Primary and secondary education

To further these objectives the government has instituted a major restructuring of the education system designed to build a simultaneous system of public and private education and vocational training, has combined public educational institutions – involving amalgamations and in some cases the closure of institutions – and has privatized a number of public enterprises. The government has also sought to stimulate non-formal education and self-instruction activities and is allowing individuals greater freedom in the choice of schools, teachers, occupations and professions. In order to expand enrolments while maintaining quality, the Ministry of Education and Training (MOET) has redesigned the curriculum and developed a series of standardized text books and other educational equipment. Considerable effort has also been made to improve the quality of teaching personnel with both wages and the required educational standard of teachers gradually being raised. To finance these developments the government has increased its budgetary allocation to education. Total expenditure on education and training was 6–8 per cent of total government expenditure between 1986 and 1989 but has progressively been increased being 12 per cent in 1995. This is a trend the government intends to continue through to 2000 when it is expected public funding to education will reach 15 per cent of total expenditure.

Increased income for education has also been generated by the government's decision to abandon full state subsidization of education. Prior to 1989, education at all levels through to grade 12 was tuition free. Parents must now pay a part of this cost and they must pay for textbooks with only the first three primary grades being fully subsidized. In 1993 the World Bank expressed concern that the imposition of fees might exacerbate the adverse trends that had characterized the education sector through the 1980s, when many of the earlier gains Vietnam had achieved in the education field appeared to be in danger of being lost. Through the 1980s enrolment rates decreased significantly with the sharpest decline occurring in the kindergarten and secondary levels. For example, between 1981 and 1991 enrolments declined from 3.18 mn to 2.73 mn at the lower-secondary level and from 0.71 mn to 0.52 mn in the upper-secondary. Likewise, the number of students enrolled in higher education declined over this period. The concerns expressed by the Bank, have recently been echoed By Ronnas and Sjoberg (1995) who have observed that there is every reason to believe that school enrolments will continue to decline. These fears, however, do not appear warranted. As can be seen from Table 8.5 enrolments at all levels of schooling have increased steadily since 1991.

Table 8.5 Number of persons attending school within country (000)

	1990–91	1991–92	1992–93	1993–94	1994–95
TOTAL	12 250 2	12 794 8	13 153	13 947 7	14 587 4
Pupils of grade	11 882 9	12 371 4	12 773 7	13 568 7	–
Pupils of complementary education	102 3	209 9	134 7	102 9	155 6
Students of technical secondary school	135 4	106 5	107 8	119	200 3
Students of colleges and universities	129 6	107	136 8	157 1	

The Bank's concerns regarding the impact of imposing fees on parents were tested by the General Statistical Office in its 1994 inter-censal study of social trends. In so doing the GSO compared the results of the 1989 census with the data generated by the later study. It was observed that if the reforms had a negative impact on parents' willingness and ability to send children to school the pro-portion of both young school-aged children that ever attended school and the percentage of the school-aged population currently enrolled should have declined. As can be seen from Table 8.6 overall there is no evidence to support the claim that access to education is declining. Both the percentage of those who ever went to school or who attended school in 1994 was higher than the percentage reported in the 1989 census. As far as primary education is concerned this might be explained as being a consequence of this level having been made compulsory but the fact that the highest growth has occurred in the non-compulsory grades largely negates this claim.

Table 8.6 Percentage who ever attended school and percentage who are currently attending school, by age

Age	% ever attended school		% currently attending	
	Census 1989	*VNICDS 1994*	*Census 1989*	*VNICDS 1994*
6	56.1	50.1	55.6	n.a.
7	78.1	78.7	77.4	n.a.
8	85.4	88.4	84.3	n.a.
9	88.9	92.5	86.6	n.a.
10	91.1	94.2	87.3	92.4
11	91.9	95.1	85.4	91.2
12	92.7	94.5	80.7	83.4
13	92.5	93.7	70.0	72.6
14	92.7	94.4	56.7	57.7
15	92.7	93.5	42.6	42.0
16	92.9	93.3	32.3	31.3
17	92.9	92.9	21.1	23.4
18	92.3	92.9	11.9	14.8
19	92.0	92.3	5.5	9.2

Source: The 1989 census results are calculated in Vietnam population census 1989. Completed Census Results, Vol. II, Hanoi: Central Census Steering Committee, 1991. The percentage who ever attended school from VNICDS are based on the household member data and the percentage who are currently attending school are based on the birth history data.

While it is true that the provision of education at all levels has improved in Vietnam over the last five years, it remains the case that the education sector continues to face substantial difficulties. In rural areas many schools are in a very poor state and villagers lack the means to repair them. Some 11.43 per cent of children ranging from 6–14 years in the rural districts have never been to school. Further, the percentage of teenagers and small children enrolled in school tends to decrease very quickly. The proportion of children enrolled that are aged 6–10 is 82.4 per cent; 11–14 is 69.2 per cent; 15–17 is 25.46 per cent; and 18–24 is 4.23 per cent. As a consequence of this high dropout rate 36.13 per cent of the work force has a very limited level of education; 30.84 per cent only finished primary school; 20.5 per cent finished lower-secondary school and 5.7 per cent finished high school.

Hope that this inadequate situation will soon improve is offered by the significant increase in enrolments that have occurred in 1996. The new school year began on 5 September and saw a total enrolment of 20 652 000 students, an increase of 13 per cent from 1995. This figure includes all pupils of infant schools, vocational schools and well as literacy and post-literacy classes. In 1996 the government aimed to ensure that much more emphasis was placed on quality of education and greatly increased the number of specialized classes for gifted children with a view to better meeting the needs of industrialization and modernization. This was also the first year after the government elected to make education a 'prime national policy' and launched a national programme of renovation and the upgrading of education at all levels. To help facilitate this development the final drafting of a new Education Law was prepared for submission to the National Assembly in 1997 as well as amendments that would strengthen the Law on Universalization of Primary Education with the object of ensuring that by the year 2000 the entire population will have completed primary education and there are no more illiterates.

2.   Technical and vocational training

In January 1992 a study by the Institute for Labour Science and Social Affairs, *Training System for Labourers in the Multi-Sector Economy*, stated that 'in carrying out the process of renovation, the Party and the State need to develop a new job-training policy with term targets and diversified forms and standards'. This development reflected the dramatic shift in the government's development strategy associated with the move to embrace the market. The change in policy is best captured by MOLISA's observation that henceforth job-training providers should strive to 'meet the requirements of all sectors (not only the state sector)' and should 'prepare workers to seek their own employment opportunities in the emergent labour market'.

Four years on it would appear that this call to arms has met with only limited success. The system of technical and vocational education has had great difficulty in turning from the supply-driven mechanism (centrally determined numbers of workers trained to predetermined skill levels to meet the requirements of the state sector) to the market-driven approach. There would appear to be at least two primary reasons for this result. First and foremost, there is an acute shortage of teachers of vocational and technical subjects. Second, foreign investors are reluctant to invest in training schools due to the lack of clear guidelines from the government. The picture is further complicated by the fact that many teachers employed in the TVA sector are technical trades workers without any formal qualifications or pedagogical skills.

The government is very much aware of the problems the TVA sector is experiencing but remains determined that the shortage of skilled labour within the economy (Vietnam has less than 4 mn vocationally trained workers, just 10.7 per cent of the total work force) will not be allowed to prove an insurmountable barrier to the industrialization and modernization processes. This resolution was made clear at the 8th Party Congress which called for a significant increase in the skilled work force to 22–25 per cent of the total labour force by the year 2000 and demanded that the TVA sector experiment with diverse forms of job-training. The new emphasis on technical and vocational training is also reflected in the government's determination to transform the current graduate training structure. In October 1996 Tran Dinh Hoan, the Minister of Labour, War Invalids and Social Affairs, declared that at the moment the ratio is 1: 1.6: 3.6 for university graduates, high school graduates and skilled workers respectively. He suggested that this is significant distortion of what is required by a commodified industrializing economy and that the emphasis will be changed with the goal being the development of a graduate ratio of 1: 4: 10 respectively.

3. Higher education

The transit from a centrally planned economy to a market economy has had a profound impact on the higher education sector. We shall not attempt to analyse the involved organization of higher education in Vietnam here. Historically, the system of higher education followed the Soviet model: teaching activities separated from research activities, few multi-disciplinary universities and many mono-disciplinary institutions all operating in a context of *lack* of integration at system level. The higher education sector has more than 100 universities and colleges and there are over 300 state research institutes or centres belonging to various ministries.

It has become accepted that cross fertilization of ideas and externalities in the use of human and non-human capital could be obtained if there were a merger of research institutes with universities and a programme of amalgamation has been set in place. In 1994, Prime Minister Vo Van Kiet signed a decree that established Vietnam National University. This university is a merger of three leading institutions (Hanoi Foreign Language Teachers, Hanoi Teacher-Training College and Hanoi University) has relative independence and autonomy, and is considered as the cornerstone of the country's higher education reform.

A shortage of learning resources combined with teaching methods and curricula inappropriate to a market economy have been also been recognized as significant problems and the government has placed a high priority on turning from the 'socialist style of education' (for example the extensive study of Marxism–Leninism, instruction in Russian language and socialist economic planning) to the 'Western approach to education'. Reflecting the significance of modernization and industrialization needs in the government's education policies concern, emphasis is placed on the development of problem-solving capacities and training in areas such as entrepreneurship, cost accounting, business management and finance. The extensive changes in personnel, policies and programmes of higher education have been prompted by (concurrent) recommendations from the World Bank and a report (Vietnam Educational Sector Analysis, 1992) by the United Nations Educational, Scientific and Cultural Organization, and the United Nations Development Program.

The needs identified by university rectors and college directors in the institutions visited by the World Bank mission in May of 1992 were the following (in rank order):

(1) Retraining and upgrading of staff;
(2) Revision of curricula;
(3) Provision of equipment and learning resources; and
(4) Provision of equipment and library resources.

It is to be noticed that the enhancement of human resources (professional development and upgrading of staff) was considered *more* important than improved physical facilities. The findings were welcomed by the government, and several recommendations were incorporated into the new policy for higher education decided upon by the Communist Party of Vietnam in January of 1993. This policy recognizes the accumulation of human capital as a driving force for the achievement of socioeconomic objectives, and emphasizes that education and training should meet the demands of national economic development. Moreover, the Decision signalled several measures conducive to an improvement of the system of higher education, including the upgrading of teaching and managerial resources and the need for the increase in higher education enrolments to be more closely linked to the needs of the economy.

Many institutions have developed an 'open admission pattern' as an alternative to Vietnam's traditional higher education institutions. The archetypical example is given by the Ho Chi Minh Open University which encourages people to enrol either to improve their job skills or study particular subjects. This institution is considered as an unparalleled success because it 'enrols more students than any other Vietnamese university'. It started [in 1990] with only 400 students in an English-language training course but today has 38 000, many in distant-learning programmes. As with all other sectors of education the financing of the new system includes the payment of fees. It is estimated that in the academic year 1991/92 national enrolment in higher education was of the order of 200 000–250 000 higher education students, and more than 50 per cent paid tuition fees and/or hostel fees. It is of interest to note that the 1996 enrolment in colleges and universities has more than doubled with respect to 1991 making it clear that, as in the school system, the introduction of fees has not reduced the overall number of students.

The ongoing metamorphosis of Vietnam's higher education structure and system is perhaps the best illustration of the dialectic nature of the process of transformation. Vietnam is today irrevocably embarked on structural change characterized by 'pragmatic dualism', that is a process of pursuing a free-market economy, while maintaining the principles of socialism. The essence of this concept is exemplified and demarcated by Le and Stolper in the following two passages:

> ... There is evidence of what appears to outsiders as the operation of contradictory forces in Vietnam's remarkable transformation, as may be seen in the following examples: the endorsement of open-market policies by the CPV [Communist Party of Vietnam], which maintains the panoply of Party ideology and apparatus; increasing acceptance of social pluralism but a central commitment to socialism; a freeing of entrepreneurial spirit but manifest evidence of a social conscience; a programme of equality and education for all and a simultaneous commitment to nurture talent and to develop excellence; new regulations for the operation of private higher education institutions and a resolution to increase, by 22 per cent, the hours that undergraduates in state universities spend formally studying the philosophy of Marxism–Leninism. How much effort is spent in resolving apparently mutual contradictions such as these is unknown. It would seem that many Vietnamese adopt a pragmatic pattern of dualism in order to achieve progress.

> The desire to stand upright as an independent nation and yet to be linked to and accepted by the wider international community is a tangible part of Vietnam's process of modernization. This contemporary pragmatic dualism has a parallel in the centuries of common border and cultural relationship with China to the north. It reaffirms the Vietnamese proverb, sometimes illustrated with a grove of mature bamboo: 'To succeed you must learn to bend with the wind'.
> *Higher Education in Vietnam: Change and Response* (1995: 23–4).

VIII.   Poverty alleviation

In its 1993 report the World Bank offered two explanations for the high dropout rate from the education system. It was suggested it might be either a consequence of the increased job opportunities that have been created by the emerging private sector or it might be a manifestation of the declining quality of the available education. Both of these possibilities appear to have some validity. The Centre for Population and Human Resources Studies reports that an examination of the relationship between education and income for 1992–93 revealed:

> It is not necessary for the job seekers to have a qualification beyond the lower secondary level, even knowing how to read and write is enough. That is to say education level from lower secondary downwards does not effect much upon employment (CPHRS, 1995: 15–16).

Likewise, the fact that the number of children enrolled in high school rose significantly as the state increased resources to the education sector suggests that there may be a good deal of truth in the World Bank's second explanation. However, care needs to be taken not to overemphasize the significance of these two factors for a third influence not mentioned by the Bank needs to be added to the equation – this is poverty.

Vietnam's shift to a commodity economy has resulted in a very significant increase in per capita income. In the 1980–1988 period average income in the rural sector was about 17 kg of rice per month. From 1989 this average increased markedly reaching 34–40 kg in 1993. As a consequence of this development the rate of poverty has been greatly reduced. *The Statistical Year Book* reports that a poverty survey undertaken in 1993 found that 51.77 per cent of the population reported that their living standard had improved since 1990. The problem of poverty, however, is far from being resolved. The poverty survey also found that overall 20 per cent of total households continue to live below the poverty line with a level of consumption of less than 2100 calories per day. Moreover, 30.72 per cent of people survey in the poverty study reported there had been no change in their living standard since 1990 and 17.51 per cent believed they were worse off.

In electing to shift to a commodity economy the government was very much aware that one cost of this decision would be an increase in income differentiation between regions and an increased polarization between rich and poor. Both of these developments have become manifest in the period since 1989. Table 8.7 illustrates the situation in 1993, where one can verify the asymmetric distribution of income between urban and rural areas. These facts represent undesirable (and perhaps inevitable) consequences of the transition

Table 8.7 Average income per household member by regions in 1993
Unit: 1000 dongs per cent

	In general	Urban areas	Rural areas	Urban/rural difference
Whole country	95.2	197.5	68	2.90
Northern mountains	65	133	50	2.66
North middle hills	79	178	70	2.54
Red river delta	89	180	71	2.54
Former Fourth region	70	170	58	2.93
South central	88	178	60	2.97
Western highland	74	140	55	2.55
Eastern south	169	25	80	3.31
Mekong river delta	102	185	85	2.18

Poverty gap by regions
Unit: times

Areas	Period	
	1989–1990	*1992–1993*
Rural areas		
North	3.96	8.60
Central	3.17	9.50
South	5.10	15.00
Northern mountains	4.40	5.30
Southern mountains	7.30	8.00
Urban areas		
North	3.20	5.90
Central	4.00	6.50
South	4.80	14.00

Source: Survey on richness and poverty carried out by the Centre for Population and Human Resources Studies.

process. Needless to say, they have negative implications for the quality of Vietnam's human resources.

The Government has responded to this increased inequality by seeking to develop policies that treat low household income as a human resource development problem that is to be resolved by investing in the poor rather than by providing relief:

> The strategic standpoint in alleviating poverty is to facilitate the poor with more opportunities and favourable conditions to emerge from poverty and integrate into the community. This is the human development point of view, rather than that of social relief and benevolent action like it used to be before (Nguyen, 1992: 22).

The fact that poverty is an HRD problem has also been emphasized by the Centre for Population and Human Resources Development which has identified three primary ways in which low income is undermining the effective development of human resources in Vietnam.

1 *Low family income reduces education opportunities of children.* CPHRD argues that is the primary reason why most farmers' children have an education level of under lower-secondary school (CPHRS, 1995: 9). In support of this assertion the Centre notes that in 1992–93 expenses for education per pupil by grade were as follows (unit 1000 dongs):

Primary school	90.6
Lower-secondary school	229.8
Upper-secondary school	533.6
Technical secondary school	556.7
Higher education	932.7

This argument is also supported by the General Statistical Office 1994 inter-censal study which revealed that parent occupation and family wealth are major factors influencing the number of years children remain within the education system. In short, the results of the survey suggest that, as in the rest of East Asia, parents in Vietnam rate education highly and are willing to invest in this field if they are given the chance.

2. *Low income leads to low expenditure on health undermining the phys-*
   ical status of the work force. Average family expenditure on health
   in rural areas is only 1.9 per cent of total income which compares
   with 3.49 per cent in the north urban areas and 2.41 per cent in
   the urban south. With families simply unable to spend more on
   health and with malnourishment and morbidity rates being
   much higher in low-income regions the government is striving to
   increase spending on public health. The health care sector of the
   economy is being reorganized, external assistance is being
   sought, a private health care system has been established, and
   hospitals now charge fees though the fee system takes into
   account the socioeconomic status of the recipient
3. *Low income limits the effect of population and family planning man-*
   agement programmes. As has been found repeatedly elsewhere, on
   the whole it is the poor who are least responsive to family planning. Poor people tend to have more children (see Table 8.8),
   they are unable to invest in the development of their competen-
   cies and hence they cannot break from the poverty cycle. In
   brief, poverty generates poverty.

The clear implication of the intimate relationship that exists
between income and human resources development is that the government must ensure there are appropriate public funds invested in
the development of the most vulnerable members of society. That
this need is recognized is made clear in the government's report to
the 1995 World Summit for Social Development. The report stated

Table 8.8 Comparison of some demographic indicators between poor and
average households

Indicators	Average level of community	Average level of poor group
Average members per household	6.01	6.13
Total fertility rate (TFR)	3.73	5.65
Crude birth rate (CBR) per cent	30.04	41.29
Crude death rate (CDR) per cent	7.06	12.00
Average life expectancy (years)	65.5	61.7
Male	63.5	59.8
Female	67.5	68.5

Source: Centre for Population and Human Resources Studies, 1995, p. 40.

that every province had been instructed to establish hunger eradication and poverty alleviation funds and to survey and constantly monitor the number of poor households and the effect of HRD and welfare programmes. In line with the policy of treating low family income as an HRD problem the government also reported that it was implementing various incentive policies designed to help poor households. These included preferential treatment in the provision of infrastructure and assistance for business development and employment generation; increased access to vocational training and technology transfer; and exemption or reduction of hospital and school fees.

IX. Employment provision

The fourth and final strategic objective in Vietnam's human resources development programme, identified by Nguyen in 1992, is employment provision. Vietnam's work force of 38.2 mn (1994) is increasing by almost one mn workers per annum. As a consequence between 1996 and 2000 employment will have to be created for some 7.5 mn extra job-seekers. Since the introduction of the 1989 reforms the government has shown a capacity to meet this challenge. In the four years 1991–94 it was able to generate the million jobs required per annum and as a consequence unemployment was reduced from 8–9 per cent in 1990 to 6–7 per cent in 1994. This is an impressive effort but will be very difficult to sustain. In January 1996 the ILO warned that its estimates suggest that while the labour force is growing at 3 per cent per annum in the countryside and 5 per cent in the urban centres the possibility of employment generation is only 2.5 per cent. The problem, moreover, is compounded by the vast pool of underemployed in the rural sector who would enter the urban labour market were more jobs available. In April 1996 Nguyen Cong Tan, Minister of Agriculture and Rural Development, reported that there were some 8 mn 'underemployed or half employed' persons in the countryside or some 30 per cent of the rural work force.

Given the severe contraction in the number of jobs in the public sector brought about as a consequence of the increased commodification of the economy, it is clear that the private sector – including household-based enterprises – must absorb Vietnam's surplus labour. To maintain the level of absorption required the government must ensure there exists an effective labour market buttressed by appropriate state and community policies. Under the centrally planned system students graduating from secondary and tertiary institutions were assigned jobs even if they did not match the individual's talents or desires. Students who did not get an education beyond the primary level were not generally allocated jobs. The Socioeconomic Stabilization and Development Strategy to the Year 2000 that was adopted by the Seventh National Congress of the Communist Party in June 1991 made it clear that an even larger group of job-seekers would henceforth be compelled to fend for themselves in the labour market. The government, however, has decided that it will not leave employment generation solely to market forces.

Employment generation must be directed towards the objective of developing and effectively using employment resources, while meeting the requirements of reform in the economy and labour force during the process of industrialization and modernization. In coming years efforts should be concentrated on reforming the structure of the rural economy so as to reduce the labour force involved in agriculture, and increase the labour force in industry, handicrafts and services (SRVN, 1995: 14–15).

To this end the government has developed a seven-point programme that is integrated with other economic development programmes which are aimed at accelerating economic growth, social stability and security, and reducing both unemployment and underemployment. To this end it will:

- *Create favourable conditions of investment.* This will involve the creation and/or development of capital, securities and labour markets and the smooth functioning of facilities for investors. It is hoped that these measures will attract about US$48–US$50 bn in capital investment to the year 2000 of which over 80 per cent will be devoted to industry and infrastructure facilities which will create more employment.
- *Re-green barren hills and uncultivated lands.* It is believed that this policy should develop some 2 000 000 hectacres of forest and 40 000–50 000 hectares of agricultural land The government will also induce investment in marine resources and a number of pro-

jects that it believes have the potential to create long-term employment while protecting the environment.

- *Provide individuals with low-interest credit.* Small credit advances are to be made to enable people to create employment for themselves, the funds for this project to be built up over time.
- *Expand the rural credit scheme so as to increase the number of peasant households receiving financial assistance.* This is a key requirement given peasant households have become independent, self-managing and self-financing and will extend this scheme which was initially established in 1991.
- *Expand vocational training and employment promotion centres.* Over the next three years all 53 provinces will be expected to establish at least one of these centres which will focus both on training and on ensuring that the labour market operates more effectively.
- Encourage organizations such as Youth, Women, Trade Unions and Peasant Association and other professional bodies to create jobs for their respective members utilizing their own finances as well as financial assistance from international agencies.

X. Conclusion

The role that human resource development has played in the spectacular economic dynamism associated with the nations of the Asia-Pacific Rim has very much been appreciated by the government and people of Vietnam. As is common to the people of Asia, the population of Vietnam has shown an enthusiastic willingness to seize the possibilities provided by education. Likewise, as in so many other areas, the government has shown an almost amazing capacity to adapt while retaining its commitment to both short-term efficiency and equity goals as well as the long-term vision of socialism. Vietnam's approach to human resource development should therefore be assessed not only in terms of the high level of basic education and the rapidly evolving higher education system, but also on the basis of its commitment to the managent of population growth and the elimination of poverty. The Vietnamese people have shown enormous resilience, fortitude and determination to overcome extreme challenges. It should be hardly necessary to add that those distinguishing features will remain ingrained in the quality of human resources in Vietnam, and pave the way for further improvement.

Notes

1. This point is forcibly made by Ogawa *et al.* (1993). The present section draws heavily on that volume.
2. The 1992 evidence on GDP per capita in rank order is as follows: Brunei (PPP$20 589), Singapore (PPP$18 330), Malaysia (PPP$ 7790), Thailand (PPP$5950), Indonesia (PPP$2950), Philippines (PPP$2250), Laos (PPP$1760), Cambodia (PPP$1250), and Vietnam (PPP$1010), where the numbers in parenthesis indicate GDP per capita converted into US dollars on the basis of the purchasing power parity (PPP) of the country's currency.
3. What we call here HCI is nothing but the statistic 'educational attainment' that appears in the Human Development Report 1995. See UNDP (1995, p. 18). It is to be noticed that the allocation of weights tends to understimate the importance of secondary and higher education. As an illustration, consider two hypothetical countries exhibiting the following values for the relevant variables:

	AL	CR
Country 1	90	50
Country 2	80	70

The value of the proxy for human capital is the *same* in both countries (HCI = 76.67). However, the combined first-second-and-third-level enrolment ratio is 40 per cent higher in Country 2 than in Country 1.
4. There are two polar cases of gender inequality aversion. If we denote by $e = 0$ the degree of aversion to gender inequality, we have: e = o (*no* aversion for gender inequality, i.e. only achievements of men get a positive weight) and e = infinity (*absolute* aversion for gender inequality, i.e. only achievements of women get a positive weight). Table 8.3 employs the same value of the parameter e as the Human Development Report 1995, namely: $e = 2$, which represents a *moderate* degree of gender inequality aversion.

References

Ashwood, N. (1994), *A Business Handbook*, Graham & Trotman, London.
Borthwick, M. (1995), *Pacific Economic Development Report 1995. Advancing Regional Integration*, Pacific Economic Cooperation Council, Singapore.
Centre for Population and Human Resource Studies, CPHRS (1995), *Analysis, Evaluation of the Relation Between Population, Migration, Human Resources and Employment (Abstract Report)*.
Department of Foreign Affairs and Trade (1996), *Country Economic Brief Viet Nam 1996*, AGPS, Canberra.
Fahey, S. (1996), *Trade Unions in Viet Nam*, Paper prepared for 'Labour history: themes, comparisons and directions' conference at University of Wollongong, 30 September–1 October 1996.
General Statistical Office, GSO (1996), *Education in Viet Nam Trends and Differentials*, Statistical Publishing House, Hanoi.

International Labour Office (1993), *Employment, enterprise development and training in Viet Nam*, International Labour Office, Bangkok.

Hansson, E. (1995), *Trade Unions and Doi Moi. The changing role of trade unions in the era of economic liberalization in Viet Nam*, Department of Political Science, Stockholm University, Stockholm.

Ministry of Higher Education and Vocational Training (1994), *Viet Nam's Vocational Training System*, Ministry of Higher Education and Vocational training.

Nguyen, H. D. (1992), *Human Resource Development in the Transformation Process to Market-Oriented Economy in Vietnam*, Vietnam Social Sciences and Humanities, 3, Hanoi, Vietnam.

Nguyen, P. (1995), *Report on Labour Statistics in Viet Nam*, Centre for Scientific Information on Labour and Social Affairs – Ministry of Labour, Invalids and Social Affairs, Hanoi.

Norlund, I. (1995), 'Labour laws and the new labour regimes. A comparison of Viet Nam and China', paper prepared for the conference 'Viet Nam – Reform and Transformation' Centre for Pacific Asia Studies, Stockholm University 31 August–1 September 1995.

Ogawa, H., Jones, G., Williamson J., eds (1993), *Human Resources in Development along the Asia-Pacific Rim*, Oxford University Press, Singapore.

Ronnas, P. and Sjoberg, O. (1995), 'Economic reform, employment and labour market policy in Viet Nam', *Labour Market Papers 9*, International Labour Office, Geneva.

Sloper, D., Can, L. (1995), *Higher Education in Vietnam Change and Response*, Institute of Southeast Asian Studies, Singapore.

Socialist Republic of Viet Nam, SRVN (1995), *Viet Nam's Country Report on Social Development*, Hanoi, prepared for the World Summit for Social Development, Copenhagen, 6–12 March 1995.

Statistical Yearbook, Central Statistical Office, Hanoi.

Thalemann, A. (1996), 'Viet Nam: Marketing the Economy', *Journal of Contemporary Asia*, Vol. 26, No. 3, 1996.

Thi, L. (1996), 'Female Workers in the Economy's Transition and the Application of New Technology, and Gender Responsive Policy', *Social Sciences*, Vol. 2, No. 52, 1996.

United Nations Children's Fund (1990), *Viet Nam The Situation of Children and Women*, United Nations Children's Fund Office of the Representative, Hanoi.

United Nations Development Programme, UNDP (1995), *Human Development Report 1995*, Oxford University Press, New York.

United Nations Educational, Scientific and Cultural Organization (UNESCO), *Vietnam Educational Sector Analysis*, 1992.

Van, P. (1995), 'The Legal Status of the Female Labourer in the New Code of Labour of the Socialist Republic of Viet Nam', *Social Sciences*, Vol. 3, No. 47, 1995.

World Bank (1993), *Viet Nam Transition to the Market: An Economic Report*, World Bank, Washington D.C.

World Bank (1995), *Viet Nam Economic Report on Industrialisation and Industrial policy*, World Bank, Washington D.C.

9
Business Ethics and Foreign Enterprises in Vietnam

Tran Van Hoa

I. Introduction

The role of ethics in business has gained increasing importance and emphasis in recent years. It has formed the core subject in many study courses on business management and public administration worldwide. With the advent of information technology, we can witness the use of ingenuity, innovation and creativity in the people to produce advancements in sciences and in the way we do business (the so-called electronic commerce), but we can also witness the situations where these characteristics can be used to produce (and detect) transgressions more easily, initially for corporate interest but ultimately for personal gains. In addition to this reason, the rise of business ethics can be said to have arisen from two important aspects of business: globalization via transnational corporations – with some disastrous scandals and unprecedented, large-scale financial and goodwill losses subsequently raising questions in the mind of both public and authorities about the ethics of business – and the introduction of Total Quality Management (TQM) where total quality does not mean simply high quality but acceptable quality and responsibility in the management of a business organization in each stage of operation (Chryssides and Kaler, 1993).

However, it is true that, due to its diverse applications and dynamic characteristics, the issue of business ethics is changeable and complex even in a homogeneous society and economic community (for example, North America and the European Economic Community). For international business crossing many nationalities and frontiers where languages, cultures, law, attitudes, economic systems, customs and practices are different, the issue of business ethics becomes more challenging and no less desirable and import ant. The case of business ethics of transnational corporations and individual business people in developing and transition economies presents, in our view, a thesis of paramount practical business interest and applications worthy of serious investigation and discussion.

The chapter focuses on the issues of business ethics for both transnational corporations and individual people doing business in Vietnam, a fast-growing transition economy and a vast market (with 7 mn people as at 1998) with huge untapped human and natural resources, and with potential applications to other similar developing or transition economies in the Subcontinent and the Asia-Pacific Rim. The chapter will point out problems and potential consequences arising from these issues. More significantly, it will also put forward the view that an ethical style of organization, management and operation by transnational corporations and business people constitutes a comparative advantage, with social and private economic benefits, that will by its nature enhance the quantity and quality of international business, both the short and long terms.

II. Foundations of ethics in business

Much of the knowledge about many important aspects of our life has come into existence only as a result of sudden enlightenment after a long search (for example, Buddhism) or of sudden discoveries either by hard work (the compass, the wheels, gunpowder, chemistry, Pasteur's bacteria, radio-communications, Einstein's equation and DNA) or by chance (fire and electricity). Some of our knowledge has come in the form of accumulated wisdom and experience nationally or transnationally acquired or of genetic endowment. Ethics, or a code of good conduct, is one of the concepts in our treasure of acquired knowledge that has a venerable and long history (see further arguments in, for example, Teulings, 1978, and Chryssides and Kaler, 1993). It is also pervasive in all aspects of human endeavour.

Ethics as an acceptable norm of conduct has been practised by philosophers through their codification of what is regarded as the ideal standard measuring behaviour, or as a good conduct or an action with fair and equitable outcomes. Ancient and modern teachers have been practising it by teaching us what is known as good and decent behaviour acceptable to the society in which we live. The church (via its canon law and in the Judaeo-Christian tradition) and other evangelists and religious practitioners (by means of, for example, the law of Moses, the Year of the Jubilees, and three of the points in Buddha's Eightfold Path) have been practising it through encouraging people to engage in moral as distinct from amoral activities under the general concept that life as a whole is simply a training ground for the development of our divine qualities. Ethics has also been practised by sociologists in their essays or treatises on what is good for individuals, associations or society, and by criminologists in their theories of institutional design and accountability (Fisse, 1993). In recent times, ethics has been used equally effectively by politicians in their electioneering campaigns to elevate the quality of their candidature or with the purpose of eventually righting a wrong, and by entrepreneurs in their domestic or international business (De George, 1993), as well as by their institutional statutory supervisors, the government commissioners, in enforcing the trade practices laws in various countries.

With the emergence of global business, especially since the successful reconstruction of the world economies after World War II, the introduction of TQM and the advent of information technology as mentioned earlier, and the appearance of and interest in developing and newly industrialized economies in South America, the Middle East, the Subcontinent and East Asia, the issues of ethics have also assumed a more prominent role. Some of these issues involve international law and its suitability and applications, transnational corporations and their motives in doing international business, a transnational code of ethics as opposed to that operational at home, and problems of economic development and exploitation of human and natural resources (see for example Hoffman *et al.*, 1994, for some aspects of these issues). These have generated numerous discussions and debates on the relationship between ethics and the setting up, management and operation of global business by transnational corporations.

In the case of some developing and transition countries, such as Vietnam or China in Asia and other similar, former Commonwealth-of-Independent-States countries in Eastern Europe, where the government and the people have been trying to adapt the practices of free-market economics to what is essentially a centrally planned economy, the issues of ethics in business are compounded, and the problems are more complex, from the perspective of both the government in these countries and transnational corporations who want to operate there.

III.   Business ethics at work

Some aspects of ethics and their interpretations in the context encountered by transnational corporations while doing business either at the organizational stage or during the operational period in Vietnam – and no doubt in other similar developing and transition economies – have been starkly reported in the media or on the Internet in recent times. A few of these cases are described below to illustrate the problems of ethics involved.

Case 1

In 1996, a female employee of a shoe factory in Vietnam, managed by a South Korean company, took the company to court after she claimed she was hit on the body with a shoe by a Korean manager at the factory; her alleged transgression: she was slow with her work. In court, the company was admonished and fined a small amount of money (about US$7). The employee concerned and her colleagues were unhappy with the court decision, and decided to take further action in a higher court. It is common knowledge among people familiar with Korean corporate management in South Korea that hitting employees is sanctioned by some management at home. But it was not the done thing in Vietnam. The case above has created an international incident, nevertheless. As a solution, to avoid further similar incidents at Korean companies in Vietnam, the government of South Korea has sent representatives from the Ministry of Trade to meet its counterpart in Vietnam to discuss and set up training programmes for Korean management staff. These will inform employees of Vietnam's acceptable labour customs and practices, among others, before their arrival or before they start work in the country.

Case 2

In 1996, the Ministry of Finance in Vietnam announced that, as a policy of government and corporate management of great urgency, it would introduce training courses in Western accounting and auditing practices to Vietnam's government officials. The implication was that Vietnam's accounting and auditing practices, while fully, operational and accepted by all in the country, were not the same as those used in Western countries or not up to international standards. In spite of these, many finance offices in Australian institutions in Australia are either unaware of the situation or aware of it but unable to adapt to it and accept it. As a result, these offices unilaterally insist in their financial transactions with Vietnam that only Australia's accounting and auditing practices are acceptable and should be used as standard, and that any transaction that does not conform to these practices will either not be accepted or will not be promptly processed. The consequences of this less than knowledgeable, arrogant attitude and a refusal to accept the existence of cultural differences by these offices in financial dealings with Vietnam has led to substantial delays in completing the transactions and the work, wasteful use of resources by all the parties involved, and unnecessary antagonisms.

Case 3

Early in April 1997, two giant US corporations in Vietnam, Nike and Reebock, signed an agreement to adhere to international labour standards in their factories. This happened at the same time as the US government achieved an agreement with the clothing industry in the US to enforce the same labour standards for all US factories whether operating at home on in other countries. These standards include a maximum of 60 hours work per week, and no employee under 15 years of age (child labour) to be employed by the factories either at home or in their factories in other overseas countries. The agreement is a giant step forward to maintain labour standards, protect the labour force, and avoid corporate exploitation especially in developing and transition economies. The agreement nevertheless has its own critics in the sense that the people in some of these countries have no choice for family reasons but to send their children under 15 years of age to work to support the family. It is in these countries that an adherence to the other requirements of the World Trade Organization (WTO) even under threats of trade sanctions may be difficult to attain at least in the short run.

Case 4

After the meeting of the congress in Vietnam in 1996, a vice-minister was reported in the media as telling foreign journalists in front of the National Assembly that foreign investors in Vietnam are evils of the West and have been exploiting the human and natural resources of the country. Half an hour later, however, the secretary-general of Vietnam's communist party also appeared in front of the National Assembly and declared that that view is not correct, foreign investors are in fact Vietnam's good friends and have helped to contribute to the country's economic progress and development especially since the introduction of Doi Moi (renovation).

The cases cited above show that the ethics of doing business (as distinct from personal ethics that may involve private greed, fraud, corruption and personal glory at the expense of others) in Vietnam (or in other similar countries) can be viewed from two perspectives: the local and the foreign. What is good or acceptable for one party or country may be bad or unacceptable for the other. Given this difference in the interpretation of the same action or event, is there a common ground as far as ethics is concerned in doing business by transnational corporations and individual business people for mutual economic and social benefits in Vietnam or other similar countries?

In the following section, we will look at a set of guidelines or value statements that have been suggested by business leaders, academics, government officials and special interest groups and that may serve as the common background to a standard code of conduct for transnational corporations in particular and for international business in general.

IV. Consensus principles of business ethics

In Australia, business ethics is encouraged by the government, relevant authorities, trade and consumers associations. The legal tool to enforce the requirements of business ethics or part of it is the Trade Practices Act and the jurisdiction for enforcement is vested in the Australian Competition and Consumer Commission (ACCC), an amalgamation of the former Price Surveillance Authority and the Trace Practices Commission. The main criteria for judging good business ethics are promotion of competition and fair trading. Any action that hinders or is likely to hinder competition in trade is forbidden and can be fined. Any action that gives rise to unfair trading is also forbidden and can be fined.

The basis for promoting competition is derived from what is contained in Adam Smith's *Wealth of Nations* (1776) in which the pursuit of self-interest by each individual is expected to rebound to the benefit of all. In this case of *laissez faire* economics, ethical considerations as set forth before *Wealth of Nations* in Adam Smith's *Theory of Moral Sentiments* (1759) were removed, and the authority of technology is asserted over morality. Adam Smith's 'so-called animal spirit' gives rise to the modern critical-rationalistic school of economics as expounded by Max Weber and then Karl Popper and Hans Albert, and this school has been known to be the leading school of thought among business economists (Schreuder, 1978).

In its essential form, the basis for promoting competition is the tenet of the economic theory of a perfect market (that is, a market without any distortion whatsoever) in both the product (the commodities produced or the services rendered) and the factors of production (capital, materials, labour and management). The economy achieves Pareto optimum (that is, maximum utilization of resources with unlimited supply of goods and services at the lowest possible costs and prices) when the market or economy is perfectly competitive. Any distortion of this situation (for example, price controls, subsidies, trade barriers and so on) will give rise to inefficient use of resources, misallocation of capital, manpower and management skills, shortage of goods and services, higher prices, private and public corruption (see Mauro, 1997), and public discontent. It also hinders domestic and international trade. It is known that international trade distortions or barriers have been responsible for great world wars with global damage in this century.

The trade practices act of a country which sets the standards of business to attain efficiency and fair trading includes, in fact, elements of the normativist school of economic thought (Schreuder, 1978). This school takes into account ethical considerations, value judgements and social responsibility in carrying out business and trade. The act the articles of which are enforced by say the equivalent of the ACCC in Australia is appropriate as a code of conduct for business in a country, and this code is further checked by either the trade or consumers' associations. However, there is still little agreement on a general code of international business ethics applicable to all transnational corporations operating in foreign countries, although the desirability and feasibility of a transnational code of conduct have been investigated and found to be positive by various authors (see Hoffman *et al.*, 1994). The two well-known exceptions to this state of affairs are the US and Sweden where laws exist to guide their transnational corporations' conduct in foreign countries.

It has been hoped by many authors that, although it is not likely in the immediate future, eventually, there will be a United Nations (UN) code of conduct (or equivalently, international policy regimes or a set of mutually accepted norms for behaviour) on transnational corporations. A draft code was adopted by the General Assembly on 13 May 1990 and a letter was transmitted from the UN Commission on Transnational Corporations to the UN Economic and Social Council. The UN draft incorporates implicitly the International Labour Organization (ILO) 'Tripartite Declaration of Principles concerning Multinational Enterprises and Social Policy' of 1977 and the UN 'Set of Multilaterally Agreed Equitable Principles and Rules for the Control of Restrictive Business Practices' of 1980, and forbids corrupt practices in emulation of the US and Swedish anti-bribery laws as mentioned above. The UN draft code can be seen as the result of a series of international codes, guidelines and declarations of various geographic and functional scopes governing business conduct in world markets, including the UN convention on international sales of goods (1980), the World Health Organization (WHO) infant formula code (1981); and the UN general consumer guidelines (1985) covering product safety and quality, promotion, distribution, education and information, redress of grievances, food, water and pharmaceuticals (Windsor, 1994, p. 165).

In the following, we summarise the 12 basic principles or 'Just Profit' consensus guidelines in a possible transnational code of conduct for international business. These so-called Vesper-Hinksey, or The San Francisco, guidelines come from an August 1990 conference in San Francisco, USA, of academics, business leaders and representatives of special interest groups (Ryan, 1994, pp. 191–9).

1. Transnational corporations commit to a long-term relationship when investing in a country and to operate in cooperation with the host community to seek beneficial impacts.

2. Transnational corporations act in ways that respect and protect fundamental human rights.
3. Transnational corporations make full and fair disclosure of all information relevant to the well being of stake-holders and the general public.
4. Transnational corporations protect the ecosystem by specifically meeting identified environmental standards and conserving natural resources through efficient use.
5. Transnational corporations produce products and services which meet adequate safety within a healthy workplace environment.
6. Transnational corporations recognize the rights of employees to organize and bargain collectively.
7. Transnational corporations seek to promote employee welfare through fair terms of employment, job security, a safe and non-discriminatory workplace and a commitment to retraining in order to prevent the event of or mitigate the impact of lay-offs or a plant closure.
8. Transnational corporations seek long-term profitability by providing quality goods and services at a fair price.
9. Transnational corporations identify and involve stake-holders at appropriate levels and phases of the decision-making process.
10. Transnational corporations provide management leadership and resources to develop and implement internal ethical guidelines.
11. Transnational corporations respect local practices and customs or adhere to the corporation's own ethical guidelines, whichever is most beneficial for the local community.
12. Transnational corporations respect international law and support the development and implementation of codes of conduct for international business which achieve broad international consensus.

In addition, the following consensus guidelines have also been suggested in the case of American business internationally:

1. Protection of the environment;
2. Integrity and honesty;
3. Standards of fairness with vendors and suppliers;
4. Providing useful products or services to customers;

5. Equity – fair and safe workplace;
6. Creativity and innovation;
7. Opportunity for people to reach their own goals while working towards company goals;
8. Quality of goods and services.

Further consensus value statements about the responsibilities of business for transnational corporations in a free-market environment were provided by the Gustavus Adolphus working group at the San Francisco conference above and include:

1. To use good management, creativity and innovation to produce useful, high-quality goods and services for customers, optimal returns to investors and contribute to creating a better world;
2. To respect the human dignity of each of its employees by providing a fair, safe and diverse workplace with opportunities for employees to develop their own potential;
3. To demonstrate long-term commitment to all stake-holders by operating with the highest ethical standards;
4. To pursue the goals above with honesty and integrity, seeking to exemplify excellence in all aspects of corporate activity.

V.   A useful model of good ethical conduct

The guidelines and value statements described above would appear to provide a good *modus operandi* for transnational corporations and individual business people in Vietnam or other similar countries. They cover social aspects of international business and industries: human resources, justice and economic distribution, cultural differences, advertising and marketing, the environment and finance; and corporate governance, industrial sociology and industrial relations. They are the transnational corporation's guidelines in so far as the transnational corporation is concerned, and the responsibility rests with these corporations to communicate them to their branch offices in overseas countries for action there. It is not difficult to see from these guidelines and value statements that some of them may not be equally applicable to all countries since they may contradict the law or regulation in some countries (for example, to support collective bargaining unionism is forbidden in some countries). In other words, since the business environment is so diverse and dynamic, no situation is inflexible. As a result, what is correct in one situation may be entirely inappropriate in another similar situation.

The fact that not all the suggested guidelines and statements are applicable to all countries where the transnational corporations operate means that a model of ethical conduct, to be useful in practice, must integrate corporate guidelines and statements with local values and beliefs. These local values and beliefs may include law and culture, ethics, business practices, customs and cross-cultural concerns.

One of such models has been suggested by Cohen and Nelson (1994) in which corporate and local values and normative beliefs are combined and manifested throughout the branches and offices of the transnational corporations. This model contains, in our view, a higher ethical standard and may be similar to what Garrott (1992) alluded to in his 'deeper approach' to developing and practising ethics in business. This model would be a good starting-point for practical applications by transnational corporations on the local scene.

Essentially, the model recognizes, respects and integrates two perspectives as its important components: corporate and local. At the corporate level, the manifestation of guidelines and value statements of business ethics is done through training, communication systems (such as memoranda, circulars or email), the process of decision-making, the existence of a code of conduct, various compliance procedures, reward systems, and monitoring and control systems. At the local level, the manifestation is done through familiarization with local legal regulations, setting up business–government relations via local representatives, understanding of the business roles and responsibilities in the country, and understanding of the roles and responsibilities of the individuals in the corporation's branches.

Based on these manifestations, corporate and local business practices are then carried out in all aspects of corporate and local management and operation. All these practices must express corporate guidelines and statements and at the same time they must reflect local interpretation.

If we assume that this model of ethical conduct combining corporate and local values and beliefs would provide a good foundation to carry on international business in general and business in Vietnam in particular, how would it be applied to or implemented by Australian enterprises doing business there or in similar countries?

VI. Implications for Australian enterprises in Vietnam

Judged from the spirit of the above guidelines and value statements, the suggested model of ethical conduct, and the implications of the four case-studies mentioned earlier in section 3, it follows that, in practical situations, the application of consensus business ethics standards and value statements is desirable and even necessary for good management and operation of international business. However, the use of even the same ethical standards can take various guises and forms in different situations even in one country such as Vietnam. Some of the possible practical manifestations of the ethical standards suggested for Australian (and other foreign) companies and individual business people operating in Vietnam are summarised below in descending order of importance and relevance from our analysis and experience at the time of writing. This order can be re-ranked if the new emerging situation warrants it and if a particular company finds it more suited to its own existing experience and resources. Further aspects of business ethics for Australian companies doing business in Vietnam were given by Longstaff (1996).

1. Understanding and respecting cross-cultural values and beliefs

Case-study 1 in section 3 brings out the problems of not understanding the value assigned to and the role played by the labour force in a socialist country such as Vietnam. In fact, the incident as reported in the media was in violation of the basic code of ethics for international business as we discussed them earlier in section 4, and also of WTO labour standards. Similar to the problem underlying the incident is the attitude of many managers of transnational corporations or individual businesses in Western or newly developed economies, especially with respect to their employees in less developing economies, in which it is assumed that 'we' are normal or standard and 'others' are not.

Vietnam is a socialist country but it has deep-rooted traditions, derived from the teachings of Confucius, which demand absolute devotion and respect to the parents. This means that leave of absence from office may be more frequently requested by employees in Vietnam for attending family matters than in Western or even other Asian countries. It is also the general belief of many in Vietnam that early in the month is a period in which a certain activity is not recommended. It is therefore not unusual for transnational corporations employees to abstain from corporate activities during this period no matter how 'unscientific' it may look to outsiders. Just as it is unreasonable to expect others to act contrary to their conscience, it is equally important to be true to one's own conscience and not to judge a country and its people by stereotypes. It is important, one may stress, to avoid showing a certain kind of behaviour (for example, the so-called corporate arrogance, see Chryssides and Kaler, 1993, pp. 517–18) in which it is claimed that our value systems should be taken as they are and therefore need not be adjusted to meet the requirements of the local situations.

2.   Understanding and respecting cross-cultural law, customs and practices

Vietnam is a developing and transition economy where average income per head was about US$250 in 1996, but the country has a long history dating back over 2000 years, and it has claimed many victories in battles against the invading armies of far superior force from as early as 43 AD, with the two Trung sisters, in order to attain personal freedom and national independence. In other words, Vietnam prides itself on this history and heritage and will protect its laws, customs and practices in international relations, in administration and in commerce with this background.

A common complaint from foreign business people in Vietnam is that the country is riddled with corruption and administrative obstacles which hinder business operation. It should be noted that this is the complaint the government of Vietnam itself is fully aware of and has been trying from the office of the prime minister down to the lowest level of bureaucracy to rectify through introducing new anti-corruption and efficiency-improving laws and decrees, through publicity in the media, and through exemplary court cases trying high-ranking officials accused of transgression. Another example is in the improvement of the accounting and auditing process through training and short courses for business and government departments. The reason is that many foreign investors, business people and international experts have claimed that the current process is giving an inaccurate picture or unreliable information in Vietnam. Foreign investors and representatives of the Australian government often complain about the problem of grease money being used in Vietnam to facilitate business activity. It should also be noted that grease money or facilitation payment is not forbidden by US anti-bribery law while bribery is. As an analogy, we can cite the case of breakfast meetings with free breakfast provided which is a common activity in corporate institutions in Australia, but to say that they are bribes to the participants is to a large extent missing the point.

3. Use of consultants for business feasibility studies and local staff for assistance in management and operation of business

For any business person who is not Vietnamese born in Vietnam and who is not familiar with ways of doing business in Vietnam, it is a real hurdle to try to comprehend the complexity of law, by-laws, legal requirements, personal and public relations, and their practices and procedures at the central and, more importantly, provincial levels where the transnational corporations and business people will have their licences submitted, scrutinized and approved (or rejected). This may explain why most businesses in Vietnam until now have been joint ventures in which the expertise of the local business people is required in combination with the foreign capital, expertise and technical know how of transnational corporations or individual investors and business people. The employment of local staff to run the business is self-explanatory. But it is on behalf of these employees that careful attention has to be paid to the manifestation of the code of ethics in relation to corporate guidelines and statements, the WTO standards and the local conditions, as well as values and beliefs in relation to the rights, behaviour and aspirations of these employees.

4. Use of experience from other transnational corporations or individual business people operating in the country

Chryssides and Kaler (1993, p. 518) recommend that people who want to do business in a country should talk to people who have already visited that country to find out the ways in which they found their experience rewarding or frustrating, the problems they encountered and, if possible, the solutions they have successfully developed. On the question of ethics issues in business that they were faced with, they should be asked for advice on how to solve it. The danger which one has to avoid here is talking to the people who may not have been right to engage in international business in the first place, who, as a result, are disenchanted with doing business in Vietnam and have a grudge against the whole system or the whole country. However, these people might still be used as devil's advocates so one can see the pros and cons of doing business in the country and draw some good lessons from them.

5.   Maintain high quality of goods produced and services provided

This advice is self-explanatory for transnational corporations and individual business people. Business is by definition an activity that will provide profits for the owner of the business. A business can be goods-producing or services-producing. If a business is not competitive in the quality of the goods it produces or in the services it provides, there is no reason why it should be in business or it would be forced to leave the industry altogether. This maxim of the economic theory of perfectly competitive markets is applied equally to state-owned and privately owned enterprises, necessary public goods (for example, national defence) excepted.

6.   Project honesty, integrity and transparency in business dealings

Shady business and its fruits, however good they may be, are frowned upon in our society. This is true both at home and in other countries. Even for two corporations with similar outcomes in terms of profits, market shares, long-term planning and growth potential, the one with a clean slate usually wins the day in the long run. In fact, a corporation with a good record of ethical activities can use it as a comparative advantage to compete with its business rivals. This can be seen as an aspect of putting in practice the concept of TQM we discussed earlier in international business. The urge not to maintain honesty, integrity and transparency may be great for out-of-country managers of international business or private investment or companies since, as has been mentioned above, there are no adequate laws to deal with the situation. To maintain these qualities, however, requires a business leader of strong and high ethical standards.

7. Effective communications between local branches and corporate head-offices at home

This advice is related to that above on the need for transparency and efficiency in the management and operation of international business. It has often been claimed that great corporate disasters are the results of inadequate communications or knowledge between the branch offices and the headquarters or between the manager and the managing director. The two widely reported court cases with adverse outcomes for the people concerned in recent times involving the Barings Bank in the United Kingdom and the Coles-Myers business in Australia are typical examples of what would happen when corporate communications are inadequate or not effective.

8. Frequents visit to the country to update oneself with new developments and their implications at the corporate level

This is important for countries such as Vietnam where according to one former ambassador from the United Kingdom to Vietnam one would not be able to recognize even the city of Hanoi after only eight weeks of absence. The diversity and dynamism of international business make it one of the most challenging and rewarding for human endeavour. Field-trips and normal visits form part of this exciting fact-finding exercise. It would provide timely knowledge on the trends, emerging issues and discussions and debates affecting international business in the country. This is particularly true for Vietnam in its transitionary progress from a socialist to a free-market economy with socialist tendencies, as local politicians and senior government officials in Vietnam often state.

9. Good citizenships in the country where the company is operating

While the sole purpose of a business is to make money in a country, it is not unusual that this business is expected to plough something back into the community and society in which it operates. The idea of good citizenship is accepted worldwide by the corporate community. Good citizenship can be expressed in the form of financial support for sporting events, youth activities, donations to charity appeals, awarding prizes for excellence in business and in services to the community, or even donating prizes to beauty contests. Donations to political parties are another form of good citizenship in some Western countries although some of these practices have been barred in some countries in recent times.

10.   The need for thinking big and long instead of small and short

A taboo in some developing and transition economies is a business that may be a fly by-night business-only for making a quick profit without a long-term commitment to the country in which it operates. While many individual investors and business people have been known to be able to make quick profits from their ventures in Vietnam in recent years, they have not been given the kind of respect and collaboration that transnational corporations and individual business people with long-term business and investment plans in the country have been receiving. As we have discussed earlier on, an international code of conduct for international business, long-term commitment to the country and the community in which a transnational corporation or individual business person operates is one of the guidelines strongly suggested for adoption and for manifestation in the local scene. This is a psychological aspect of international business.

References

Chryssides, G. D. and Kaler, J. H. (1993), (eds), *An Introduction to Business Ethics*, Melbourne: Chapman & Hall.

Cohen, D. V. and Nelson, K. A. (1994), 'Multinational Ethics Programs: cases in Corporate Practice', in Hoffman, W. M., Kamm, J. B., Frederick, R. E., and Petry Jr, E. S. (eds), *Emerging Global Business Ethics*, London: Quorum Books.

De George, R. T. (1993), *Competing with Integrity in International Business*, New York: Oxford University Press.

Garrott, G. R. (1992), *Ethics in Business: A Deeper Approach*, Hobart: Institute of Business Ethics.

Fisse, B. (1993), *Corporations, Crime and Accountability*, Cambridge: Cambridge University Press.

Hoffman, W. M., Kamm, J. B., Frederick, R. E., and Petry Jr, E. S. (eds) (1994), *Emerging Global Business Ethics*, London: Quorum Books.

Longstaff, S. (1996), 'The Ethics in Doing Business in Vietnam', *International Workshop on Trade, Investment and Business in Vietnam*, University Conference Centre, Sydney, 20 November.

Mauro, P. (1997), 'Why Worry About Corruption?', Washington: International Monetary Fund.
Ryan, L. V. (1994), 'Incorporating "Just Profit" Guidelines in Transnational Codes', in Hoffman, W. M., Kamm, J. B., Frederick, R. E., and Petry Jr, E. S. (eds), *Emerging Global Business Ethics*, London: Quorum Books.
Schreuder, H. (1978), 'The Social Responsibility of Business', in van Dam, C. and Stallaert, L. M. (eds), *Trends in Business Ethics: Implications for Decision-Making*, Boston: Kluwer.
Teulings, C. H. I. E. M. (1978), 'Standards and Values in the Business Enterprise', in van Dam, C. and Stallaert, L. M. (eds), *Trends in Business Ethics: Implications for Decision-Making*, Boston: Kluwer.
van Dam, C. and Stallaert, L. M. (1978) (eds), *Trends in Business Ethics: Implications for Decision-Making*, Boston: Kluwer.
Winsdor, D. (1994), 'Toward a Transnational Code of Business Conduct ', in Hoffman, W. M., Kamm, J. B., Frederick, R. E., and Petry Jr, E. S. (eds), *Emerging Global Business Ethics*, London: Quorum Books.

10
Environmental Regulation and Standards: Implications for Trade in Vietnam

Subhabrata Bobby Banerjee

I. Introduction

Environmental issues are playing an increasingly important role in global trade. Recent trends indicate that an increasing number of firms are spending money and resources on minimizing their environmental impact. Examples of this phenomenon abound in the business press: McDonald's launched a major waste reduction effort in alliance with the Environmental Defence Fund aimed at reducing waste by 80 per cent in five years (Allen, 1991). Procter & Gamble has invested in projects ranging from new, less environmentally harmful technologies to packaging modifications and industrial composting. Under pressure from environmental groups, Procter & Gamble pledged to spend USD20 mn annually to develop composting facilities for disposable nappies (Coddington, 1993). While these examples are from firms in industrialized countries, environmental concerns are a global issue: it is especially critical in the case of developing countries like Viet Nam where industrial expansion is increasing rapidly.

Most environmental problems facing the world today can be traced back to industrialization. It is therefore no surprise that the impetus for addressing environmental issues facing industry arose from the industrialized countries. Increased government regulation and rising public concern for the environment are some important factors that have compelled firms to pay more attention to environmental issues.

In this chapter I will discuss the relationship between environmental concerns and business activity and how firms can integrate environmental issues into their strategic planning process. Using the ISO 14 000 set of standards as a framework for environmental management, I will discuss the role of environmental regulation and standards, and how these relate to the environmental policies of the World Trade Organization. I will also discuss the implications of these policies for trade in Viet Nam and other developing countries.

II.   Environmental concerns, economic growth and the business firm

Economic accounting systems under the neoclassical economic paradigm do not directly address environmental costs of economic growth. The current economic paradigm presents a distorted picture of the economic situation by ignoring environmental damage. Macroeconomic indicators like GNP and GDP do not reflect the costs of environmental damage. Indonesia is a case in point. Touted as a model for all Third World countries to follow, Indonesia had an annual GNP growth rate of 7.1 per cent in 1990. However, after accounting for resource depletion (Indonesia's primary industry is timber), the growth rate declines to less than 4 per cent (Passel, 1990). One of the world's worst environmental disasters, the Exxon-Valdez oil spill, actually showed up as a *gain* in the United States' GNP because of the products and services involved in the clean-up (Reilly, 1990). Traditionally, environmental costs have been treated as 'externalities' arising from economic activity, and these costs are typically not borne by the producer and are thus not included in the market transaction. Public policy actions frequently attempt to internalize these externalities by estimating the external cost of pollution and by applying pollution taxes (Petulla, 1980). Governmental monitoring and control of the ecological impact of business activity is a process that is designed to minimize the negative consequences of environmental damage. These macro level actions attempt to address societal concerns about environmental issues and have strategic implications for business firms that are manifested at the micro level. Thus, environmental public policy along with rising public concern for the environment are forcing many companies to respond to environmental issues.

In the industrialized countries, pollution standards are becoming stricter and firms are required to spend more money in conforming to these standards. In the United States, the Clean Air Act standards for air pollution and acid rain emissions cost business USD21 bn annually (*Business Week*, 1990). Tougher legislation can affect a firm in two ways: first, the cost of compliance can become prohibitive. It is estimated that the Fortune 500 companies spend over USD350 bn each year on environmental compliance (Gill, 1995). Given these legislative factors, many senior managers of firms perceive that a more effective strategy is to reduce emissions at the start instead of complying with clean-up and pollution control regulations (Kirkpatrick, 1990).

Second, legislation can require substantial changes in product or package design or distribution channels. For example, several leading automobile manufacturers currently incorporate the Design for Environment process by including disassembly as a factor in their product design process (McCrea, 1993). A proposed German regulation involves manufacturers of electronics to take back used equipment (Green MarketAlert, 1993). This can involve significant investments in channel structure as well as product design to include disassembly as a factor. The industrialized countries all have comprehensive environmental policies already in place and this process has already begun in the developing regions of the world. However, as will be discussed later, this process is fraught with problems and fails to recognize the unique environmental conditions in developing countries.

Public concern is also forcing firms to address the environmental impact of their business activity. In some cases public perceptions of a company's environmental impact can lead to direct change in strategy. For years, McDonald's was the target of environmentalists as a large producer of solid waste and user of environmentally unsafe packaging. As environmental awareness grew, so did the negative public image of McDonald's. McDonald's abandoned their 'clamshell' polystyrene box after years of constant complaints by their customers and lobbying by environmental groups. Their initial response was to set up a recycling programme for polystyrene. However, due to operational problems and the public's negative perception of polystyrene, the recycling programme did not prove to be effective. McDonald's alliance with the Environmental Defence

Fund proved crucial in influencing public perception of their waste reduction activities. Despite investing in recycling programmes for polystyrene, McDonald's decided to replace the clamshell box with paper wrap, due to continued consumer pressure and the advice of its new environmental partner (Simon, 1992). The joint effort resulted in the development of 42 separate waste reduction initiatives and McDonald's is now in the process of integrating environmental concerns with corporate strategy (Green Business Letter, 1993).

Environmental concerns have also yielded unexpected benefits to business firms. For instance, there are numerous cases where the installation of new environmentally friendly technologies has reduced costs for firms. New production processes and manufacturing changes in several firms (AT&T, Carrier, 3M, to name a few) have resulted in unexpected cost savings while meeting environmental protection goals (Naj, 1990). A strategy of source reduction instead of pollution prevention has proven to be more advantageous for firms. Procter & Gamble used a dual source reduction strategy for the product (Downy softener) and the package (refillable pouch). The refillable package was found to be more cost-effective than the recycling option and led to a 95 per cent in reduction in waste (Simon, 1992).

Preventing environmental damage is less expensive than cleaning up and can be cost effective in the long run. The 3M company, which has a corporate wide programme called 'Pollution Prevention Pays', realized the cost advantages of source reduction over conventional pollution control measures like smokestack scrubbers. Their strategy was to reduce emissions before they were created with a view to cut costs and develop a stronger competitive position (Ottman, 1993). The Pollution Prevention Pays programme has saved 3M over USD1 bn since 1975 (Kirkpatrick, 1990). Several such case studies have shown that environmental costs were transformed into cost savings leading to competitive advantage for the firm (Porter, 1995).

Thus, purely financial reasons can motivate firms to focus on environmental activities. For instance, in the chemical industry in the US, spending on environmental compliance is between 3 per cent and 4 per cent of sales per year (or about USD10 bn per year). A strategic focus by firms in this industry to reduce costs of environmental compliance is manifested by their change in approach to environmental issues. In the industrialized countries, environmental management has evolved from mere compliance during the 1970s to the development of pollution reduction programmes and pollution prevention programmes in the 1980s and is now poised to become an integral part of company strategy (Buchholz, 1993; Coddington, 1993).

Constant innovation in cleaner technologies and products can enable firms to differentiate their product based on their environmental friendliness. This may allow the firm to command a premium price for their products and thus provide the competitive advantage. New marketing opportunities have, and will continue to emerge, due to recognition of environmental problems. For instance, Pacific Gas and Electric dropped their proposed expansion plans for new nuclear power plants and decided that energy conservation was a more profitable investment. Environmental concerns were key issues driving this strategy. Also, Dupont used its technical knowledge derived from their in-house pollution prevention programme to set up a consulting operation. This new business is expected to yield annual revenues of USD1 bn by the year 2000 (Kirkpatrick, 1990). New strategic markets that have emerged due to environmental concerns are growing rapidly. The environmental services sector has been growing at more than 20 per cent annually over the past five years (Newman and Breeden, 1992).

Environmental concerns are being integrated into the strategic planning process of firms, especially firms in those industries facing strict legislation. A survey of 311 US firms in diverse industries indicated that legislation, public concern and the need for competitive advantage were important factors that determined the degree of strategic focus on environmental issues (Banerjee, 1998). As shown in Figure 10.1, the process of integrating environmental concerns throughout the organization was facilitated by top management, who were influenced by these three factors. Type of industry also influenced the degree of environmental responsiveness: industries with greater environmental impact tended to be faced with stricter legislation and thus paid more attention to environmental issues.

One method of integrating environmental concerns in strategic planning involves employing the Total Quality Environmental Management (TQEM) approach as advocated by the Global

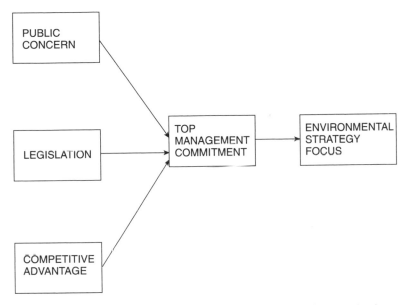

Figure 10.1 Factors influencing environmental strategic focus in business firms

Environmental Management Initiative (GEMI), a group consisting of 20 leading companies in the US. TQEM draws on the 1980s change in business philosophy to 'total quality management', which received widespread acceptance as a tool for improving corporate performance. In the 1990s, GEMI proposed applying TQM tools to environmental management and corporate environmental strategies (GEMI, 1992). The meaning of 'quality' was expanded to include environmental quality as well as product and process quality. A major implication of this conceptualization is the integration of efforts within all business functions to improve environmental performance. In many cases, TQEM has led to an enhancement of product quality and corporate performance as well (GEMI, 1992).

For example, in order to comply with German environmental legislation, the Polaroid Corporation needed a significant reduction in their packaging for their new camera. The reduction in packaging meant that the product needed to be more durable to withstand possible damage in shipment. Driven by both regulatory pressures and a marketing strategy emphasizing the environmental friendliness of the new package, Polaroid scientists redesigned the camera to make it more rugged, thus enhancing product quality (McCrea, 1993).

Combining 'quality' and 'environmental' concerns can also lead to significant cost advantages for companies, and many firms have made waste reduction a part of their corporate quality efforts. Firms like Xerox, Procter & Gamble, IBM, DuPont, DEC, AT&T, Allied Signal and 3M have reduced pollution and lowered costs in diverse industries (Smith, 1991).

In the examples discussed above, business firms performed a variety of activities in order to reduce the environmental impact of their products and processes. These activities involved different levels of investment, both financial and managerial, and had different strategic implications for the firm. However, aligning environmental strategies with corporate strategies is by no means an easy task. A recent survey of 220 senior executives in US companies conducted by Booz-Allen & Hamilton indicated that a vast majority of managers thought that environmental issues were 'extremely important' to their firm (Newman and Breeden, 1992). However, only 7 per cent of those surveyed claimed to understand fully the environmental problems faced by their company. The survey found that most companies restrict their environmental activities to the manufacturing process and do not address environmental issues at the strategic level where competitive advantage can be created. The survey also found that companies that effectively managed environmental issues, as indicated by integration of environmental concerns throughout the organization, received support from the highest echelons of management, and publicly demonstrated their environmental efforts. It is no coincidence that these firms belong to industries that are faced with strict environmental regulation in both domestic and international markets.

As of now there is no global environmental standard for manufacturing processes. Most countries have their own federal guidelines and environmental standards. The ISO 14 000 series was developed in the early 1990s in an attempt to standardize environmental performance in industries. The next section will discuss the salient features of this system.

III.   ISO 14 000

In an attempt to develop a set of standards for environmental management, the International Standards Organization created the ISO

14 000 series outlining the required components of an environmental management system. Closely related to the ISO 9000 series dealing with quality standards, the 14 000 series are aimed at implementing a total environmental control system that is designed to manage, measure and improve the environmental areas of firms' operations (Tibor, 1996).

The basic aspects of the ISO system involve:

- Developing an environmental policy that reflects the firm's environmental goals;
- Developing objectives and targets that quantify those goals;
- Implementation of an environmental programme to achieve the specified objectives;
- Monitoring and measuring the environmental programme;
- Conducting an ongoing audit and review of the programme.

It is important to note that the standards developed by the ISO are *process* standards, not performance standards (EPA, 1996). Similar to the ISO 9000 series that evaluates the quality control system in organizations, the 14 000 series is geared toward developing an environmental management system. Just as Total Quality Management or the ISO 9000 quality system is expected to result in better product quality and a more efficient process, an environmental management system is expected to improve the environmental performance of a firm in terms of emissions reduction and other environmental impacts. The ISO 14 000 system does not prescribe accepted levels of pollution: those are governed by national or state legislation; it does not prescribe performance standards by industry or region. It develops the process standards of an environmental management system and provides a certification system for organizations that want to set up such a system.

What benefits can a firm expect from ISO 14 000 certification? As discussed in the previous section, consumers all over the world are becoming more environmentally conscious and public policy initiatives on environmental protection are on the rise. The ISO certification will provide firms with a strategic advantage in addressing environmental issues and demonstrating their concern for the environment. It will also reduce the need for multiple environmental inspections at different levels as dictated by local, national and international laws. While the certification is voluntary at this time, it is possible that governments and international organizations like the WTO could adopt these standards, making it imperative for firms to be ISO-certified if they want to do business with member countries. However, as will be discussed later, these polices can have negative environmental and other consequences in developing regions of the world. International competition is another issue: in several countries a firm must be ISO 9000 certified in order to do business. Just as these quality standards are forcing many firms to be ISO 9000 certified, competitive and regulatory forces may require companies to seek ISO 14 000 environmental management certification. Several multinationals require ISO-certified suppliers and this could have a ripple effect in a variety of industries. Other benefits include cost reductions due to a more efficient manufacturing process, reduced costs of environmental compliance, reduction in raw material and energy use, customer satisfaction and an enhanced public image.

The relatively high certification costs of the programme could be one problem in the implementation of the system. Estimated certification costs for large US firms range from USD100 000 to USD1 mn per plant (EPA, 1996), and for smaller firms the costs could vary between USD50 000 to USD100 000 (Sissell, 1995). The actual cost depends on the size of the firm's operations, its current environmental management programmes and its experience with prior certification programmes such as the ISO 9000 system. The process of registration can also be cumbersome and involves audits by a number of third-party agencies. However, this is a one-off cost and can be viewed as an investment that will yield some of the benefits described earlier.

IV.   Requirements of ISO 14 000

ISO 14 000 is a fairly complex process and requires a number of procedures. The broad areas covered are: policy setting, environmental impact assessment, objectives and targets, implementation, monitoring, and management review (EPA, 1996).

1.   Policy

Several large corporations already have environmental policies. ISO 14 000 requires that the environmental policy should include a commitment to pollution prevention, a commitment to comply with relevant legislation, a system of environmental objectives and a commitment that the policy will be implemented and communicated to all employees. The environmental policy of the firm should also be accessible to public scrutiny. An example of a policy, developed by Church & Dwight Co. Inc, one of the world's largest manufacturers of baking soda is shown in Figure 10.2.

2. Environmental impact assessment

After the policy is developed, the extent of the firm's environmental impact is assessed. This impact could be assessed in terms of emissions released during manufacturing, energy usage, use of raw materials, or any aspect of production, consumption and disposal of their products. Identifying and interpreting environmental impacts forms the basis of setting objectives and targets to minimize these impacts. The scope is fairly broad and deals with environmental impacts of the firm's manufacturing plants, impacts of their products or services, as well as environmental impacts of their contractors or suppliers.

3. Objectives and targets

The policy and environmental impact details are then operationalized into measurable objectives and targets. These objectives and targets are designed to facilitate achievement of the environmental policy statement. ISO 14 000 requires that the objectives should be specific, measurable and should also incorporate time frames for achievement. Objectives could involve reduction of emissions by a specified percentage over a specified period of time, reduction in use of energy and raw materials, reduction in packaging content, increase in the recycled content of the package, increase in percentage of waste recycled and so on.

4. Implementation

Developing a total environmental management system to implement the environmental policy is the next stage of the process. This involves a series of activities at different levels of the organization. It identifies key personnel in the organization who are responsible for implementing the system. It involves setting procedures for external communication (to the public, government, customers, suppliers)

Church & Dwight Corporate Environmental Policy

Our corporate environmental policy is to produce quality products which, in the totality of their lifecycles, have minimum impact on the environment. We will be a model of corporate environmental responsibility in this regard. Our carbonate-based technologies and products enable us to be a leader in toxics reduction and source reduction programmes, especially as they relate to our nation's air and water resources.

To fulfil this policy, we make the following commitments:

1. *We will understand the environmental impact of our technologies and products, and take scientifically sound steps to minimize them.*

2. *We will implement, as part of our Quality Improvement Process, an Environmental Improvement Process which will help ensure that minimization of environmental impact continues to be part of our corporate culture.*

3. *We will develop products and processes which can be demonstrated to have a more favourable impact on air and water quality than most existing products and processes by focusing on the toxics reduction and source reduction capabilities of carbonates.*

4. *We will help educate our consumers and customers on environmental issues and the environmentally responsible distribution, use and disposal of our products and packaging.*

5. *We will assist environmental stake-holders in the development of environmentally responsible policies, programmes and communications.*

6. *We will regularly measure and review our environmental performance against these commitments.*

Figure 10.2   Example of an environmental policy

Source: From Coddington, 1993.

on the firm's environmental activities, developing record-and document-control procedures, handling regulatory requirements, developing environmental training procedures for all employees, management of hazardous and non-hazardous materials and wastes, implementing procedures concerning procurement and vendor control, and internal environmental communication and employee awareness.

5. Monitoring and auditing

This stage involves measuring, monitoring and evaluating the environmental management programme. Regular audits of the system are also specified by ISO 14 000. Monitoring is expected to highlight problem areas and gaps between targets and achievement to enable the application of corrective action. Environmental audits can either be done internally or through third-party auditors. Every aspect of the environmental management system is audited, from internal operations to the firm's suppliers or vendors. Audit findings are reported to top management and the necessary corrective action taken.

6. Management review

The final stage is management review, a process that reviews the environmental management system. The results of the audit are reviewed and necessary changes in policy and procedures are made in the review process. This stage provides the feedback loop to the policy-setting stage and ensures that the process aims at continuous environmental quality improvement.

Obtaining ISO 14 000 certification has important implications for world trade. Developing countries without the necessary technology to standardize their environmental performance will be at a disadvantage compared to the industrialized nations with well-developed environmental policies. The WTO Committee on Trade and the Environment is currently studying the implications of an international system of standardization with a focus on developing countries. The lack of globally accepted pollution standards (which the ISO does not aim to provide) and the emergence of the WTO as a powerful trade body has led to some paradoxical situations where environmental protection efforts are classified as a 'restrictive non-tariff barrier'. In the next section, I will highlight some issues facing the WTO Committee on Trade and the Environment.

V. Environmental policies of the World Trade Organization

The WTO Committee on Trade and Environment was established after the Uruguay Round of GATT in April 1994. The main task of the Committee is to 'identify the relationship between trade measures and environmental measures in order to promote sustainable development' (WTO Trade and Environment Bulletin No. 2, 1995). As part of the process of removing 'protectionist' trade measures, the Committee for Trade and Environment was set up to examine the effect of environmental standards and environmental measures such as environmental taxes, subsidies, duties and charges on trade. It looks at 'the effect of environmental measures on market access, especially in relation to developing countries, in particular to the least developed among them, and environmental benefits of removing trade restrictions and distortions' (WTO, 1995). The establishment of the WTO has important consequences for Third World nations and several environmental groups and non-government organizations have criticized the policies of the WTO because of the negative economic and environmental consequences to the developing world. The WTO is supposed to examine the 'environmental benefits of removing trade restrictions'. What these so-called benefits are unclear. At one level, imposition of environmental standards by a country can be termed as a non-tariff barrier that must be removed. This would result in a downward levelling of environmental standards which is in opposition to the aims of sustainable development.

For instance, the WTO encourages environmental standards in trade. However, if a particular country has a higher standard of environmental protection, this would be termed an unfair trade practice and the country would be penalized. If, however, the standards were lower it would be termed as 'free trade' and obtain the 'most favoured nation' status. Through the dispute resolution mechanisms in the WTO, it is possible for a country's environmental standards to be challenged and changed to meet the requirements of the WTO agreement.

For Third World nations like Viet Nam, the current climate of economic liberalization can have some negative environmental consequences. Unlike GATT, the WTO has powers over agricultural goods, trade and investment in services, foreign investments and intellectual property rights including the patenting of life-forms (Khor, 1993). 'Liberalization' implies accelerated exploitation of natural resources in these regions apart from rapid industrialization which involves transfer of technologies that could be environmentally harmful. Several Third World scholars have pointed out that this process would strengthen the industrialized countries' techno-logical domination over the developing world, resulting in a loss of autonomy by Third World governments to set their own environmental standards (Khor, 1993; Shiva, 1993). Technology plays an important role in the development of 'global' standards and the fact that only the industrialized countries are involved in the process of setting standards poses some problems on the global appropriateness of these measures. In many cases, developing countries do not have the necessary facilities for product testing or inspection of hazardous goods. Information on why certain products are banned in the West and on the environmental consequences of these products is not readily available. At the May 1995 meeting of the WTO Committee, several delegates from developing countries in Asia and Latin America listed examples of cases where due to lack of information or testing facilities many pharmaceutical products were sold to these countries after the expiry date of the product had passed (WTO, 1995).

The balance between environmental sustainability and preserving what the WTO calls an 'open non-discriminatory multilateral trading system' is not easy to find, especially if the needs of developing countries are taken into account. Several 'trade measures' approved by the WTO are often in direct contrast to national environmental policies (Shiva, 1993). Probably the most cited example in this context is the infamous Dunkel Draft arising from the Uruguay Round of GATT which included life-forms and bio-diversity under Intellectual Property Rights control. Traditional bio-diversity rights to seeds which belonged to farmers in the Third World are now under the purview of Intellectual Property Rights. Countries like India, which does not recognize patents in the area of bio-diversity, were compelled to sign the agreement despite initial resistance so as not to be labelled 'discriminatory' by GATT.

VI. Implications for Viet Nam

As an economy in transition, Viet Nam will see rapid industrialization in the next few years and consequently face heavy pollution loads. It is therefore imperative that appropriate environmental policies be developed and more important, be enforced in the industrial and agricultural sectors. The industrial sector currently accounts for about 22 per cent of Viet Nam's GDP and is expected to rise to 38 per cent in the next few years (World Bank Report, 1995a). Accelerating industrial output without suitable environmental protection measures can create serious environmental problems. The Ministry of Science, Technology and Environment (MOSTE) established in 1992 and its subsidiary body, the National Environment Agency (NEA), established in 1993 are the main policy-making institutions in Viet Nam, responsible for preparing a national Environmental Action Plan to address the environmental consequences of industrialization. These institutions also serve the crucial role of screening potential industrial projects in terms of environmental impact. While at the current time the economic focus is on exploiting the labour surplus, industrial expansion will ultimately lead to importing technologies and heavy industries that cause more severe environmental problems. The problem is exacerbated by the nascent stage of Viet Nam's environmental policy, the difficulties involved in enforcing such policy, and the lack of trained personnel in environmental management (World Bank Report, 1995a).

The policy framework being developed in Viet Nam is similar to the one used currently in the industrialized countries and focuses on pollution prevention rather than on pollution control. It is important that prevention policies rather than conventional 'end-of-pipe' control methods be used as the latter tend to be inefficient and costly. It is also important that natural resources be preserved in the new climate of economic liberalization: attempting to follow the path of the newly industrializing countries (Indonesia, Korea, Taiwan) should not (as it did in those countries) come at the cost of resource destruction, especially the loss of forest cover due to high export demand for timber.

As in many other developing countries, environmental policy in Vietnam follows the Western framework. Attempts to internalize environmental costs follow the 'polluter pays principle' and utilize a combination of regulatory policies and incentives that put taxes on resource use (World Bank Report,1995b). The basic problem given the rapid economic changes that are taking place, is a lack of institutional infrastructure, especially the enforcement infrastructure. Developing policy is one matter; having the resources to implement and enforce that policy in a rapidly expanding economy is another issue.

In conclusion, I will highlight four important areas of environmental policy that are relevant for Viet Nam and other developing economies in transition. First, policy efforts should be aimed at conserving bio-diversity in the region. There are too many cases where economic liberalization has resulted in loss of bio-diversity in developing regions. Environmental policy in the area of land-use and sustainable agriculture should be developed at both the macro and micro levels and land use planning at the local level must involve consultation with small farmers and communities.

Second, policy-makers should allocate sufficient resources for training in environmental management and develop sound environmental management procedures for industry. Environmental impact assessment, pollution prevention, source reduction, energy conservation and utilization of alternative energy sources, and recycling are some aspects of environmental management that should be examined and standards should be developed for all these areas. Training is an important area in environmental management and both policy-makers as well as industry personnel should be adequately trained in environmental management. Environmental management should be viewed as a system of continuous improvement and should be subject to periodic review at both organization and industry levels.

Third, appropriate environmental legislation should be developed and enforced. While advocates of market forces claim that environmental legislation is costly and unnecessary, evidence in the industrialized countries indicates that legislation is a driving force for business firms to improve their environmental performance. National laws and standards on emissions and conservation are required to ensure that economic growth does not come at the expense of the environment. In addition, policy-makers should work with industry experts to develop incentives and joint research projects to minimize environmental impact. One of the principles of the ISO 14 000 system is to comply with all existing local, state and national regulations. Governments can develop and legislate performance standards that the ISO system is expected to deliver and use the system to achieve and better these standards.

Fourth, policy efforts should focus on creating public awareness of environmental issues. Both government and non-government organizations have an important role to play in this area. Environmental education is important because in many countries throughout the world, public concern for the environment has resulted in the creation of new laws protecting the environment. Many organizations have corrected poor environmental practices and improved their environmental performance because of public pressure. An informed and environmentally conscious public is necessary to develop and enforce effective environmental policy. Apart from providing information, policy-makers should also seek public participation in environmental management.

Perhaps the most critical factor in the future of developing countries like Viet Nam in the current economic climate is their ability to participate in global trade without eroding national sovereignty and losing control over their natural resources (Khor, 1993). Several policies under consideration by the WTO, particularly those relating to domestic self-sufficiency, intellectual property rights, and technology, are not consonant with the needs of developing countries. How these policies are played out in the years to come will determine what sort of future developing countries can expect. While 'subsistence' economies play no part in the new economic order, policies of economic liberalization should ensure that economic growth in the 'new' economies does not expand the hegemony of the industrialzed countries and neither should it result in the elusive search for 'quality of life' as it has in the industrialized countries of the world.

References

Allen, Frank Edward (1991), 'McDonald's to Reduce Waste in Plan Developed with Environmental Group', *The Wall Street Journal*, 2 February 1991.

Banerjee, S. (1998), 'Corporate Environmentalism: Perspectives from Organizational Learning', *Management Learning*, 29(2), 147–164.

Buchholz, Rogene A. (1993), *Principles of Environmental Management: The Greening of Business*, Englewood Cliffs, NJ: Prentice Hall.

Business Week (1990), 'Environment: The Greening of Corporate America', 23 April, 96–103.

Coddington, Walter (1993), *Environmental Marketing: Positive Strategies for Reaching the Green Consumer*, Washington D.C., McGraw-Hill, Inc.

EPA (1996), *What is ISO 14 000?*, Washington D.C., Government Printing Office.

Gill, Kevin (1995), 'Environmental Costs and Environmental Solutions', *Honeywell: The Journal*, Waltham MA. October.

GEMI (1992), *Total Quality Environmental Management: The Primer*, Washington, D.C., Global Environmental Management Initiative.

Green Business Letter (1993), 'Win-Win: The Emerging Era of Corporate-Environmentalist Partnerships', 1–5.

Green Market Alert (1993), 'The Office Electronics Industry', 4 (4), 5 April.

Khor, Martin (1993), 'Free Trade and the Third World', in *The Case Against Free Trade: GATT, NAFTA, and the Globalization of Corporate Power*, Washington, D. C. Earth Island Press.

Kirkpatrick, David (1990), 'Environmentalism: The New Crusade,' *Fortune*, 12 February, 44–52.

McCrea, Charles D. (1993), 'Environmental Packaging and Product Design', paper presented at the 1992–1993 'Professional Development Series: American Marketing Association' Boston MA. 22 April.

Naj, Amal Kumar (1990), 'Some Companies cut Pollution by Altering Production Methods', *The Wall Street Journal*, 24 December, A1.

Newman, John C., and Kay M. Breeden (1992), 'Managing in the Environmental Era: Lessons from Environmental Era', *The Columbia Journal of World Business*, 27 (3 & 4), 210–21.

Ottman, Jacquelyn A. (1993), *Green Marketing: Challenges and Opportunities for the New Marketing Age*, Lincolnwood: Il, NTC Business Books.

Passel, Peter (1990), 'Rebel Economists Add Ecological Cost to Price of Progress', *The New York Times*, 27 November.

Petulla, Joseph M. (1980), *American Environmentalism: Values, Tactics, Priorities*, Texas, A&M University Press.

Porter, Michael E. (1995), 'Green and Competitive: Ending the Stalemate', *Harvard Business Review*, 73 (5), 120–34.

Reilly, William K. (1990), 'The Green Thumb of Capitalism: The Environmental Benefits of Sustainable Growth', *Policy Review* (Fall), 16–21.

Shiva, Vandana (1993), 'Biodiversity and Intellectual Property Rights', in *The Case Against Free Trade: GATT, NAFTA, and the Globalization of Corporate Power*, Washington, D.C. Earth Island.

Simon, Francoise L. (1992), 'Marketing Green Products in the Triad', *The Columbia Journal of World Business*, 27 (3 & 4) (Fall & Winter), 268–85.

Sissell, Kara (1995), 'Fitting in ISO 14 000: A Search for Strategy', *Chemical Week*, 157 (17), 39–42.

Smith, Emily T. (1991), 'Doing it for Mother Earth', *Business Week*, 44–9.

Tibor, Tom (1996), *ISO 14 000: A Guide to the New Environmental Management Standard*, Boston MA: Irwin Publishing.

WTO (1995), *Trade and Environment Bulletin No. 2*. New York, NY.

World Bank Report (1995a), *Viet Nam: Economic Report on Industrialization and Industrial Policy*, Report No. 14645-VN. New York, NY.

World Bank Report (1995b), *Viet Nam: Environmental Program and Policy Priorities for a Socialist Economy in Transition*, New York, NY, June 1995.

11
South Korea's Economic Growth, Trade and Development: Contemporary Problems and Prospects

Charles Harvie

I. Introduction

In December 1996 South Korea achieved its long-held objective of membership of the Organisation for Economic Cooperation and Development (OECD), the Paris-based club of the world's richest nations. This represented a watershed moment and a clear recognition of how much this nation of some 44 mn people has achieved since it embarked on its first five-year economic plan in 1962, when it had a per capita income of only US$87. By the end of 1996 it had grown into the fifth largest economy in Asia after Japan, China, India and Indonesia, the world's twelfth largest trading nation, and attained a per capita income of over US$10 000. Its membership of the OECD made it the tenth largest economy in the rich nations' club (see Table 11.1).

While the material achievements of South Korea are impressive the development of its political and economic organizations have not kept pace, and there is a clear need for reform in a number of key areas including that of the labour market, financial markets and the banking sector, the industrial sector, small- and medium-sized enterprises and trade and investment. In recent years the government has come under intense pressure from its trading partners to open up its economy to both trade and foreign investment. There is also strong pressure at home for leaders to keep up the fight against

Table 11.1   The OECD's largest economies, 1995

OECD rank	Country	GNP, US$, bn, PPP*
1	United States	7062
2	Japan	2782
3	Germany	1643
4	France	1210
5	Italy	1127
6	United Kingdom	1115
7	Canada	658
8	Mexico	656
9	Spain	584
10	South Korea	527
11	Australia	360

* Purchasing Power Parity
Source: Asiaweek

corruption, protect consumers and curtail the power of the large business organizations (the chaebols) that still dominate the economy. Membership of the OECD will exert a profound impact on the way that business is conducted in Korea both at home and abroad, and it will intensify foreign pressure, as well as domestic, for further liberalization of the economy. Korea's economic success story is, therefore, standing at a major crossroads, with the country facing as many challenges after its membership of the OECD as it did to become a member of this organization. Keeping the reform process going, and bringing the country's institutions up to the level of those in advanced countries, has become the pivotal agenda of President Kim Young Sam's government. While progress to date has been gradual, it is the government's objective that by the year 2000 about 97 per cent of South Korea's economy, including the rapidly growing service sector, will be open to foreign investment.

The remainder of this chapter proceeds as follows. In section 2 a brief review is conducted of the achievement of the four original 'Tiger' economies, including that of South Korea, as well as the so called 'new Tiger' economies. It briefly discusses the concern over the recent slowdown in economic growth and exports in these economies, and evaluates whether this is a temporary or permanent phenomenon. Section 3 conducts an overview of Korea's evolving economic development strategy, while section 4 conducts a brief overview of the recent macroeconomic performance of the Korean economy. Sectoral developments are discussed in section 5, while contemporary economic problems and reforms are identified in section 6. Section 7 identifies the significance of the Korean economy in the context of global trade and investment developments. Section 8 analyses the trade and investment relationship between Korea and Australia and prospects for their further development, while section 9 presents a summary of the major conclusions derivable from this chapter.

II.   South Korea and the East Asian economic miracle

Over the past twenty to thirty years the East Asian economies have achieved an unprecedented period of rapid and sustained growth of output. The original four 'Tiger' economies (Hong Kong, Singapore, South Korea and Taiwan) have almost all now joined the ranks of developed economies in terms of GDP per head (Hong Kong and Singapore are both richer than the UK, their former colonial master). In addition, and more recently, China, Indonesia, Malaysia and Thailand have also experienced rapid growth although from a much lower level of income, while the Philippines, as a much later starter, has also demonstrated its ability to join the race (see Table 11.2). However, these rapidly growing East Asian economies

Table 11.2   East Asian economies' GDP per capita, and real growth rates (per cent), 1970–96

	GDP per head*, 1995, US$	1970–79	1980–89	1990–96
Hong Kong	23 900	9.2	7.5	5.0
Singapore	22 600	9.4	7.2	8.3
Taiwan	13 200	10.2	8.1	6.3
South Korea	11 900	9.3	8.0	7.7
Malaysia	10 400	8.0	5.7	8.8
Thailand	8 000	7.3	7.2	8.6
Indonesia	3 800	7.8	5.7	7.2
China	3 100	7.5	9.3	10.1
Philippines	2 800	6.1	1.8	2.8
Rich industrial countries	19 400	3.4	2.6	2.0

* At purchasing power parity
Source: IMF, ING Barings, national statistics.

have recently experienced a dramatic decline in their export growth rates to only 5 per cent during 1996 (see Figure 11.1), which compares very poorly with the 20 per cent growth rates achieved in 1994 and 1995. In addition, Malaysia, South Korea and Thailand are experiencing current account deficits of between 5–8 per cent of GDP. South Korea was severely disrupted by strikes during the early part of 1997, with work stoppages causing an estimated US$3.15 bn in lost output with a subsequent loss of exports. The stock markets in Bangkok and Seoul have plunged, while the financial systems in general throughout the region are looking weak. These developments are reflected in the average GDP growth rate in the region slowing from almost 9 per cent in 1995 to 7 per cent in 1996. Some commentators have even compared the economies of Indonesia, Malaysia, the Philippines, South Korea and Thailand to that of Mexico prior to its balance-of-payments crisis in December 1994 (*The Economist*, August 1996, pp. 57–8). Does this signal the end of the Asian economic miracle or are these concerns exaggerated?

An influential 1993 report entitled 'The East Asian Economic Miracle', compiled by the World Bank, identified a number of key factors behind the region's remarkable economic success: inexpensive labour combined with high human capital and a strong work ethic; high domestic savings rates that stimulated domestic investment and capital stock accumulation; the establishment of macroeconomic stability; implementation of agricultural reform; the adoption of an outward orientation in terms of export-led growth and the attraction of foreign investment and technology; and finally increased labour productivity arising from technological innovation. Some economists, led by Paul Krugman (1995), argued that the World Bank had overestimated Asian innovation and productivity. Krugman argued that Asia's rapid expansion was unsustainable because it was based primarily on inputs of education, capital equipment, labour and technology borrowed largely from the west, and not on gains in efficiency. Further, East Asia's growth relied primarily on 'perspiration rather than inspiration', and the region had displayed little total factor productivity (TFP), a measure of overall economic efficiency in terms of capital and labour, that was the source of sustainable development. He argued that when resource inputs reached saturation levels, Asia's miracle would start to fade. The recent slowdown in output and export growth was therefore structural and inevitable.

On the other hand, more optimistic economists have given little weight to the argument that something is structurally wrong in the miracle economies. Instead they argue that the recent economic slowdown is cyclical. Sooner or later the cycle will turn and the Asian miracle will restart. A number of reasons have been advanced to explain the recent cyclical slowdown in both economic growth and growth of exports by the East Asian economies. First, demand from North America and Europe has been weak as the rate of growth of industrial production slowed in 1995 and early 1996. Historically, Asian exports tend to move closely in line with the strength of the developed economies. Secondly, the recent appreciation of the US dollar, to which many Asian currencies are in effect linked, has depressed exports. The US dollar's weakness in 1994–95 helped to boost exports but in 1996 the effect was reversed. The US dollar rose by 50 per cent against the yen from a low point in April 1995, eroding the competitiveness of many East Asian exporters against Japanese products. This was particularly detrimental to an economy such as South Korea's, whose product demand is highly price sensitive. Thirdly, there was a slump in the world semiconductor market, with memory chip prices falling by more than 80 per cent in 1996. This had a particularly severe impact upon South Korea and also Singapore, since electronics account for a sizeable proportion of their exports. In addition the steel and petrochemical industries have been plagued by global over capacity. Finally, regional demand and hence intra-Asian trade, which accounts for an increasing share of East Asian countries' total trade, was curtailed by tight monetary policies being applied in the overheating economies of China, Malaysia and Thailand, resulting in a discouragement of imports.

The argument that Asia's export slowdown was caused largely by cyclical factors rather than an underlying loss of competitiveness, is also supported by other evidence. First imports fell as sharply as exports. Hence if competitiveness had been the problem, imports would have accelerated. South Korea's annual rate of export growth slowed from 30 per cent in 1995 to 4 per cent in 1996, but its import growth also slowed from 32 per cent to 11 per cent. The second piece of evidence is that the export growth of other developing countries, such as in Latin America, also slowed in 1996. As a result, East Asia's share of American and Japanese imports hardly changed in volume terms.

Even if the pessimist's viewpoint is regarded as being exaggerated, and even if the main causes of the recent slowdown were cyclical, the slowdown has revealed several structural problems which need to be overcome if East Asia is once again to achieve and sustain rapid economic growth. The problems, and the policies required, will vary from country to country. In the case of South Korea, it is too heavily concentrated on a few industries, such as electronics and petrochemicals. There is a need for the economy to be opened up to more competition, for the power and bias towards the indebted industrial conglomerates (the chaebols) to be reduced, and for labour and capital market rigidities to be relaxed. In contrast to South Korea, the economies of Hong Kong, Singapore and Taiwan have flexible labour markets, less government intervention, and small, nimble firms. Taiwan is pushing ahead with deregulation more swiftly than South Korea and its more flexible industrial policy is more suited to fast-changing business conditions.

To the extent that a country's long-term growth potential is a reflection of its stage of development, the growth rate of the East Asian economies will inevitably tend to slow. This has already happened in the original four tigers. Nevertheless their growth is likely to remain faster than the industrial economies' average of around 2.5 per cent so long as savings remain high, economies are kept open and education remains a priority. The original tigers are likely to see growth slow to an average of 5–6 per cent over the next decade, while China, Malaysia, Thailand and Indonesia should be able to grow by 7–8 per cent over the next ten years.

III. Korea's evolving economic development strategy

South Korea has passed through four stages of economic development and is currently in the midst of a fifth. Unlike several of the larger economies in East Asia, which evolved from protectionist inward-looking trade regimes toward relatively open economies, Korea did not possess a sufficiently large domestic population to contemplate a strategy other than export-led development. Its performance has been described as forced growth, since it did not stem from exploitation of natural resources, an influx of labour, flows of speculative capital or the adoption of new means of production. Instead growth resulted from a systematic state initiated programme of importing raw materials and intermediate goods for processing and export with value added. However, as the economy has evolved the extent and nature of government intervention is being questioned both domestically and overseas, with increasing emphasis being placed upon the need for economic reform and liberalization of the economy. This will be essential as the country enters the next stage of economic development resulting in its further integration into the global economy.

Korea's stages of economic development

(a)   *War, reconstruction and land reform (1950–60)*

Korea had a relatively well-developed infrastructure at the end of World War II, but the partitioning of the peninsula by US and Soviet forces severed economic links between the heavily industrialized North and the agricultural South. The war exacted a heavy toll, in the form of 1.5 mn fatalities and the destruction of two-thirds of the South's industrial capacity. With a poor natural resource base and one of the world's highest population densities, South Korea was almost entirely dependent on US aid after the war. Despite the war devastation it did assist South Korea to prepare for an industrial take-off, by loosening the country's rigid social structure and opening the way for fundamental change in attitude by the population. Although developmental efforts in the 1950s included several false starts, progress was made in reconstruction including the restoration of transportation and communication networks. The government was also successful in completing a land reform programme which had stalled before the war.

(b)   *Export take-off (1961–73)*

Under the auspices of President Park, an aggressive export promotion was combined with import protection at home. South Korean policy-makers maintained close control over trade, the exchange rate and financial policy, as well as aspects of industrial decision-making. In contrast to other controlled economies, such instruments were used with the primary objective of pursing export-led growth. During this period the trade regime was biased in favour of exports as a whole, but was essentially neutral with respect to the composition of exports. However, the first instruments of export promotion were highly discretionary. Exporters were supported with multiple exchange rates, direct cash payments, permission to retain foreign exchange earnings to import restricted commodities, and permission to borrow in foreign currencies. This system not only avoided hampering exporters with restrictions on capital and intermediate inputs for their own use, but it also gave access to favourable exchange rates in the heavily protected domestic markets. As discretionary incentives were gradually replaced by more automatic instruments, exporters received significant exemptions from import controls. Tariff exemptions were given to indirect as well as direct exporters, and there were generous wastage allowances on imported intermediaries. These enabled exporters to avoid distortions from protection and in some cases to benefit from the protection of the domestic market.

Support for exports was also channelled through the state-controlled banking system. State objectives were implemented through bank-directed credit and interest rate subsidies, which were extensively and explicitly earmarked for particular activities or industries. Following explicit government directives, banks increasingly used export performance as the criterion of creditworthiness.

(c)   Heavy and chemical industries (HCI) drive (1973–79)

The heavy and chemical industries (HCI) drive represented a major policy shift away from the neutral incentives of the take-off period, to a commitment by government to steer resources into specific sectors to rapidly alter the industrial structure. Special legislation singled out six strategic industries – steel, petrochemicals, non-ferrous metals, shipbuilding, electronics and machinery – to receive support, including tax incentives, subsidized public services and preferential financing. The government chose the first three sectors to enhance self-sufficiency in industrial raw materials, while the latter three were meant to be developed into technology-intensive export industries. Policy-based lending made a significant contribution to the rapid expansion of Korean industry, and particularly manufactured exports. Most of the directed lending to priority industries translated into investments in equipment.

Unlike other governments that attempted to build a heavy industry sector, Korea was at least partly successful. One reason for this was that the government made clear from the outset that these industries were expected to become internationally competitive. As a result, projects tended to be forward-looking with only current technology imported, and US-trained Korean scientists and engineers were recruited. However, interventions were so pervasive that bottlenecks emerged, large-scale debts were incurred, and labour-intensive industries in addition to small- and medium-sized firms were starved of credit. When the second oil shock of 1979–80 hit, inflation was already high, and the exchange rate had appreciated, capacity utilization in the HCI sector was low, and exports were faltering. The government decided to alter course.

The cost of such extensive and highly subsidized directed credits during the drive was substantial, and likely to increase as development proceeded. Directed credits burdened banks with non-performing loans, interfered with the financial system's efficient operation, hindered the growth of financial savings, and sometimes threatened macroeconomic stability. Korea was initially able to weather these difficulties partly because its closed capital markets at the time enabled the government to suppress interest rates on deposits, thereby funding the subsidies for loans to corporations. In addition, relatively easy credit in international capital markets and Korea's strong relationship with two key lenders, Japan and the United States, helped to ensure the availability of foreign capital, which was either then funnelled into directed credit or went to bail out troubled enterprises unable to repay subsidized loans. The costs of the HCI drive are still not known, but are thought to have been high.

(d)   Functional incentives and liberalization (1980–90)

The world recession of 1980–81 produced major difficulties for Korea. The resulting high real interest rates and decline in demand in the industrial economies, meant that Korean firms which were highly leveraged and heavily committed to the US market suffered severely. As Korean firms found themself in some difficulty, so too did the banks. A major crisis was averted by the government due to a sharp lowering of real interest rates on deposits and loans, resulting in a substantial transfer of wealth from savers (mostly households) to borrowers (mostly firms). Such a forceful financial repression worked because of the effectiveness of the foreign exchange controls which were in place. Households, unable to exchange domestic currency for foreign currency, had to accept the temporary negative real interest rates.

During this period support for strategic industries was curtailed and abruptly reversed. The currency was devalued, and credit allocation policies switched, with a termination of large-scale preferences to the HCI sector. The five-year economic plan drafted in 1979 recognized that the complexity of the economy was exceeding the government's management capacities. The plan's emphasis on indicative planning and a greater role for the market was eventually translated into a range of financial and import liberalization programmes. Since 1979 intervention has focused on the restructuring of distressed industries, support for the development of technology, and the promotion of competition.

(e)   Financial sector and other economic liberalization (1990–)

The key to Korea's future industrial policy lies in its approach to financial sector reform. The government has been coping with the after-effects of the HCI drive during the 1970s and has been particularly active in bailing out sunset and over-leveraged industries. The remnants of past policies are part of the price Korea is paying for prior interventions policies and for the failure to establish an independent financial sector. The Korean government's intervention policy, most notably the HCI promotion, has often been evaluated from the perspective of the success or failure of industrial policy. Another important approach in evaluating intervention policy, however, would be to estimate the fiscal/financial cost associated with intervention. Government intervention incurred direct costs in the form of subsidies to strategic sectors through policy loans and tax exemptions especially during the 1973–79 period of HCI promotion. Intervention incurred indirect costs in the form of accumulated non-performing loans and the resulting portfolio difficulties of commercial banks. As the Korean government abandoned HCI preferences during the traumatic economic adjustments of 1979–81, the direct costs of interest subsidies all but disappeared. However, as the Korean government opted to bail out the struggling heavy machinery, shipbuilding, overseas construction and shipping industries in the mid 1980s, the non-performing loans of commercial banks accumulated rapidly and accordingly bank profitability seriously deteriorated. It has taken almost a decade to begin to deal with the indirect costs in the form of accumulated non-performing loans and squeezed bank profitability. Not until 1993 did the Korean government announce a medium-term plan to transfer policy loans, which then still accounted for more than 40 per cent of total domestic credit, to separate accounts and to handle their financing through the budget at yet to be determined costs.

The government has traditionally maintained tight control over Korea's economic development, through targets and priorities established under successive five-year plans and an associated network of administrative controls. However, with an almost twelve-fold growth in the absolute size of the economy in the past 30 years, it is recognized that policies of administrative guidance and discriminatory regulation have become unsuitable for ensuring a continued fast pace of economic development. More emphasis is now being put on private sector initiatives with increasing reliance on signals from the market. The current Five Year Plan (1993–97) stresses the provision of strong incentives for participation in economic development, and the fair distribution of the burdens and benefits of economic development among participants. The plan emphasizes institutional reforms and the adoption of new approaches and ways of thinking to meet the challenges of a new era. Major areas identified for institutional reform include the fiscal system, the financial sector and administrative regulations. President Kim Young Sam has repeatedly stated his intention to improve the competitiveness and productivity of the Korean economy, and is placing priority on the 'globalization' of Korea as it moves into the ranks of the developed nations. Policy measures being developed include enhancement of infrastructure investment, incentives to encourage both outward and inward investment flows, and the liberalization of domestic financial markets which facilitated Korea's entry into the OECD.

In his New Year 1996 national policy address, President Kim Young Sam declared six national priority policies to take Korea into the next century. First the reunification of the country, secondly to strengthen the economy, thirdly to keep inflation to about 4.6 per cent in 1996, fourthly to redress the growing imbalance between a booming heavy industry and a declining light industry, fifthly to improve the prospects of small- and medium-sized enterprises

(SMEs), and finally to develop social infrastructure. However, despite the repeated commitment to further deregulation, the government's policies towards the chaebols, which remain the main generators of growth, has been inconsistent. However, the government has reaffirmed its commitment to encourage the chaebols to focus on their own areas of expertise, and has done so by signalling its opposition to any attempts by the chaebols to expand outside those areas. For example Hyundai was denied permission to move into steel production on the basis that its profitability would be endangered when there was sluggish demand for steel.

Korea's membership of the OECD has accelerated the pace for deregulation of the financial markets. In 1996 it was announced that the ceiling on foreign stock ownership was to be increased to 20 per cent from its previous level of 15 per cent. The government also announced that it was preparing schedules for the full deregulation of domestic foreign exchange and capital transactions in 1999. The government also plans to reinvigorate its programme to revise labour legislation, including the controversial law banning third-party intervention in labour disputes. OECD members are likely to pressurize for further deregulation in this area.

IV. Korea's recent macroeconomic performance

Over the period 1990–95 Korea achieved an average annual real GDP growth rate of 7.9 per cent (see Table 11.3). In the early part of the 1990s real GDP growth was over 9 per cent but experienced a sharp decline over the period 1992–93 before increasing again in 1994 and 1995. The main sources of growth in 1994 and 1995 were a strong export performance, assisted by a high yen which gave Korean exporters a competitive advantage over Japanese exporters, a boom in construction and domestic infrastructure investment and steadily rising private consumption. As Table 11.3 indicates growth across all sectors of the economy remained strong in 1994 and 1995, with the exception of agriculture in 1994. It is apparent that the primary source of growth was derived from the manufacturing sector, however in 1994 and 1995 the services sector was making an increasingly significant contribution. Industrial output overall grew by 11.9 per cent in 1995 driven largely by growth in the heavy industry and chemical sectors, on the back of the previously

Table 11.3 Macroeconomic indicators 1990–95

	1990	1991	1992	1993	1994	1995
Nominal GDP (US$ Billion)	253.6	294.1	307.9	322.8	380.7	455.6
GDP real growth rate (%)	9.5	9.1	5.1	5.8	8.6	9.0
Per capita GNP (US$)	5833	6757	7007	7466	8483	10 076
Real growth in sectoral output (%):						
manufacturing	9.7	9.1	5.1	5.0	10.4	10.7
construction	23.7	11.3	−1.9	5.3	4.7	9.8
agriculture	−4.6	−0.4	6.0	−2.9	1.6	2.8
services	9.9	10.9	6.9	7.6	10.8	10.0
Interest rate (%) corporate bond yields	13.3	13.4	16.0	12.6	12.9	13.8
CPI (%)	8.6	9.3	6.2	4.8	6.3	4.5
Unemployment (%)	–	2.3	2.4	2.8	2.4	2.0

Sources: Bank of Korea; Korea Development Institute.

mentioned strong export performance. Light industry, however, registered growth of only 0.9 per cent in 1995.

In terms of other macroeconomic developments consumer price inflation (CPI) has generally been on a downward trend during the period of the 1990s, falling to 4.8 per cent in 1993 but rising in 1994 to 6.3 per cent before then falling to 4.5 per cent in 1995. The latter fell within the government's target of 5 per cent and arose from stable agricultural prices and increased imports. Price stability was the government's primary focus during 1996. Unemployment remained low during the 1990s falling to 2 per cent in 1995 from 2.4 per cent in 1994. Despite the fact that the economy had reached full employment, wages rose less than expected. An increasing labour shortage in the manufacturing sector resulted in the government instituting policies to increase the participation of women and older people in the work force, as well as agreeing to increase the number of foreign temporary workers. Korean interest rates, nominal and real, have remained relatively high during the period of the 1990s, a reflection of the country's heavily protected financial markets. The corporate bond yield varied between 12.6–16 per cent over this period. This created problems for heavily leveraged companies and represented a further financial burden to less favoured small- and medium-sized enterprises.

Table 11.4 indicates that during the period of the 1990s Korea has been running current account deficits with the exception of 1993. More recently in 1995 its current account deficit reached US$8.3 bn (1.8 per cent of GDP) a noticeable increase from the US$3.9 bn (1 per cent of GDP) in 1994. This sizable increase in the deficit was due to a US$3.5 bn deficit on invisible trade, a third of which arose from spending by Korean travellers, as well as the continued rise in imports of capital and consumer goods. The growth in capital goods imports derived largely from increased facility investment, itself a consequence of a large surge in business activity of 1994. The growth of exports was relatively modest in the early 1990s but heavy industry contributed significantly to a 30.3 per cent growth in exports to the value of US$125 bn in 1995, with semiconductor, automobile and chemical exports increasing by 37.5 per cent. The export volume of light industry rose at a much lower rate, with growth recorded at 14 per cent. According to the Korea Trade Promotion Corporation (KOTRA), the country became the world's

Table 11.4 Trade, balance of payments and the exchange rate (US$ Bn) 1990–95

	1990	1991	1992	1993	1994	1995
Merchandise exports (fob)	63.1	69.6	75.2	81.0	93.7	123.2
Merchandise imports (fob)	65.1	76.6	77.3	79.1	96.8	127.9
Trade balance	-2.0	-7.0	-2.1	1.9	-3.1	-4.7
Invisibles balance	-0.5	-1.6	-2.6	-2.0	-2.0	-3.5
Current account balance	-1.7	-8.3	-3.9	1.0	-3.9	-8.3
(% of GDP)	-0.7	-2.8	-1.3	0.3	-1.0	-1.8
Exports (fob)	65.0	71.9	76.6	82.2	96.0	125.1
(% change on previous year)	4.2	10.6	6.5	7.3	16.8	30.3
Imports (fob)	66.1	77.2	77.4	79.4	96.9	128.0
(% change on previous year)	13.6	16.8	0.3	2.6	22.0	32.1
Gross external debt	31.7	39.3	42.6	44.1	56.9	79.0
Net external debt	4.9	12.5	11.0	8.0	13.0	18.2
Foreign exchange reserves	14.8	13.7	17.1	20.2	25.6	32.7
Exchange rate:						
(US$–Won)	716.4	760.8	788.4	808.1	788.7	774.7
(AUD–Won)	–	582.0	543.0	585.0	611.0	575.6

Sources: IMF; Bank of Korea; Korea Development Institute.

ninth largest trading country in real trade volume and was the world's third best performer in terms of export growth. In 1995 exports to the US increased by 17.4 per cent to US$24.1 bn and to Japan by 26.1 per cent to US$32.5 bn. Exports to South East Asia rose by 40.1 per cent to US$32.5 bn, reflecting the region's improved purchasing power derived from high economic growth. Exports to the EU reached US$16.3 bn, an increase of 47.4 per cent from 1994. Exports to China also rose markedly to US$9.1 bn.

Imports, with the exception of 1992 and 1993, have also grown rapidly during the 1990s, but most noticeably over the period 1994–95. Imports increased in 1995 by 32 per cent to the value of US$128 bn, fuelled by increases in imports of capital goods (32.5 per cent), industrial materials (32.6 per cent) and consumer goods (27.8 per cent). Developments in Korea's import structure reflect the country's restructuring efforts. As its production capability shifts to a higher value-added scale so too do import items become higher value-added, a phenomenon which is currently causing an increasing trade deficit with developed countries. In 1995, the deficit with developed countries stood at US$29.1 bn, compared with a trade surplus of US$19.2 bn with developing countries. In 1995 developing countries emerged as Korea's largest export destination, accounting for 50.1 per cent (US$62.6 bn) of total exports.

Korea has traditionally been sensitive to bilateral trade imbalances, especially with Japan. The balance of trade deficit with the US was US$6.29 bn in 1995 compared with a US$1.02 bn deficit in 1994. The trade imbalance between Korea and Japan remains a major cause of concern to Korea, and this reached a record US$15.57 bn in 1995 compared to a deficit of US$11 bn recorded in 1994. The Korean government has made it clear that it will progressively dismantle restraints on imports from Japan, but unless this is linked to increased international competitiveness of domestic goods the trade balance with Japan is likely to deteriorate further.

Korea's gross external debt has been steadily increasing throughout the 1990s, with big increases occurring as the country's trade balance blows out. Gross external debt increased by 39 per cent in 1995, compared to the previous year, reaching some US$18.2 bn. The increase was due to the rising trade deficit, and expanded borrowing from overseas to meet increasing facility investment. The country's foreign exchange reserves have continued to increase rapidly throughout the 1990s, and by the end of 1995 had increased to US$33.2 bn. Korea's foreign reserves, which were approximately equal to Australia's in 1988, had become more than twice as large.

The Korean currency (the won) experienced a continual depreciation against the US dollar during the early part of the 1990s, and with the weakening of the dollar itself against the Japanese yen implied a gain in competitiveness for Korean products relative to those of Japan. However, from 1994 the won began to appreciate against the dollar, and with the dollar strengthening against all major international currencies suggested a loss of international competitiveness of Korean products. The strengthening of the won against the yen has major implications for Korea's competitiveness *vis-à-vis* Japan in Asian markets. This was considerably improved by the yen appreciation in the early 1990s, but has since been steadily eroded. The effects of this are being felt in export demand for goods such as steel, chemicals, consumer electronic products, petroleum products and plastics. Some benefits will, however, flow to the more technologically advanced Korean industries that are substantial importers of sophisticated Japanese capital goods and technology, but the Korean government's policy of encouraging the development of the domestic capital goods industry may be set back.

The country's economic performance in 1996, however, indicated a noticeable deterioration over that of 1995. The country's current account deficit blew out to a record US$23.7 bn, and GDP growth slowed to 6.8 per cent, the country's gross foreign debt increased to almost US$100 bn arising from the financing of the current account deficit, and the won depreciated considerably relative to the US dollar. The major reasons for the growing trade and current account deficits have been the global semiconductor slump, which began in 1995 and has seen a significant decline in prices and demand. Semiconductor exports are important to Korea. In addition, lower prices for steel and a weaker Japanese yen and declining per capita productivity have had an adverse impact upon export revenues and competitiveness. Meanwhile, imports of capital and consumer goods continue to grow rapidly as does the country's imports of commodities such as oil, gas and grain which are at record levels. The bad news for the country continued into the early part of 1997, when it experienced its worst labour unrest in history. Over a number of weeks workers across the nation struck to protest against a new law making lay-offs easier, in conjunction with restricting union activities. The work stoppages caused an estimated US$3.15 bn in lost output. Soon after this the country experienced the Hanbo debacle. On 23 January South Korea's second biggest steel company imploded under a US$5.9 bn debt, which took out its entire parent group the fourteenth largest Korean conglomerate. The Bank of Korea's swift injection of 6 trillion won (US$7 bn) in liquidity prevented a possible chain reaction of bankruptcies. This made South Korea's already shaky financial system even more so, with many banks becoming loan shy, the yield on benchmark three-year corporate bonds being unlikely to drop below the prevailing 12.2 per cent. In addition, with the additional liquidity in the system, inflationary concerns deepened and the government's CPI target of 4.5 per cent for 1997 looked unlikely. The anticipated decline in GDP growth will inevitably result in an increase in unemployment from its then prevailing rate of 2.4 per cent. The current account deficit is also not anticipated to decline much from its massive blowout in 1996. In 1997 the government's top priority will be to focus upon a reduction of the current account deficit, with major ramifications for its trade partners should this be attempted through a reduction in imports.

V. Sectoral developments

1. Manufacturing

The manufacturing sector remains the backbone of the economy, with real growth at 5 per cent and above for the period of the 1990s. During 1994 and 1995 production rose by over 10 per cent, the largest increases since 1988. Strong export growth of semiconductors, automobiles, equipment and machinery and strong domestic demand for food and beverages underpinned this growth. However, there are increasing concerns about the disparity between the strong heavy industry sector with its high growth rates, and a declining light industry sector which includes most SMEs. In an effort to address this disparity, the government has announced a number of initiatives designed to redress light industry's most pressing problems, including that of a labour shortage, dependence upon imported capital goods, and access to credit. However, the light manufacturing sector in Korea continues to face considerable difficulties. Labour-intensive SMEs, the backbone of the Korean manufacturing sector in the 1980s, which for several years have been faced with steep wage increases, high interest rates and limited access to bank loans, are no longer competitive. The government's decision to establish the Small and Medium Business Administration (SMBA) should provide a mechanism to coordinate policies affecting SMEs, and the government also plans to rejuvenate the manufacturing sector through financial deregulation designed to provide competitive sources of funding to SMEs.

The Korean steel industry enjoyed buoyant activity in 1995, with domestic demand for steel increasing by 11.5 per cent compared to 1994, due to high facility investment, especially in the automobile, machinery and electronic sectors. As facility investment decreases, the Korean Iron and Steel Association expects domestic demand to fall, and steel-makers will have to look overseas for a larger proportion of sales. Korean steel production capacity is projected to reach over 40 mn tons on a crude steel basis in 1996 and to near 50 mn tons by 1998, with both construction and expansion of more production facilities. The government continues to oppose the entry of a second blast furnace steel producer.

Korean shipbuilders won orders worth US$6.8 bn in 1995 for a total tonnage of 7.13 mn, which was more than a quarter of all orders worldwide. The shipbuilding industry is one of the few which is unlikely to be touched by the economic slowdown, however, the yen depreciation will intensify competition between Japanese and Korean shipbuilders. The industry in Korea will continue to register healthy levels of growth as maintenance or refitting orders continue over the next ten years.

Construction continues to play an important role in the growth of the economy, recording a growth rate of 9.8 per cent in 1995 compared to 4.6 per cent in 1994. Construction growth has been fuelled by the expansion of production facilities, and the outlook is good for both domestic infrastructure projects and overseas construction. As investment in social overhead capital projects within the region continue to rise, Korea is well placed to take advantage of opportunities. The industry is anticipated to receive orders worth US$20 bn a year by 1999. Orders for overseas construction projects in 1996 were US$14 bn, with the majority of orders received from South East Asia.

The automotive industry continues to be a major strength of the economy. In 1995 international demand continued to grow, with exports benefiting from the appreciated yen and effective market diversification efforts of automotive manufacturers. Korean car-makers recorded growth of 41.8 per cent in exports of automobiles, excluding knockdown exports. Domestic car-makers plan to expand their production capacities by increasing facility investment and technology innovation. Domestic demand slowed in 1995, due to a high car-supply ratio and the longer life of Korean cars due to their improved technology. Pressure from the US, and to a lesser extent the EU, has broken down some of the formal barriers for foreign cars in Korea, but imports will probably expand slowly as long as the government and Korean consumers persist in perceiving foreign cars as luxury items.

The electronics sector recorded exports of US$26.2 bn in 1995. This is another market that has benefited from a high value for the yen, as well as an improved brand image overseas for Korean electronics products. International demand for semiconductors has continuously surged, making it the single biggest item among Korea's exports. However, the recent slump in the global market, as referred to previously, arising from market saturation and declining prices for semiconductors is of concern to Korean producers.

2. Agriculture

The agriculture sector continues to play a decreasing role in the economy, although it recorded positive growth rates in 1994 and 1995. Agriculture's share of GDP was 6.6 per cent in 1995, and has been on a steady downward trend for three decades reflecting Korea's transition to an industrial economy. The number of people employed in the farming and fisheries sector has been steadily declining, reaching 2.7 per cent in 1994, and is expected to drop further as the sector restructures. The government's priorities for the sector in 1996 were on its modernization with assistance given to improving the internal distribution network, acquisition of technology, improving export performance and generally enhancing its competitiveness. Although the agriculture sector remains heavily protected, the country imports considerable amounts of agricultural products. This sector has the potential for further substantial growth and thereby presents significant opportunities for Australia.

3. Services

With the continued expansion of domestic disposable incomes, greater market sophistication and liberalization, this sector is expected to continue to expand rapidly. Services now account for 41.2 per cent of GDP and experienced growth of 10 per cent in 1995, a slight drop from the growth of 10.8 per cent recorded for 1994. Particularly strong growth occurred in the telecommunications sector, due to the increasing popularity of cellular phones and pagers. The Uruguay Round services outcome requires the opening up of 78 business lines in 8 fields including: government procurement; finance; communications; tourism and environmental services, which will lead to potential market opportunities in Korea in a range of service areas covering finance, transport, education and professional services such as medical, legal and accounting services.

VI.   Contemporary economic problems and reform

Recent economic developments in the Korean economy suggest that the country is facing a number of economic difficulties, as reflected in its recent growth slow-down of output and exports, which will need to be overcome if the country is to re-establish the high rates of economic growth to which it has become accustomed. This will require further economic reform in a number of key areas. Key problems and the need for reform exists in regard to: the need for restructuring of the economy; a pressing need to overcome difficulties in the banking sector and for further financial sector reform; the implementation of labour market reform; external difficulties and the need to maintain further trade reform; the potential reunification of the country should North Korea implode.

1.   Economic restructuring

A key component of any reform process will be the curtailment of the power of the chaebols, which have provided the basis of the country's success in the past. The country's economic structure is still heavily biased in favour of the chaebols, which account for the bulk of the country's industrial output. In 1994, large corporations, defined as firms with more than 300 employees, accounted for 46.1 per cent of South Korea's national production and 49.7 per cent of value-added production. However, they only employed

28.5 per cent of the national work force and accounted for just 0.8 per cent of the total number of South Korean businesses. The concentration of economic power in the country is therefore somewhat extreme, making it difficult for smaller companies to grow properly. For many years the government encouraged this top-heavy structure. In the 1970s and 1980s South Korea's military rulers used chaebols such as Hyundai, Daewoo and Samsung to develop the economy, allocating scarce credit and resources along with instructions as to which industrial sectors companies should enter, the government's strategy being that economic growth would take too long if it focused on small companies. Hence the chaebols were cultivated with official support. But now that the conglomerates are big enough to stand on their own, government aid needs now to be shifted to smaller companies. However, the government will not commit itself to direct financial support, which the authorities believe would be futile, and violate its pledge to the OECD to uphold free market principles, but rather to improving the general business environment for small businesses.

If such reform is successful it will have a profound impact upon South Korea's industrial landscape, as chaebols have long used their privileged access to credit to fund aggressive investment and expansion regardless of the risk. Proposals by the government to curtail their access to unlimited credit is likely to bring such empire building to an end. Breaking up the tightly-knit industrial structure characterized by the chaebols will be a key part in the process of moving the Korean economy into a position of maturity in the international economic community, since the economy is seriously over-reliant on a few industrial sectors in which chaebols have concentrated their development. The country still depends on heavy industry at the expense of light industry, and manufacturing at the expense of services. Exports are also dominated by a few key items such as cars, ships, steel, petrochemicals and semiconductors. But remaking the economy's industrial structure will not be easy, as opposition exists both within industrial and government circles. Korea's membership of the OECD, however, will provide the government with the stimulus to overcome existing bureaucratic and corporate obstacles, and create the conditions necessary to implement economic reforms to deregulate an economy that has long been subject to state controls. In the future Korea's development and prosperity will depend on accelerating the evolution of its companies away from a dependence on cheap labour and imported technology and equipment, toward innovation-intensive industries.

In order to develop light manufacturing as well as the services sectors of the economy, reform is most clearly needed in the context of the small- and medium-sized firms which tend to dominate light manufacturing industries and offer the most potential in terms of developing the services sector. However, rising wage costs (see Table 11.5), high interest rates and competition from newly emerging economies have combined to worsen the prospects for small- and medium-sized firms, which employ around 70 per cent of the

Table 11.5   Hourly labour costs in manufacturing (US$) 1985 and 1995

Country	1985	1995
Germany	9.60	31.88
Japan	6.34	23.66
France	7.52	19.34
United States	13.01	17.20
Italy	7.63	16.48
Canada	10.94	16.03
Australia	8.20	14.40
Britain	6.27	13.77
Spain	4.66	12.70
South Korea	1.23	7.40
Singapore	2.47	7.28
Taiwan	1.50	5.82
Hong Kong	1.73	4.82
Brazil	1.30	4.28
Chile	1.87	3.63
Poland	na	2.09
Hungary	na	1.70
Argentina	0.67	1.67
Malaysia	1.08	1.59
Mexico	1.59	1.51
Czech Republic	na	1.30
Philippines	0.64	0.71
Russia	na	0.60
Thailand	0.49	0.46
Indonesia	0.22	0.30
China	0.19	0.25
India	0.35	0.25

Source: Morgan Stanley.

total work force. As many as 14 000 small businesses went bankrupt in 1996 because of tight credit, primarily caused by the large portion of bank lending taken up by the chaebol-linked firms. However, in 1996 the Ministry of Trade, Industry and Energy established the SMBA to supply up to 2 trillion won (US$2.6 bn) in low interest loans to small- and medium-sized companies. But that measure is seen as little more than a temporary step, and small businesses still complain about the pace of deregulation. Hence more reform, as well as a more rapid pace, is required in this area.

2. Banking and financial sector reform

On 9 May 1996 the government issued a policy paper seeking to impose more transparency on companies, and to cut into the chaebol's near monopoly on bank financing. The most controversial proposal was seen as being the one which would phase out in five years the system that allows one chaebol-linked company to issue credit guarantees to another firm in the group. This change would effectively bar chaebol companies from monopolizing credit from group-linked banking institutions as they currently do. In general the extent and pace of deregulation required in the banking system must be seen as pressing. The success of such a deregulatory programme will depend crucially upon how swiftly it loosens its bureaucratic control over banks, by giving them greater freedom and autonomy. The domestic banking system is in a very weak position because domestic banks are severely burdened with sizeable loans to chaebol firms that carry preferential interest rates, a procedure, as mentioned previously, which has been conducted in the country over many years. An opening up of South Korea's financial markets will force the banks to enhance their competitiveness, and the performance of their loans, or face bankruptcy. If they are to strengthen themselves, the low interest subsidy loans to affiliated companies need to be eliminated. Reform of the chaebols is therefore closely linked with desperately needed reform of the country's banking system. An added difficulty has arisen from the Hanbo debacle of 23 January 1997, which has had a profound impact upon an already weak banking system. Without the intervention by the Bank of Korea many bankruptcies would have arisen.

A key test of South Korea's full acceptance into the club of industrialized nations will be the nation's ability to open up its financial markets. The government has been liberalizing slowly. Foreigners are now able to own South Korean securities worth up to 20 per cent of any quoted company's equity, but the authorities have been extremely cautious about deregulating international capital flows. They fear that such a move would invite outside investors, attracted by Korea's relatively high interest rates, and contribute to an appreciation of the domestic exchange rate in the short term, which would result in a loss of international competitiveness as well as contributing to domestic inflationary pressure. The other side of that concern is that artificially high interest rates impose a heavy penalty on the local economy, especially entrepreneurs needing start-up capital. This is most prevalent in the case of small- and medium-sized enterprises producing light manufactured goods. These enterprises, as mentioned previously, are precisely the ones the government should be attempting to encourage.

3. Labour market reform

The Korean economy has recently been experiencing a decline in international competitiveness arising from the strengthening value of the won, a decline in per capita productivity and increasing wage costs (see Table 11.5) relative to its regional rivals. In Korea workers only obtained the right to strike in the late 1980s, and have since pushed hard for wage increases. Labour costs in certain industries now match those in the more developed nations. Some chaebols are, as a consequence, establishing plants overseas, such as in Europe, where they can negotiate long-term deals linking wage increases to inflation and productivity and not union strength. As Korea further opens up its economy under obligations to the OECD and the World Trade Organization, thereby becoming further integrated into the global economy, domestic concerns will grow about its international competitiveness and labour costs. For many companies, especially the small- and medium-sized enterprises, the ability to lay off workers and hire temporary staff will be important if Korean companies are to maintain a competitive edge and to provide employment. Staying internationally competitive will require a flexible and fluid work force, or else the country will slip behind rivals such as Taiwan and Japan.

As with Japan in the early 1990s, rising costs and a strong currency have encouraged many Korean firms to set up production facilities elsewhere in Asia. In Japan additionally, a prolonged recession forced many companies to dismantle their lifetime employment systems, retrench work forces and introduce promotions based more on merit than seniority. The position of many dynamic small- and medium-sized firms benefited from this shake-out. Similar developments in Korea are likely from its own labour reforms. Giving firms greater power over whom they can hire and fire will be of major benefit to small firms, who cannot afford to pay large labour bills or the cost of a labour tribunal in order to retrench workers. That, in turn, could inject greater dynamism into the economy as small firms get the opportunity to expand.

One major benefit of a flexible labour pool is that retrenched workers can be rechannelled into the more dynamic sectors of the economy. But the government will have a key role to play in this process. Re-training programmes will be essential to enable workers to be re-employed in the high tech and service industries. Korea requires to move up the high tech ladder, and this will require a movement away from the dependence on the heavy industries which currently dominate the economy. The government will also require to expand the existing safety net, in the form of unemployment insurance, to assist those workers made redundant during this important transition process. The recent antagonism towards the government's labour reforms suggests the need to explain the necessity and aims of economic restructuring to a sceptical public and political opposition, rather than presenting it as a *fait accomplis*.

4.   External difficulties and further trade reform

As mentioned above Korea has recently experienced a noticeable deterioration in the growth of its exports, combined with continuing substantial imports of capital and consumer goods. Exports are uncomfortably dominated by a few key items such as cars, ships steel, petrochemicals and semiconductors (see Table 11.6). The top ten export items accounted for 53 per cent of the total value of shipments in 1995, up from a 50 per cent share in 1994. These in addition to other manufactured goods accounted for 85 per cent of exports. Substantial imports of machinery and equipment have also been apparent for the economy during the period of the 1990s, and as a proportion of total imports this has been increasing. Such imports have been essential to expand and upgrade production

Table 11.6 Korea's exports and imports by commodity groups

	1990	1991	1992	1993	1994	1995
Major exports (% of total exports)						
Machiner/equipment	37.7	36.6	41.6	44.9	49.0	52.5
Manufactured goods	52.4	46.0	46.5	42.5	38.0	32.7
Chemicals	3.3	3.7	4.4	6.0	6.6	7.1
Mineral fuels	1.1	1.1	2.1	2.3	1.8	1.9
Major imports (% of total imports)						
Machinery/equipment	32.7	32.8	33.3	33.9	36.5	36.6
Manufactured goods	21.5	20.7	22.6	21.7	23.5	38.5
Mineral fuels	12.4	15.9	15.6	18.0	15.1	7.4
Raw materials	14.2	12.2	10.9	10.6	9.2	8.7
Chemicals	11.6	10.3	10.0	9.8	9.5	9.7

Source: National Statistical Office.

facilities, and they have contributed considerably to the country's worsening trade balance. As with exports, imports of machinery and equipment in addition to other manufactured goods dominate contributing 75 per cent of total imports. The global slump in the semiconductor market, weakening steel prices, rising labour costs, declining per capita productivity and the weakening of the Japanese yen, have all combined to reduce the growth of export values. This in conjunction with record imports of commodities contributed to the record current account deficit of US$23.7 bn in 1996. This persistent external shortfall has required more overseas borrowing, resulting in a rapid build up of foreign debt. Gross foreign debt increased to around US$100 bn by the end of 1996, almost double the same figure in 1994. Some commentators contend that South Korea's current account and foreign debt situation is similar to that of Mexico before the 1994 peso crisis. However, such fears do appear to be exaggerated, although the Korean government put reducing the current account deficit as its top policy objective for 1997 with a reduction of imports emerging as its main strategy.

However, despite these more recent adverse developments in its trade and current account balances, it will be vital that further progress is made in the opening up of the economy. In this regard much progress has been made by Korea in reducing tariff barriers over the past eight years (see Table 11.7), and this should be maintained. The economic reforms already alluded to, in conjunction with further reductions in tariffs barriers, will be vital to enhance the international competitiveness of domestic companies, and to enable the economy to take the fullest advantage of its further integration into the global economy.

5. Reunification of the country

Another major concern to the South Korean authorities would be the collapse of the North Korean economy, which would require the South to take on the burden of a sudden reunification of the country. This would likely lead to a flood of migration into South Korea and with it a requirement for large expenditures by the South Korean government to stabilize the situation. With the North Korean economy in desperate shape the likelihood of reunification becomes ever more likely. The prospects of such a scenario has

Table 11.7   International tariff barriers, 1988 and 1996

Average tariffs % Country	1988	1996
Australia	15.6	5.0
Canada	3.7	1.6
Chile	19.9	11.0
China	39.5	23.0
European Union	5.7	3.6
Hong Kong	0	0
Indonesia	18.1	13.1
Japan	4.3	4.0
Korea	19.2	7.9
Malaysia	13.6	9.0
Mexico	10.5	9.8
New Zealand	14.9	5.7
Philippines	27.9	15.6
Singapore	0.3	0
Taiwan	12.6	8.6
Thailand	31.2	17.0
USA	4.2	3.4

Sources: Manila Action Plan for APEC, European Union.

forced the South Korean government to provide food aid to the North to bring about an economic 'soft landing'. If this does not occur it could create major problems for the current reform drive of the South Korean government, and the long-term economic future of a reunified Korea. According to a South Korean presidential committee, it could cost up to US$1.2 trillion over several years to bring the North Korean economy up to the level of South Korea's. In the North, with a population of 23.3 mn, income per capita has been estimated at US$957, compared to the South's US$10 067 in 1995. The experience of Germany would suggest that the process of economic reunification is an extremely costly and prolonged process, with major problems in the interim in terms of government finance, rising unemployment, difficulties on the current account and the need for overseas borrowing. Such a task has been an immense drain on the resources of one of the world's richest nations, and without these same resources the task facing South Korea would be even more immense.

VII. Korea's international trade and investment

1. Trade

International trade for Korea, as with the other tiger economies, has been a key component of its economic success. Today Korea has emerged as a major trading nation as indicated by Tables 11.8 and 11.9. Table 11.8 shows that Korea was the world's twelfth largest exporter by value in 1995 at US$125.1 bn, with a 2.5 per cent share of world exports, while Table 11.9 shows that the country was the world's eleventh largest importer by value with US$135.1 bn equivalent to 2.7 per cent of world imports. As mentioned previously South Korea's economy is seriously over-reliant on a few industrial sectors in which chaebols have concentrated their development. The country's heavy dependence on heavy industry at the expense of light industry, and manufacturing at the expense of services is most clearly demonstrated by the country's export reliance upon a few key items such as cars, ships steel, petrochemicals and semiconductors. The country's major trading partners are indicated in Table 11.10. From this it can be seen that the major partners consist

Table 11.8 World's major exporters by value, fob, 1995, US$ bn

Rank	Country	Exports, US$ bn	% of total world exports
1.	USA	584.7	11.7
2.	Germany	502.7	10.0
3.	Japan	443.1	8.8
4.	France	286.7	5.7
5.	United Kingdom	241.8	4.8
6.	Italy	231.3	4.6
7.	Netherlands	195.5	3.9
8.	Canada	192.2	3.8
9.	Hong Kong	173.8	3.5
10.	Belgium	151.2	3.0
11.	China	148.8	3.0
12.	South Korea	125.1	2.5
13.	Singapore	118.3	2.4
14.	Taiwan	111.6	2.2
15.	Spain	91.7	1.8
23.	Australia	53.1	1.1

Sources: IMF, WTO.

Table 11.9   World's major importers by value, cif, 1995, US$ bn

Rank	Country	Imports,US$ bn	% of total world imports
1.	USA	771.0	15.1
2.	Germany	448.0	8.8
3.	Japan	335.9	6.6
4.	France	275.0	5.4
5.	United Kingdom	263.8	5.2
6.	Italy	204.1	4.0
7.	Hong Kong	192.8	3.8
8.	Netherlands	176.1	3.5
9.	Canada	168.4	3.3
10.	Belgium	142.0	2.8
11.	South Korea	135.1	2.7
12.	China	129.1	2.5
13.	Singapore	124.5	2.4
14.	Spain	115.0	2.3
15.	Taiwan	103.7	2.0
22.	Australia	61.3	1.2

Sources: IMF, WTO.

Table 11.10   Major trading partners (% of total trade)

	1990	1991	1992	1993	1994	1995
USA	29.5	26.9	24.4	21.7	21.2	21.0
Japan	22.6	23.1	21.8	19.0	19.6	19.1
EU	12.8	12.8	11.3	11.8	12.0	13.2
China	1.7	2.1	2.9	4.0	5.9	6.4
Hong Kong	3.2	3.3	3.6	4.4	4.4	4.4
Australia	2.6	2.6	2.6	2.7	2.5	2.5
Saudi Arabia	1.5	1.8	2.8	2.8	2.4	2.5

Source: National Statistical Office.

primarily of the developed economies of the USA, Japan and the EU, which together constituted over half of Korea's total trade (53.3 per cent) in 1995. It is also apparent from this table the increasing significance of China as a trading partner.

Trade between Korea and China has grown at a rate of approximately 30 per cent per annum since 1988. Trade volume between the two countries reached US$16.54 bn in 1995. Korean exports to China amounted to US$9.14 bn in 1995, representing an increase of 47.4 per cent from 1994. Imports reached US$7.4 bn, an increase of

35.9 per cent from 1994. Export growth was led by petrochemicals, industrial equipment and machinery. Imports were mainly composed of basic and light industry products. This trade pattern reflects the two countries' complementary industrial structure, which will be maintained for some time as China's economy develops. Trade between Korea and the EU reached US$34.5 bn in 1995. Exports to the EU increased by 47.4 per cent reaching US$16.3 bn and imports by 24.4 per cent amounting to US$18.2 bn. Korea and the EU have initialled a Framework Agreement for Trade and Cooperation, which is designed to strengthen relations in a wide variety of fields including science and technology, services and agriculture. In addition Korea–Russian trade volume also grew rapidly in 1995, which is anticipated to be maintained. For 1995, total Korean exports to Russia amounted to US$1.762 bn, 40 per cent higher than in 1994, while imports from Russia increased by 50 per cent during 1995 to US$2.266 bn.

2. International investment

The extent of foreign direct investment in Korea and Korean investment overseas is contained in Tables 11.11 and 11.12. Table 11.11 suggests that the extent of foreign investment in Korea is very small by comparison to that elsewhere in the region, and is indicative of the general perception by overseas investors that Korea is not an attractive country within which to invest. Among the reasons cited for this perception are high wage rates, expensive finance, abuse of intellectual property rights, requirements that profits be reinvested and excessive government regulation. Such a problem will need to be given high priority by the authorities in the future, given the important role which such investment could play in the attraction

Table 11.11   Foreign direct investment in Korea (US$ mn)

	1990	1991	1992	1993	1994	1995
USA	317	296	379	341	311	645
Japan	236	226	155	286	428	418
Europe	207	824	282	307	407	475
Others	43	50	128	110	170	403
Total	802	1396	894	1044	1316	1941

Source: Ministry of Finance and Economy (MFE).

Table 11.12   Korea's outward foreign investment (US$ mn)

	1990	1991	1992	1993	1994	1995
North America	438	459	392	390	573	546
China	16	42	141	262	631	814
Asia (exc. China)	296	428	519	223	1080	1641
South America	36	42	36	44	49	na
Europe	95	90	144	190	428	611
Others	93	97	127	152	175	na
Total	971	1158	1359	1257	2305	3059

Sources: Bank of Korea; Ministry of Trade, Industry and Energy.

and upgrading of technology used in the country. In 1995, inflows of foreign direct investment amounted to 578 projects/transactions valued at US$1.9 bn, an increase from US$1.3 bn in 1994 and almost double the flow since 1993. It is dominated by that from the developed economies, in which the USA, Japan and Europe contributed 79 per cent of total FDI inflows in 1995. By sector, investment in manufacturing increased most dramatically to US$883.5 mn (a 120 per cent increase in two years), while investment in other sectors increased but at a much steadier rate (15 per cent over two years). US companies were the largest investors in 1995, with 161 projects/transactions valued at US$645 mn.

In an effort to restructure industry by inducing strategic high-tech transfers from advanced countries, Korea is now attempting to attract FDI and encourage Korean corporations to enter into strategic alliances with foreign companies. Korea increasingly regards FDI as an essential element in strengthening its economy and obtaining transfers of advanced technology. In late 1994 the government reaffirmed its policy of encouraging foreign investment in Korea by reducing corporate tax on foreign invested firms, relaxing regulations on foreign ownership of land and simplifying approval procedures. Particular effort has been concentrated on attracting more Japanese investment in the areas of auto parts, electric/electronic parts, and machinery industries, as Japanese manufacturers have diversified their production bases to overseas countries in order to reduce increased production costs incurred by the strong yen.

As a consequence of an easing of its regulatory regime, investments made by Korean companies overseas reached US$10.2 bn at the end of 1995, focused mainly in North America where investments were 14.2 per cent of the total investment. However, in terms of recent Korean investment overseas an increasingly clearer pattern is beginning to emerge, as indicated in Table 11.12, with investment changing away from traditionally favoured destinations such as the USA to South East Asian countries and China. Asia, other than China, was the recipient of US$1.6 bn investment funds, 53.6 per cent of total Korean investment overseas, in 1995, compared with only US$296 mn in 1990 or 30 per cent of the total. China has increasingly emerged as a major recipient of investment by Korean firms, which increased from only US$16 mn in 1990, or 1.6 per cent of the total, to US$814 in 1995 equivalent to 26.6 per cent of the total. This overseas investment development is indicative of the increasing concern labour of intensive manufacturing industries such as textiles, footwear and fabricated metals in particular, dominated by small- and medium-sized firms, over a loss of competitiveness resulting from rising domestic wages. Hence, to offset a decline in price competitiveness, Korean companies have sought to relocate some of their less competitive manufacturing and assembly facilities in lower-cost countries such as China, Vietnam, Indonesia and recently North Korea. China in particular is seen as the most desirable country for investment because of its proximity, cheap labour and huge market potential. Asia therefore received 80 per cent of total Korean investment overseas in 1995, compared with only 32 per cent in 1990. The relative significance of the USA as a destiny for such investment by Korean firms has clearly declined, while on the other hand that of the EU has also noticeably increased. The government has complemented this process of 'restructuring' by providing financial incentives for Korean companies to upgrade their domestic production facilities with improved technology.

From 10 October 1995, all Korean companies have been required to source at least 20 per cent of projected investment capital in overseas projects of US$100 mn or more from internal sources or from their own capital, reserves or cashflow. The policy is designed to slow Korea's increasing foreign debt, and also to allay government concerns that companies may over-extend themselves. The US$100 mn barrier will certainly hinder the investment plans of the top four chaebols – Samsung, Hyundai, Daewoo and LG – who had planned to invest at least US$20 bn over the period 1996–2000, and whose moves offshore could have caused major problems at home.

VIII.   Australia/Korea international trade and investment prospects

1.   Trade prospects

The bilateral trading relationship between Korea and Australia has been developing strongly. A major reason for this has been the strong complementarity in the economic relationship, in which there is still significant potential for further diversification and expansion. Should the strong growth of the Korean and Australian economies be maintained, it will provide opportunities for exporters in both economies. Primary products continue to dominate Australia's exports to Korea. Major Australian export items include gold, coal, iron ore and concentrates alumina, wool, car engines and wheat, with Korea's exports to Australia consisting primarily of manufactured goods and of machinery and transport equipment (see Table 11.13). Total two way Korea–Australia trade over the period 1995–96 was worth AUD8.9 bn (an increase of AUD1.6 bn or 21.9 per cent from the previous year). During 1995–96 Australia's exports to Korea were worth AUD6.6 bn, an increase of 24.5 per cent over the period 1994–95. Over the period 1995–96 Australia imported goods worth AUD2.3 bn from Korea. The balance of merchandise trade therefore remains firmly in Australia's favour, with a surplus of AUD4.3 bn over the period 1995–96. Korea is now Australia's second largest export market, accounting for almost 8 per cent of total Australian merchandise exports, and is also Australia's ninth largest source of imports and its fourth largest trading partner.

With Korea's rapidly expanding per capita income and greater propensity to import, the prospects for continued expansion of trade between the countries is good. Increasing opportunities for trade exist in markets including foodstuffs, consumer goods and timber houses, the demand for which is being driven by factors such as expanding disposable incomes, changing community standards and economic restructuring and opening. Industry demand is also giving rise to market development opportunities for Australia in a range of other areas including computer software, automobile components and other engineering products.

Table 11.13   Australia-Korea trade by commodity 1995–96

Commodity classification	Exports by Australia AUD mn	Imports by Australia AUD mn	Trade balance AUD mn
0. Food & live animals	234	18	+216
1. Beverages & tobacco	2	–	+2
2. Crude materials, inedible, except fuels	1076	13	+1063
3. Mineral fuels, lubricants and related materials	1101	14	+1087
4. Animal & vegetable oils, fats and waxes	6	–	+6
5. Chemical & related products, nes*	99	170	–71
6. Manufactured goods, classified chiefly by material	745	539	+206
7. Machinery & transport equipment	405	1322	–917
8. Miscellaneous manufactured articles	101	154	–53
9. Commodities & transactions not classified elsewhere	2838	63	+2775
(of which gold-non-monetary)	(2187)	(–)	(+2187)
TOTAL	6607	2293	+4314

* Not elsewhere specified
Source: ABS, International Merchandise Trade Australia.

Tourism is another excellent example of trade growth driven by market liberalization, with the lifting of restrictions on overseas travel by Korean citizens. Korean tourists to Australia have increased rapidly from 12 000 in 1990 to over 160 000 in 1995, and this figure is expected to increase to over 250 000 per annum by the end of the decade. The growth rate in inbound tourism from Korea has been a major factor in the agreement reached to increase air services. In July 1996 Ansett Airlines was allowed to join other airlines, Quantas, Korean Air and Asiana, providing direct Korea–Australia air services.

With the structure of the Korean economy changing rapidly, both the government and business are searching aggressively for state of the art technology to modernize industry and build international competitiveness. Although Korea, traditionally, has been dependent on the US, Japan and Europe as the source of industrial technology and know-how, it is now seeking to multiply and diversify its sources of supply. This will provide Australian producers with increased opportunities in high technology areas, including information technology, environmental management technology and advanced engineering and design.

There is also a growing number of young Koreans wishing to further their education abroad, particularly in English language education. During 1995 the Australian embassy in Seoul issued almost 6200 student visas compared with 3968 in 1994, with more than three quarters of these being for English language courses. The establishment in October 1995 of an Australian International Education Office to coordinate and market Australian education and training services in Korea, has strengthened Australia's standing in the market.

Currently Australia has a small but active participation in the Korean financial sector, with two Australian banks having offices in Seoul (ANZ and the National Australia Bank). With the rapid growth and continuing liberalization of Korea's services sector, including that in finance, opportunities are broadening. For example the ANZ Bank recently signed an accord on banking services with the Korean Exchange Bank, which will provide general reciprocal banking services, including investment banking, custodian services and other immigration-related services.

2. Investment prospects

Compared with trade the investment linkages between Australia and Korea are modest, although Korean investment in Australia has recently increased significantly. In October 1995, a consortium including a range of Korean investors was awarded the major Wyong coal development contract by the New South Wales government. This represented a major breakthrough for Korean investment in Australia. In December 1995, the Queensland government and Korea Zinc announced that Korea Zinc intended to build a zinc smelter and refinery in Townsville. This will be the biggest single Korean investment so far in Australia, at AUD500 mn in the first stage and growing possibly to AUD1 bn. There has also been the purchase by Korean companies of beef cattle and other farming operations. Korea's Yukong oil company is participating in a joint venture with Australian and US companies to explore for oil off the northwest coast of Australia. As Korean companies further seek to globalize their operations, Australia can expect to benefit from a much stronger and more diverse portfolio of Korean outward investment. Prospects for Korean investment in Australia are particularly good in the beef and coal mining sectors, as well as in tourism.

Australian investment in Korea is presently minimal, the most notable contribution being the capitalisation of the two Australian banks in Korea–ANZ and the National Australia Bank. Korea, as indicated previously, has generally been regarded as a tough place for the foreign investor, and Australia is not alone in having very modest investments in the country. The investment climate, however, is likely to improve progressively over the next five years as financial deregulation continues. Australian investors will then be able to take full advantage of Korea's strengths: a powerful and rapidly growing economy, strategically located in North Asia and containing a manufacturing sector second only to Japan's in modernity and product range in Asia.

IX. Summary and conclusions

The South Korean economy has come a long way over the past thirty years. However, the economic development policy in the past, emphasizing extensive government intervention and the development of large conglomerates in the heavy industry sector, appears to have run its course. Such a development strategy has contributed to the rapid growth of the economy but has also resulted in an economy with a bias towards heavy rather than light manufacturing industry, a bias towards manufacturing rather than services, and a bias towards conglomerates rather than small- and medium-sized enterprises. The latter are responsible for the employment of some 70 per cent of the work force and should represent a dynamic component of the economy. However, rising labour costs and difficulty in getting access to bank credit, traditionally dominated by the chaebols, have stunted their development. The country also has a heavy reliance upon exports of a few key manufactured goods such as cars, ships, steel, petrochemicals and semiconductors. Developments during 1995 and 1996, declining semiconductor and steel prices, indicate the dangers of being so reliant upon a relatively few products.

The prospects for the Korean economy over the next few years remain generally favourable, and this has been enhanced by its recent membership of the OECD which will expand its internationalised industrial and administrative structures. However, there is a continuing need for the implementation of economic reforms by the government, with the objective of enhancing the international competitiveness of the Korean economy. The main strengths of the economy include: entrepreneurial strengths across a wide range of manufacturing, especially in the chaebols; a well-educated and motivated work force; a growing level of research and development expenditure; a high savings rate (around 36.2 per cent of GNP); regional linkages, especially to China and South East Asia favouring the export sector; and potential for further rapid growth in domestic demand through increased infrastructure investment and personal consumption. However, a number of problems remain, including the need for: economic restructuring of the economy; banking and financial sector reform; labour market reform; the need to overcome pressing external difficulties including a large current account deficit and an associated rapid accumulation of external debt; overcoming economic and political instability in North Korea; overcoming allegations of corruption against high-ranking officials in government and in the leading chaebols. The growth of domestic labour costs will inevitably erode competitiveness in the international market, and contribute to an outflow of investment to China and South East Asia by labour-intensive manufacturing industry. The value of the Japanese yen, will also exert a major influence over the competitiveness of Korean products as against Japanese products in Asian markets.

In the longer term the challenges are even greater. Korea must continue to reform its financial sector, remove the burden of excessive business regulation, provide a more favourable environment for foreign investment and further restructure its economy away from declining manufacturing and agricultural industries and towards services and more high-tech, sophisticated manufacturing products. There is increasing concern about the sustainability of the niche Korea occupies as a highly industrialized, but still relatively low (per capita) income economy. This concern increases the urgency for further restructuring and improvement in technological capabilities. Concern has also been expressed over the ability of Korean firms to develop the design quality control and marketing capabilities for successful adaptation to these new challenges. They are endeavouring to follow the Japanese route but the time available to them for the needed structural adjustments will inevitably be shorter, because of greater competition from other countries following the same strategy.

References

Asiaweek, Asiaweek Limited Hong Kong (various).
Australian Bureau of Statistics (1996), *Balance of Payments and International Investment position Australia 1994–95*, catalogue no. 5363.0, June.
Australian Bureau of Statistics (1996), *International Merchandise Trade Australia*, catalogue no. 5422.0, June quarter.
Department of Foreign Affairs and Trade (1996), *Country Economic Brief Korea*, Canberra, Australia, May.
Far Eastern Economic Review, Review Publishing Co. Ltd, USA (various).
International Monetary Fund (1996), *International Financial Statistics*, Washington, DC, USA (various).
Krugman, P. (1995), 'The Myth of the Asian Miracle', *Foreign Affairs*, Vol. 73, No. 6.
The Economist, Economist Newspaper Ltd, UK (various).
World Bank (1993), *The East Asian Economic Miracle*, Washington, DC, Oxford University Press.

12
General Comments and Conclusions

Tran Van Hoa

In the preceding chapters, we have provided the reader with the findings of a thorough analysis of recent local and international data on trade, investment and business, and official and private forecast trends to explore, in an integrated framework, the prospects for commerce and cooperation for Australian and other foreign companies and business individuals in Vietnam and, to a lesser extent, the Mekong Basin and East Asia. The areas of study are comprehensive and conform to the full cycle of business, in the sense that they cover practically everything important from the embryonic stage of whether a business exists or is feasible for development to the beyond end-use stage where the environmental and labour impacts of business itself within the international framework of the WTO, ILO and ISO are discussed. Other relevant and significant areas of study are: the amended law on foreign investment in Vietnam and its implications for business, fields of priority investment and ways to promote them; a survey of the business environment in Vietnam; trade with East Asia; prospects for trade in the Mekong Basin subregion; human resource development issues and priorities with their implications for international business in Vietnam; business ethics and its implications for foreign enterprises; and environmental regulation and standards. Economic achievements and problems of another developing Asian country which, since December 1996, has been admitted to the Organization for Economic Cooperation and Development (OECD), namely South Korea, are also discussed; bringing home some lessons in the economic development in East Asia with potential applications to Vietnam and others in the ASEAN.

From our discussions, it transpires that the prospects for trade, investment and business in Vietnam are outstanding both for transnational corporations and for individual investors and business people. These conclusions come from a number of factors and perspectives which have been presented and discussed.

First, Vietnam is a fast developing and transition economy where the government and the people have put together their physical, human, legal and administrative resources to achieve a free market (ostensibly with socialist orientations or features), national modernization, economic reforms, an open economy, and rapid development and growth. Second, Vietnam is a vast market (76 mn people as at 1996) on the demand side but it also has huge untapped natural and human resources on the supply side. Third, Vietnam is a member of the ASEAN and strategically situated in the Mekong Basin region with development potential recognized by the international community. This means that Vietnam as an economic base can provide a trade link for Australian and other foreign countries to the ASEAN and Indochina and Southern China markets. Fourth, Vietnam has a politically stable regime and threats of armed aggression (chiefly from China) are low.

Fifth, Vietnam has a comparatively cheap source of educated labour and abundant power resources. Sixth, with its high economic growth rates consistently attained in the decade or so and similarly predicted in the future to 2020, Vietnam's income per head has been increasing fast and this will provide the base for high consumption or demand for goods and services and trade. Seventh, Vietnam has a strong support from international countries, organizations and institutions to help it in its modernization and development process. Finally, Vietnam has been given a high business confidence score (that is, 9 out of 10) in the Asian Business confidence index calculated from surveys (*Investment in Vietnam*, Internet, 25 April 1997).

It is true, even now, that bureaucratic impediments in Vietnam are rampant, the country's infrastructure is out-dated, its law especially in the fields of business and investment is inadequate, and government intervention in business is rife. It should be noted that, to rectify these problems, serious efforts by the government of Vietnam have been made with international experts' advice and capital to streamline bureaucracy, to improve infrastructure, to draft new law, to privatize many of the state-owned enterprises, and to move closer to a free market economy. In addition, what has been perceived as Vietnam's setbacks (lack of adequate infrastructure, need of training for the labour force, lack of development in the manufacturing industry for exports, trade deficit and so on) could turn into opportunities (infrastructure construction, training, technology transfer in manufactures, enhancement of exports to Vietnam and so on) for foreign companies and individual business people.

It has often been claimed by Australian representatives and corporate managers in Australia and overseas that Vietnam is the graveyard for foreign businesses. But this is in contradiction to the successes by such companies as Telstra and the ANZ and numerous other small- and medium-sized foreign companies operating in Vietnam. It reflects the fact that investment and business in Vietnam is, due to the country's early stage of economic development, a long-term proposition, and not a short-term adventure for a quick windfall or abnormal profits. It also reflects the facts one should know about while doing business in Vietnam, a country unlike any other country in Asia in either a transition or developing stage.

In *An Insider's Quick Guide to Starting a Business in Vietnam*, Sheridan (*Investment in Vietnam*, Internet, 25 April 1997) offers a range of advice to the interested business community: have caution and patience (though too much caution and patience can lead to missed opportunities); the law in Vietnam is not transparent but it is also not static; be flexible with traditional legal concepts and in business transactions; pay special attention to the local customs and attitudes in the first business meeting; contracts in Vietnam should not be more than three pages long; friendly, honest (sometimes brutally honest) and polite discussions will be most fruitful; oral negotiations are lengthy due to time-delays for translation, false starts when misunderstandings occur, and a Vietnamese tradition of 'never agreeing until it's agreed'.

To do business in a country whose traditions, culture, language and ways of doing things are different from what we have been accustomed to in our own country may not be an easy job for a novice or the inexperienced. Our model of business management and operation incorporating business values and statements of both the transnational and local corporations and business people could be used as a good starting-point for doing business in Vietnam.

After all, it is the potential commercial gain from good trade, investment and business prospects, and the excitement of a good challenge that make a venture into Vietnam a truly high calibre adventure. This is in addition to the gain from enhancement of commerce for mutually social and economic benefits and from the promotion of regional political stability through commercial and political cooperation.

Index

accounting and auditing
practices 168
accounting standards 66
agricultural products 13
animal spirit 170
ANZ Bank 64
applied economic modelling
xiv
aqua-product 60
ASEAN xiii, 9, 82, 103
ASEAN Free Trade Association
(AFTA) 103
ASEAN–Mekong Basin
Development Cooperation
113
Asia-Pacific Economic
Cooperation (APEC) xiii,
82
Asia Pacific Rim 130
Asian approach 80
Asian Development Bank 110,
115
Australia–Korea trade 234–5
Australia Vietnam Business
Council 16
Australian Competition and
Consumer Commission
(ACCC) 169
Australian Research Council
xiii

banking 61
Barings Bank 179
beneficial spillovers 133
BHP Petroleum 108
bio-diversity 197
birth rate 142
build–operate–transfer 107
bureaucracy 68, 125
business contracts 67

business cooperation contracts
106
business economics 61
business environment 63, 66,
72, 79
business ethics 164
business management 164

capital-attracting programme
54
capital-raising 16
cattle husbandry 60
cement factories 57
centrally planned system 72
CEPII–CHELEM 6
chaebols 205, 220
chemicals 19
China 7
Closer Economic Relation
(CER) 13, 103
classification of sectors 22
Commonwealth of
Independent States (CIS)
10, 166
Council for Mutual Economic
Assistance (CMEA) 86
coffee 15, 61, 102
cold storage 19
Coles-Myers 179
College of Advanced Health
Studies 18
combined enrolment ratio
136
commercial opportunities 66
competition 16, 99
computers 58–9
consensus principles 169
consultancy 59
corporate strategies 121
corporate tax rates 107

corridor of commerce   110
corruption   71
cotton   61
cross-cultural value   175–6
crude oil   15, 64, 102
current account balance   84–6

death rate   142
Department of Foreign Affairs
    and Trade (DFAT)   10
developing countries   123
development assistance   123
devil's advocates   178
discriminatory costs   72
dispute resolution   67
distribution system   104, 122
Doi Moi   1, 82

East Asia Analytical Unit   xvi
economic arbitration courts   67
economic reform   120, 129
economies of scale   122
education   66
Education Law   150
efficiency   20
electrical products   19
electrification   117
embargo   82
employment promotion centres
    161
energy   111, 117
environment impact   184, 191
environmental compliance
    186
environmental protection   49,
    112
export   49
export development   99
export–import taxes   52
export processing zones   107
externalities   183

failure rates   65
facilitating procedures   71
family planning   142, 158
fertility rate   142
finance   61

food processing   17
foodstuff   59
foreign currency restrictions   71
foreign direct investment (FDI)
    15, 43, 79, 87, 103, 105, 232
foreign investment policy   106
foreign ownership   106
forestry   47, 57
free-market   12, 69

gender-empowerment measure
    139
gender-related development
    index   138
golden quadrangle   114
grease money   177
Greater Indochina   20
growth theory   132
ground representation   75–6
Gustavus Adolphus value
    statements   173

Hanbo debacle   223
health   66
health care   145
hi-tech industries   57
Hong Kong   13
housing development   62
human capital   135, 203
human capital index   135
human development index
    138
human resources development
    61, 111, 121, 130
hydropower   118

import and export duties   107
India   8
Indochina   9, 114
Indochina Project Management
    Company   69
industrial innovation   133
industrial zones   107
informatics   58–9
information technology (IT)
    18, 59, 105, 164
infrastructure   16, 66, 111, 124

initiative overload   114
inter-branch committee   50
international business   180
International Consulting and
    Training Center (ICTC)
    18, 55
international investment   231
International Labour
    Organization (ILO)   171
Internet   19
intervention policy   209
investment strategy   61
irrigation   52
iron steel   19
ISO 9000   189
ISO 14000   183, 188–9

Japan   7
joint ventures   19, 65
Judaeo–Christian tradition   166
just profit consensus   171

Korea Trade Promotion
    Co-operation (KOTRA)   213

labour costs   120–1
labour force conditions   50
land management   62
land rent   49
Latin America   8
Law on Foreign Investment
    44, 106
Law on Universalization of
    Primary Education   150
lay-offs   217
learning curve   65
legal infrastructure   68
less developed countries   43
leverage   68
liberalization   208–9
literacy   135

machinery   19, 46
market-oriented economies   122
mass media   21
master plans   49, 59
medical sector   105

medicaments   19, 99
medicines   63
Mekong Basin   110
merchandise exports   91
merchandise imports   91–4
microeconomic reforms   74
mineral exploitation   62
Ministry of Labour, Invalids and
    Social Affairs (MOLISA)
    134
Ministry of Planning and
    Investment (MPI)   46, 54
Ministry of Science, Technology
    and Environment (MOSTE)
    196
mountain and remote areas   51

natural resources   103, 111,
    120, 166
New South Wales Vietnam
    Chamber of Commerce
    xvi
Newly Industrialized Countries
    (NICs)   13
North American Free Trade Area
    (NAFTA)
niches, identification   16

Official Development Assistance
    (ODA)   52, 54
one-door policy   48
open admission pattern   153
Organization for Economic
    Cooperation and
    Development (OECD)   200
outward-oriented development
    53

Pacific Economic Cooperation
    Council (PECC)   136
partner-identification   16
partnerships   123
personal relationship   76, 125
pioneer investors   73
plastics   46
policy-sensitive growth   133
political patronage   70

Pollution Prevention Pays programme   185
pollution standards   184
post   58
poverty   155–9
pragmatic dualism   154
pricing policy   19
printing   19
privatization   61
property rights   72
public administration   164

realized investment capital   45
regional strategy   122
Research Institute for International Business   xiv
restructuring   233
reunification   22
rice planting   60
rural infrastructure   59

satellite stations   58
seafood products   13, 60, 102
sectoral prospects   57
security market   61
semi-skilled labour   126
short-term players   78
skilled manpower   17
Small and Medium Business Administration (SMBA)   218, 223
small- and medium-size enterprises   208, 210–1
social pluralism   154
socialist style of education   152
soft credit loan   52
soft landing   228
state management   48
state-owned enterprises   52, 104
steel products   63
strategic planning   186
strategies   74–5
sugar   19, 60
systemic deficiencies   66

taxation system   71
tea planting   61

technological transfer   49
telecommunications   19, 57–8, 99, 111, 118–19
Telstra   64
textiles   15
Total Quality Environmental Management (TQEM)   186–7
Total Quality Management   4, 164
tourism   57, 111, 121, 236
trade deficit   11
trade developments   89
trade flows   88
trade openness   14
trade promotion   16
trade strategy   20
training   17
transnational corporations   165, 171–2
transport   58, 111, 116

United Kingdom   6
United States   6
universalization   146

Vesper–Hinksey guidelines   171
Viet kieu   78
Vietnam Chamber of Commerce and Industry   16, 55, 103
Vietnam's Post Office   58
vocational education   146
vocational training   150–1

water resources   119
water supply   66
Western-style market system   73
wheat   19
work care   45
work insurance   45
World Trade Organization   xiii, 83, 168

Year of the Jubilees   166